Study Guide Accounting

THE MANAGERIAL CHAPTERS

NINTH EDITION

Helen Brubeck
San Jose State University

Prentice Hall

Boston   Columbus   Indianapolis   New York   San Francisco   Upper Saddle River
Amsterdam   Cape Town   Dubai   London   Madrid   Milan   Munich   Paris   Montréal   Toronto
Delhi   Mexico City   São Paulo   Sydney   Hong Kong   Seoul   Singapore   Taipei   Tokyo

VP/Editorial Director: Sally Yagan
Editor-in-Chief: Donna Battista
Director of Marketing: Kate Valentine
Director of Editorial Services: Ashley Santora
VP/Director of Development: Steve Deitmer
Editorial Project Managers: Rebecca Knauer
  and Nicole Sam
Editorial Assistant: Jane Avery
Development Editor: Shannon LeMay-Finn
Director of Product Development, Media:
  Zara Wanlass
Editorial Media Project Managers: Allison Longley
  and Sarah Peterson
Production Media Project Manager: John Cassar
Marketing Manager: Maggie Moylan
Marketing Assistant: Kimberly Lovato

Senior Managing Editor, Production:
  Cynthia Zonneveld
Production Project Manager: Lynne Breitfeller
Permissions Project Manager: Hessa Albader
Senior Operations Specialist: Diane Peirano
Senior Art Director: Jonathan Boylan
Cover Design: Jonathan Boylan
Cover Photos: Sideways Design\Shutterstock;
  iStockphoto; Bruno Ferrari\Shutterstock;
  Francesco Ridolfi\Dreamstime LLC -Royalty Free
Composition: GEX Publishing Services
Full-Service Project Management:
  GEX Publishing Services
Printer/Binder: Courier Kendallville
Cover Printer: Courier Kendallville
Typeface: 10/12 Sabon

Credits and acknowledgments borrowed from other sources and reproduced, with permission, in this textbook appear on appropriate page within text.

10 9 8 7 6 5 4 3 2

Prentice Hall
is an imprint of

www.pearsonhighered.com

ISBN-13: 978-0-13-256929-3
ISBN-10: 0-13-256929-9

Contents

Students will have more "I Get It!" moments

Students understand (or "get it") right after the instructor does a problem in class. Once they leave the classroom, however, students often struggle to complete the homework on their own. This frustration can cause them to give up on the material altogether and fall behind in the course, resulting in an entire class falling behind as the instructor attempts to keep everyone on the same page.

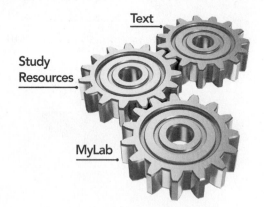

With the *Accounting, Ninth Edition* Student Learning System, all the features of the student textbook, study resources, and online homework system are designed to work together to provide students with the consistency and repetition that will keep both the instructor and students on track by providing more "I Get It!" moments inside and outside the classroom.

Replicating the Classroom Experience with Demo Doc Examples

The Demo Doc Examples, available in chapters 1 through 4 of the text, consist of entire problems, worked through step-by-step and narrated with the kind of comments that instructors would say in class. Demo Docs will aid students when they are trying to solve exercises and problems on their own, duplicating the classroom experience outside of class.

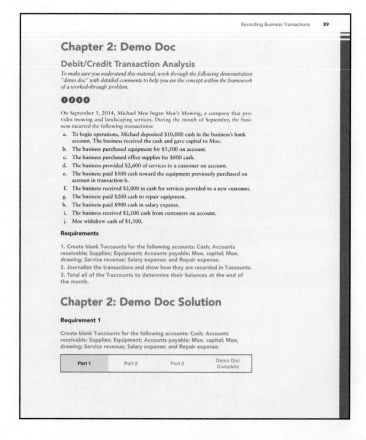

with *Accounting* and MyAccountingLab!

Consistency and Repetition Throughout the Learning Process

The concepts, materials, and practice problems are presented with clarity and consistency across all mediums—textbook, study resources, and online homework system. No matter which platform students use, they will continually experience the same look, feel, and language, minimizing confusion and ensuring clarity.

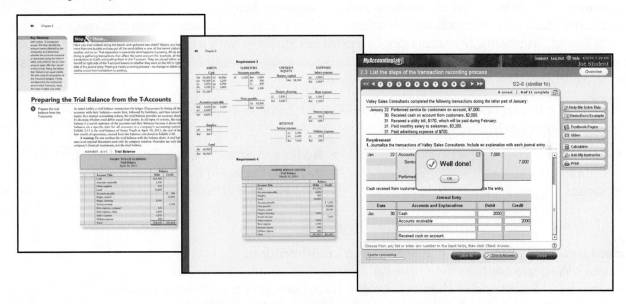

Experiencing the Power of Practice with MyAccountingLab: myaccountinglab.com

MyAccountingLab is an online homework system that gives students more "I Get It!" moments through the power of practice. With MyAccountingLab students can:

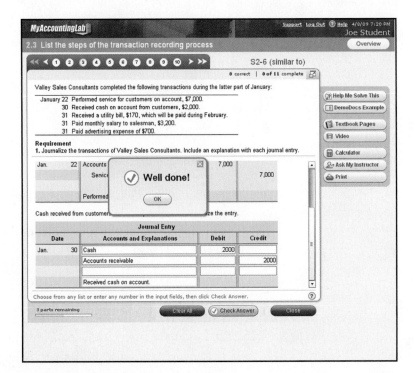

- work on the exact end-of-chapter material and/or similar problems assigned by the instructor.
- use the Study Plan for self-assessment and customized study outlines.
- use the Help Me Solve This tool for a step-by-step tutorial.
- watch a video to see additional information pertaining to the lecture.
- open the etext to the exact section of the book that will provide help on the specific problems.

Student Resources

For Students

MyAccountingLab ®

myaccountinglab.com Online Homework and Assessment Manager
MyAccountingLab is Web-based tutorial and assessment software for accounting that gives students more "I Get It!" moments. **MyAccountingLab** provides students with a personalized interactive learning environment where they can complete their course assignments with immediate tutorial assistance, learn at their own pace, and measure their progress.

In addition to completing assignments and reviewing tutorial help, students have access to the following resources in **MyAccountingLab**:

- Pearson eText
- Data Files
- Videos
- Demo Docs

- Audio and Student PowerPoint® Presentations
- Working Papers in Both Excel and PDF
- MP3 Files with Chapter Objectives and Summaries
- Flash Cards

Student Resource Web site: pearsonhighered.com/horngren
The book's Web site contains the following:
- Data Files: Select end-of-chapter problems have been set up in different software applications, including Peachtree 2010, QuickBooks 2010, and Excel
- Excel Working Papers
- Online Chapter Materials (Special Purpose Journals and Investments)

14 The Statement of Cash Flows

WHAT YOU PROBABLY ALREADY KNOW

If you find yourself short of cash occasionally, it is not uncommon to wonder where all of the money has gone. You probably already know that you need to keep track of all cash received and spent for a period of time to find out the answer. Not only does that show you the *amount* of money coming in and going out, but you will also identify the *source* of the cash received and the *use* of the cash spent. Identifying the cash activities in your life helps you to predict your future cash flows based on past history, review the decisions you have made in your financial life that result in the creation and disbursement of cash, and assess your ability to meet future financial obligations. The same issues are important to a business. In this chapter, we will see how the statement of cash flows provides this information for an entity.

Learning Objectives/Success Keys

 Identify the purposes of the statement of cash flows.

The statement of cash flows helps to do the following:

- Predict future cash flows. Recall from Chapter 13 the concept of income from continuing operations and special items. Those results are used to make predictions about the future.

- Evaluate management decisions. The cash-flow result of management's decisions is reflected in the statement of cash flows.

- Predict ability to pay debts and dividends. Investors and creditors will review past cash flows to assess the risk of nonpayment of debt and dividends.

2 Distinguish among operating, investing, and financing cash flows.

The statement of cash flows includes all transactions that increase or decrease Cash. These items are included in one of the following three categories:

- Operating—Activities that affect the income statement and current assets and current liabilities on the balance sheet. These transactions include inflows such as cash receipts from customers, interest, and dividends. Outflows include cash paid to employees and suppliers. *It is most important to have a positive net cash inflow for this activity.*

- Investing—Activities that affect long-term assets. These transactions include cash inflows from the sale of plant, property, and equipment; investments; and the collection from long-term loans. Outflows include the cash payment to purchase plant, property, and equipment; make investments; and make loans.

- Financing—Activities that affect long-term liabilities and stockholders' equity. These transactions include cash inflows from the sale of stock and issuance of long-term debt. Cash outflows include the payment of dividends and the repayment of debt.

Refer to Exhibit 14-2 (p. 664) for the relationship between the activity categories and the balance sheet classifications.

3 Prepare the statement of cash flows by the indirect method.

The **indirect method** reconciles from net income on the income statement to cash from operating activities. The schedule begins with accrual-basis net income and identifies the adjustments or items of difference to convert from the accrual basis of accounting to a cash basis for operating activities. Some of the adjustments include the following:

- eliminating such noncash expenses as depreciation, depletion, and amortization—these expenses need to be added to net income to eliminate the expense from net income.

- eliminating the gains or losses included in net income—gains need to be deducted from net income and losses need to be added to net income to eliminate these from net income. The full proceeds of sales are included as an investing activity.

- changes in the current assets and current liabilities—review the "Changes in the Current Assets and the Current Liabilities" section in the main text for the rules. Review the rationale for the rules.

This can be a challenging concept. Review carefully the "Cash Flows from Operating Activities" section of the main text and Exhibit 14-4 (p. 666).

4   Identify noncash investing and financing activities.

Companies can engage in investing or financing activities that do not involve cash. These transactions are not included in the main body of the cash flow statement, but are reported in a separate schedule.

5   Analyze cash flows.

Free cash flow is the amount of cash available from operations after paying for planned investments in long-term assets and after paying cash dividends to shareholders.

6   Prepare the statement of cash flows by the direct method (Appendix 14A).

The **direct method** lists the amount of cash receipts and cash payments from operating activities by major category. The FASB recommends the direct method, but most corporations use the indirect method, which requires less work. *Review the direct method of presenting operating activities in Exhibit 14A-4 (p. 703).*

7   Prepare the indirect statement of cash flows using a spreadsheet (Appendix 14B).

Sometimes a worksheet can be helpful in preparing an indirect method statement of cash flows, particularly when the accounting information is unwieldy.

Demo Doc 1

Statement of Cash Flows (Indirect Method)

Learning Objectives 2, 3

Indirect Method

Tanker, Inc., had the following information at December 31, 2013:

TANKER, INC.
Balance Sheet
December 31, 2013

Assets	2013	2012	Change	Liabilities	2013	2012	Change
Current:				Current:			
Cash	$ 700	$1,160	$(460)	Accounts payable	$ 680	$ 530	$150
Accounts receivable	300	420	(120)				
Inventory	800	750	50	Long-term notes payable	660	815	
Prepaid insurance	120	90	30				
				Total liabilities	$1,340	$1,345	
Furniture	1,500	1,400					
Less acc. depn.	(400)	(475)		**Stockholders' Equity**			
Net	1,100	925		Common stock (no par)	$1,800	$1,800	
				Retained earnings	880	200	
Total assets	$3,020	$3,345		Less treasury stock	(1,000)	0	
				Total equity	$1,680	$2,000	
				Total liabilities and equity	$3,020	$3,345	

TANKER, INC.
Income Statement
Year Ended December 31, 2013

Sales revenue	$3,400
Less cost of goods sold	(1,750)
Gross margin	$1,650
Depreciation expense	$ (110)
Insurance expense	(230)
Other operating expenses	(390)
Gain on sale of furniture	80
Net income	$1,000

Other Information

- Every year, Tanker declares and pays cash dividends.

- During 2013, Tanker sold old furniture for $90 cash. Tanker also bought new furniture by making a cash down payment and signing a $200 note payable.

- During 2013, Tanker repaid $500 of notes payable in cash and borrowed new long-term notes payable for cash.

- During 2013, Tanker purchased treasury stock for cash. No treasury stock was sold.

Requirement

1. Prepare Tanker's statement of cash flows for the year ended December 31, 2013, using the indirect method.

Demo Doc 1 Solution

Requirement 1

2 Distinguish among operating, investing, and financing cash flows

3 Prepare the statement of cash flows by the indirect method

Prepare Tanker's statement of cash flows for the year ended December 31, 2013.

Part 1	Part 2	Part 3	Demo Doc Complete

Operating Activities

We first set up the statement of cash flows with the proper title and then start with operating activities.

Net Income

The first item is net income. Because net income is positive, it is added to the Cash balance. Therefore, we add (that is, positive number) $1,000 on our cash-flow statement.

Depreciation Expense

Net income includes depreciation expense, which must be removed because it is a 100% noncash item. Remember, no cash was "spent" for depreciation, yet it was still deducted to arrive at the net income number. Because depreciation expense was *subtracted* to calculate net income, we *add* it back to remove it.

Gain on Sale of Furniture

After depreciation, we must look for gains and losses on disposal of long-term assets. These are treated in a manner similar to the depreciation. No cash was "earned" for the gain, yet it was still added to arrive at the net income number. The gain on sale of furniture was *added* to calculate net income, so we *subtract* it to remove it.

Accounts Receivable

After looking at net income and the depreciation and gain adjustments, we need to incorporate the changes in current assets and current liabilities.

The increases and decreases in these accounts do not tell us whether to add or subtract these items on the cash-flow statement.

The first current asset (other than cash) is Accounts Receivable. On the balance sheet we see:

Assets	2013	2012	Change
Current:			
Cash	$700	$1,160	$(460)
Accounts receivable	300	420	(120)

We must add the $120 decrease in Accounts Receivable. There are two ways to reason this out:

1. Accounts Receivable went down. Why? Tanker is collecting more of the cash that its customers owe. How does this affect Cash? It increases Cash; therefore, we should add the number on the cash-flow statement.

2. Accounts Receivable went down. This is a decrease in an asset, which is a credit. If this credit is balanced out by the Cash account, that will be a debit to Cash, which is an increase. If Cash is increased, we should add the number on the cash-flow statement.

Notice that in both of these cases, we are adding or subtracting on the cash-flow statement because of the item's effect on *cash flow. It doesn't matter if Accounts Receivable went up or down; what matters is how that affects cash flow.*

Inventory

Let's try the two ways with the next current asset: Inventory. On the balance sheet, we see:

Assets	2013	2012	Change
Current:			
Cash	$700	$1,160	$(460)
Accounts receivable	300	420	(120)
Inventory	800	750	50

During the year, Inventory increased by $50.

1. Why did Inventory increase? Tanker is purchasing inventory with cash. Therefore, this has a negative effect on cash flow.

2. If Inventory is increased, this is an increase in an asset, which is a debit. If this is balanced out by Cash, then Cash is credited, which is a negative effect on cash flow.

Prepaid Insurance

The last current asset is Prepaid Insurance. On the balance sheet, we see:

Assets	2013	2012	Change
Current:			
Cash	$700	$1,160	$(460)
Accounts receivable	300	420	(120)
Inventory	800	750	50
Prepaid insurance	120	90	30

During the year, Prepaid Insurance increased by $30.

1. Why did Prepaid Insurance increase? Tanker paid more insurance costs in advance. This has a negative effect on cash flow.

2. If Prepaid Insurance is increased, this is an increase in an asset, which is a debit. If this is balanced out by Cash, then Cash is credited, which is a negative effect on cash flow.

Accounts Payable

The last part of operating activities is to look at the changes in current liabilities. The only current liability in this question is Accounts Payable. On the balance sheet, we see:

Liabilities	2013	2012	Change
Current:			
Accounts payable	$680	$530	$150

During the year, Accounts Payable increased by $150.

1. Why did Accounts Payable increase? Tanker is not paying all of its bills. This means that it is holding onto its cash, which is a positive effect on cash flow.

2. If Accounts Payable is increased, this is an increase in a liability, which is a credit. If this is balanced out by Cash, then Cash is debited, which is a positive effect on cash flow.

We total these numbers, and we are finished with operating activities. The completed operating activities section would appear as:

Operating activities	
Net income	$1,000
Depreciation expense	110
Gain on sale of furniture	(80)
Decrease in accounts receivable	120
Increase in inventory	(50)
Increase in prepaid insurance	(30)
Increase in accounts payable	150
Total cash flow provided by operating activities	$1,220

2 Distinguish among operating, investing, and financing cash flows

3 Prepare the statement of cash flows by the indirect method

Investing Activities

Part 1	Part 2	Part 3	Demo Doc Complete

Investing activities looks at cash purchases and cash disposals of long-term assets. This means that we need to know how much cash was paid to purchase new furniture and how much cash was received when Tanker sold some of the old furniture. Do we have any of these numbers right away? Yes, we are told in the question that Tanker signed a $200 note payable to purchase new furniture. We also know that the old furniture was sold for $90 cash.

Before we do anything else, we should point out that the $200 note payable is a <u>noncash transaction</u>. Although we will *need* to use it in our analysis, it will *not* appear on the main body of the cash-flow statement. Instead, it will appear in a note for noncash investing and financing activities:

Noncash investing and financing activities	
Purchase of furniture with note payable	$200

We need to calculate the *cash* Tanker paid to purchase new furniture. To do this, we need to analyze the Furniture (net) T-account:

Furniture (net)			
Bal 12/31/12	925		
	increases	decreases	
Bal 12/31/13	1,100		

We know that the Furniture (net) account increased and decreased. What caused that account to increase? Well, it would increase if Tanker bought new furniture. So obviously the cash paid *and* the note signed for new furniture went into this account.

What would cause the Furniture (net) account to decrease?

If Tanker sold furniture, we would decrease the account, *but* it would be decreased by the *book* value (that is, the *net* amount) of the furniture sold. Remember, the book value is another term for *net* value. We are looking at net value in the T-account, so the Furniture (net) account decreases by its *net/book* value.

We know that some furniture was sold, so obviously this decrease occurred.

We know that this furniture was sold for $90 cash, but this is *not* the net book value (NBV) of the furniture sold. This amount is still unknown.

However, we can calculate this amount using the gain/loss formula:

Gain or loss on sale of fixed assets = Cash received on sale of fixed assets – NBV of fixed assets sold

For this example, this becomes

Gain on sale of furniture = Cash received on sale of furniture – NBV of furniture sold

So: $80 = $90 – NBV of furniture sold.
Therefore, the NBV of furniture sold is $10.

What else would decrease Furniture (net)? Well, when Tanker takes depreciation expense, don't we decrease the net value of its assets? We know from the income statement that depreciation expense is $110. Let's now put all of the numbers in and see what comes out:

Furniture (net)			
Bal 12/31/12	925		
Cash purchases	X		
Noncash purchases	200		
		NBV furniture sold	10
		Depreciation expense	110
Bal 12/31/13	1,100		

So X = Cash paid to purchase furniture = $95.

To summarize, this is how we find missing information for long-term assets:

1. Set up a T-account for the net value of the asset.

2. Fill in as much information as you can in the T-account (such as beginning and ending balances, depreciation expense, and purchases or net book value of disposals).

3. Solve for any missing information.

4. If there is more than one number missing, or if the missing information is not the number you need, use the gain/loss formula to calculate any remaining information.

Now we can put our two numbers, $90 and $95, into the statement of cash flows. *Cash* purchases of equipment were $95. Did this cause Cash to increase or decrease? Obviously, it is a decrease because Tanker *paid* cash, so we will subtract it. Cash received on sale of equipment is $90, which is an increase to Cash, so we will add it.

Remember that for investing activities, we *cannot* combine these two items. They *must* be listed separately because they are two separate transactions.

Totaling these numbers completes investing activities.

The completed investing activities section would appear as

Investing activities	
Cash paid to purchase new furniture	$(95)
Cash proceeds from sale of furniture	90
Total cash flow provided by investing activities	$ (5)

2 Distinguish among operating, investing, and financing cash flows

3 Prepare the statement of cash flows by the indirect method

Financing Activities

Part 1	Part 2	**Part 3**	Demo Doc Complete

Financing activities deals with long-term liabilities (debt) and equity accounts. First, we will look at long-term liabilities.

There are new notes payable (for which Tanker received cash) and Tanker repaid some other notes.

Notes Payable

We need the cash numbers involved so that we can put them into the cash-flow statement. Do we have any of them immediately available to us?

Yes, we are told that Tanker repaid $500 of notes payable.

We also know that Tanker took out a noncash note (to purchase furniture) of $200. This noncash transaction has already been recorded in the note to the cash-flow statement (discussed under investing activities).

Knowing this, let us analyze the Notes Payable T-account:

Notes payable		
	Bal 12/31/12	815
decreases	increases	
	Bal 12/31/13	660

What would cause this account to increase? Well, it would increase if Tanker took out new notes payable. What would cause it to decrease? It would decrease if Tanker paid off some of the notes. Let's put in that information:

Notes payable			
		Bal 12/31/12	815
Note repayments	500		
		New cash notes	X
		New noncash notes	200
		Bal 12/31/13	660

So we can calculate that new cash notes = X = $145.

Now we can put these numbers into the cash-flow statement. *Cash* received from new notes was $145. This increased Cash, so it has a positive effect on cash flow. Cash paid to repay old notes was $500. This decreased Cash, so it has a negative effect on cash flow.

Treasury Stock

Now we must analyze the changes in Tanker's equity. Tanker had some activity with treasury stock during the year. We know that Tanker purchased treasury stock.

Treasury stock		
Bal 12/31/12	0	
	increases	decreases
Bal 12/31/13	1,000	

What could cause this account to go up? It would go up if Tanker purchased treasury stock. What could cause it to go down? It would go down if treasury stock were sold. We know that there was no treasury stock sold, so looking at this again

Treasury stock			
Bal 12/31/12	0		
Treasury stock			
Purchased	X		
		Treasury stock sold	0
Bal 12/31/13	1,000		

So we can calculate that treasury stock purchased = X = $1,000. This means that cash was paid by Tanker, which is a negative effect on cash flow.

Dividends

The other account in equity is Retained Earnings. The two major transactions impacting Retained Earnings are net income and dividends.

Net income was already listed in the operating activities section, so all that remains to be included in the financing activities section is dividend activity.

The Retained Earnings account looks like this:

Retained earnings		
	Bal 12/31/12	200
decreases	increases	
	Bal 12/31/13	880

What makes Retained Earnings go up? It goes up when Tanker earns net income. What makes it go down? It goes down when Tanker pays dividends. Putting this information in

Retained earnings		
	Bal 12/31/12	200
Cash dividends paid X	Net income	1,000
	Bal 12/31/13	880

So cash dividends paid = X = $320. These were paid in cash so this has a negative effect on Cash.

Totaling these numbers completes financing activities. The completed financing activities section would appear as

Financing activities	
Cash proceeds from new notes	$ 145
Cash repayment of old notes	(500)
Cash purchase of treasury stock	(1,000)
Cash dividends paid	(320)
Total cash flow provided by financing activities	$(1,675)

Now we must combine operating activities, investing activities, and financing activities to get the total cash flow (the change in cash during the year).

Next, we show the Cash balance from the prior year (December 31, 2012) and add it to total cash flow to get this year's Cash balance (December 31, 2013).

TANKER, INC.
Statement of Cash Flows
Year Ended December 31, 2013

Operating activities	
Net income	$ 1,000
+ Depreciation expense	110
– Gain on sale of furniture	(80)
+ Decrease in accounts receivable	120
– Increase in inventory	(50)
– Increase in prepaid insurance	(30)
+ Increase in accounts payable	150
Total cash flow provided by operating activities	$ 1,220
Investing activities	
Cash paid to purchase new furniture	$ (95)
Cash proceeds from sale of furniture	90
Total cash flow provided by investing activities	$ (5)
Financing activities	
Cash proceeds from new notes	$ 145
Cash repayment of old notes	(500)
Cash purchase of treasury stock	(1,000)
Cash dividends paid	(320)
Total cash flow provided by financing activities	$(1,675)
Total cash flow (change in Cash balance)	$ 460
Cash, December 31, 2012	$ 1,160
Cash, December 31, 2013	$ 700
Noncash investing and financing activities	
Purchase of furniture with note payable	$ 200

Part 1	Part 2	Part 3	**Demo Doc Complete**

Demo Doc 2A

Statement of Cash Flows (Direct Method)

Learning Objectives 1, 2, 6

Direct Method

Use the information for Tanker, Inc., in the previous question:

TANKER, INC.
Balance Sheet
December 31, 2013

Assets	2013	2012	Change	Liabilities	2013	2012	Change
Current:				Current:			
Cash	$ 700	$1,160	$(460)	Accounts payable	$ 680	$ 530	$150
Accounts receivable	300	420	(120)				
Inventory	800	750	50	Long-term notes payable	660	815	
Prepaid insurance	120	90	30				
				Total liabilities	$1,340	$1,345	
Furniture	1,500	1,400					
Less acc. depn.	(400)	(475)		**Stockholders' Equity**			
Net	1,100	925		Common stock (no par)	$1,800	$1,800	
				Retained earnings	880	200	
Total assets	$3,020	$3,345		Less treasury stock	(1,000)	0	
				Total equity	$1,680	$2,000	
				Total liabilities and equity	$3,020	$3,345	

TANKER, INC.
Income Statement
Year Ended December 31, 2013

Sales revenue	$3,400
Less cost of goods sold	(1,750)
Gross margin	$1,650
Depreciation expense	$ (110)
Insurance expense	(230)
Other operating expenses	(390)
Gain on sale of furniture	80
Net income	$1,000

Requirements

1. Prepare the operating activities section of Tanker's statement of cash flow using the direct method.

2. How is the information a cash-flow statement provides different from the information an income statement provides?

Demo Doc 2A Solutions

Requirement 1

2 Distinguish among operating, investing, and financing cash flows

6 Prepare the statement of cash flows by the direct method (Appendix 14A)

Prepare the operating activities section of Tanker's statement of cash flows using the direct method.

Part 1	Part 2	Demo Doc Complete

We need to list all of the cash transactions involved in Tanker's day-to-day business operations. To do this, we should look at the income statement to get an idea of what these transactions are.

Cash Received from Customers

What is the first item on the income statement? Revenues. How does this translate into a cash transaction? Revenues should result in customers giving Tanker cash, so the appropriate line on the direct method cash-flow statement is "cash received from customers."

For each income statement account that is not 100% cash, there is always a balance sheet account to record the related accrual. In this case, Accounts Receivable (on the balance sheet) takes care of revenues when cash has not yet been collected.

Accounts receivable		
Bal 12/31/12	420	
	increases	decreases
Bal 12/31/13	300	

What could cause this account to increase? It would increase if Tanker had more sales. What could cause it to decrease? It would decrease if Tanker collected the cash. We know from the income statement that sales were $3,400, so

Accounts receivable			
Bal 12/31/12	420		
Sales revenue	3,400		
		Cash collected	X
Bal 12/31/13	300		

X = cash collected from customers = $3,520. This is the amount for the direct method cash-flow statement.

Cash Paid to Suppliers

The next line on the income statement is cost of goods sold. How does this relate to a cash transaction? In order to get the goods Tanker sold, it must buy the items from a supplier and pay for them. So the appropriate line on the cash-flow statement is "cash paid to suppliers." Accounts Payable is the balance sheet account that takes care of bills to suppliers that have not yet been paid.

Accounts payable		
	Bal 12/31/12	530
decreases	increase	
	Bal 12/31/13	680

What could cause this account to increase? It would increase if Tanker had more bills (that is, if Tanker were to purchase inventory from its suppliers). What could cause it to decrease? It would decrease if Tanker paid the cash it owed to the suppliers. However, we don't know how much inventory was purchased.

We can figure this out using the inventory formula from Chapter 6:

$$COGS = \text{Beginning inventory} + \text{Purchases} - \text{Ending inventory}$$
$$\$1,750 = \$750 + \text{Purchases} - \$800$$
$$\text{Purchases} = \$1,800$$

Putting this into the Accounts Payable T-account

Accounts payable

	Bal 12/31/12	530
Cash payments X		
	Inventory purchases	1,800
	Bal 12/31/13	680

X = Cash payments to suppliers = $1,650. This is the amount for the direct method cash-flow statement.

The next item on the income statement is depreciation expense. Because we know that this is 100% noncash, we can ignore it for the direct method.

Cash Paid as Insurance

Next is insurance expense. This would result in "cash paid as insurance." To calculate this number, we need to analyze the Prepaid Insurance account.

Prepaid insurance

Bal 12/31/12	90		
	increases	decreases	
Bal 12/31/13	120		

What could cause this account to increase? It would increase if Tanker paid more insurance in advance. What could cause it to decrease? It would decrease if Tanker incurred that insurance expense. We know from the income statement that insurance expense was $230.

Prepaid insurance

Bal 12/31/12	90		
Cash payments	X		
		Insurance expense	230
Bal 12/31/13	120		

X = Cash paid as insurance = $260. This is the amount for the direct method statement of cash flows.

Following insurance expense are other expenses. Let's leave this until the end.

After this is the gain on sale of furniture. This is noncash and, therefore, does not impact a direct method cash-flow statement.

Other Cash Expenses

Now we come back to other expenses. Are there any other current asset or current liability accounts with which we have not yet dealt? No, we have analyzed all of them. This means that there is no accrual portion (that is, no *noncash* portion) of these expenses. So we can just assume that they were *all paid in cash*. Therefore, the last line in the operating activities section is "other cash expenses" of $390.

Operating activities	
Cash collected from customers	$ 3,520
Cash paid to suppliers	(1,650)
Cash paid for insurance	(260)
Other cash expenses	(390)
Cash flow provided by operating activities	$ 1,220

Notice that the "cash flow provided by operating activities" of $1,220 is the *same* total we calculated under the indirect method. It is *always* the case that cash flow from operating activities is the same under the direct and indirect methods. This is a good check to confirm that our calculations were correct.

Remember that the investing and financing activities are the same under both methods. So the rest of Tanker's cash-flow statement (investing activities to the end) would be identical to what is shown in Demo Doc 1.

Requirement 2

How is the information a cash-flow statement provides different from the information an income statement provides?

Part 1	Part 2	Demo Doc Complete

The income statement shows the determination of net income. Net income is calculated on an accrual basis.

This means that net income not only includes cash transactions *but also* includes noncash transactions. We record revenue earned and expenses incurred *regardless* of whether or not cash has been received or paid.

The cash-flow statement shows the determination of cash flow (that is, the change in the Cash balance during the year). Because the cash-flow statement distills all transactions down to their cash components only, it is missing certain noncash transactions that are included in net income. Cash flow is actually net income *under the cash basis of accounting*.

So the primary difference is that the income statement is prepared under the accrual basis of accounting, whereas the cash-flow statement is prepared under the cash basis of accounting.

Part 1	Part 2	Demo Doc Complete

Quick Practice Questions

True/False

_____ 1. The statement of cash flows helps to inform the reader about all of the differences between net income and cash flows from operations.

_____ 2. A company may have net income but still have a net cash outflow.

_____ 3. Cash payments for interest expense would be classified as a financing activity.

_____ 4. Free cash flow is a measure of cash adequacy that focuses on the amount of cash available from operations after paying for planned investments in long-term assets.

_____ 5. Purchases of plant assets for cash would be classified as a financing activity.

_____ 6. Under the indirect method, depreciation expense would be subtracted from net income in the operating activities.

_____ 7. The majority of U.S. corporations use the direct method in preparing the statement of cash flows.

_____ 8. Under the indirect method, the acquisition of land through the issuance of common stock would be an investing activity on the statement of cash flows.

_____ 9. When using the indirect method, a loss on sale of equipment is added to net income under the operating activities.

_____ 10. Interest received on a bond investment would be shown as an investing cash inflow.

Multiple Choice

1. Which of the following statements is *incorrect?*
   a. A statement of cash flows is a basic financial statement required by GAAP.
   b. A statement of cash flows is dated for a period of time as opposed to a point in time.
   c. One purpose of a statement of cash flows is to predict future cash flows.
   d. The statement of cash flows may be combined with the stockholders' equity section of the balance sheet.

2. The operating activities section has a relationship with which part of the balance sheet?
   a. Current assets and current liabilities
   b. Long-term assets
   c. Stockholders' Equity and all liabilities
   d. Stockholders' Equity and long-term liabilities

3. Dividend payments would be included in which section of the statement of cash flows?
   a. Operating activities
   b. Financing activities
   c. Investing activities
   d. Dividend payments are not included on the statement of cash flows.

4. Cash dividends received would be included in which section of the statement of cash flows?
   a. Operating activities
   b. Financing activities
   c. Investing activities
   d. Cash dividends received are not included on the statement of cash flows.

5. The purchase of treasury stock would be included in which section of the statement of cash flows?
   a. Operating activities
   b. Financing activities
   c. Investing activities
   d. The purchase of treasury stock is not included on the statement of cash flows.

6. Activities that create revenues and expenses are included in which section of the statement of cash flows?
   a. Investing activities
   b. Operating activities
   c. Financing activities
   d. Noncash investing and financing activities

7. Where are noncash investing and financing activities reported?
   a. The financing activities section of the statement of cash flows
   b. The investing activities section of the statement of cash flows
   c. Both (a) and (b) are correct.
   d. An accompanying schedule to the statement of cash flows

8. Where is the gain resulting from the sale of equipment shown under the indirect method?
   a. In the operating activities section as a deduction
   b. In the operating activities section as an addition
   c. In the investing activities section as an addition
   d. In the financing activities section as a deduction

9. Wilson Company's 2013 income statement reports depreciation expense of $25,000. How would depreciation be shown on the statement of cash flows using the direct method for 2013?
   a. As an addition under financing activities
   b. As a deduction under operating activities
   c. As an addition under operating activities
   d. It would not be reported.

10. Which of the following would be shown as a deduction to net income under the operating activities section using the indirect method?
    a. Depletion expense
    b. Increase in Accounts Payable account balance for the period
    c. Increase in Inventory Balance for the period
    d. Decrease in Accounts Receivable account balance for the period

Quick Exercises

14-1. Your best friend just lost his job because the company he was working for went bankrupt. He was complaining to you that even though the company had been profitable for three years in a row, it still went out of business. He asks you how this can happen.

Requirements

1. Explain the most likely reason for the company's declaring bankruptcy. Could your friend have seen it coming? How?

2. Discuss the four purposes of the statement of cash flows.

14-2. State whether each of the following events should be classified as an operating activity (O), investing activity (I), financing activity (F), shown in a separate schedule of noncash investing and financing activities (N), or not disclosed on the statement of cash flows (NA).

_____ a. Received cash from sale of equipment
_____ b. Paid for a three-year insurance policy on property
_____ c. Paid cash for salaries
_____ d. Paid for supplies purchased on account
_____ e. Received stock dividends
_____ f. Purchased delivery vehicles for cash
_____ g. Retired notes payable by issuing common stock
_____ h. Received cash interest
_____ i. Issued common stock for cash
_____ j. Issued preferred stock in exchange for land

14-3. Using the following data, prepare the operating activities section of a statement of cash flows for Asakura Corporation for the year ended December 31, 2013. Assume the indirect method is used.

Decrease in salary payable	$ 1,500
Increase in accounts payable	2,000
Decrease in accounts receivable	3,500
Net income	108,000
Increase in inventory	5,800
Decrease in prepaid expenses	1,200
Depreciation expense—Equipment	5,000
Depreciation expense—Buildings	7,500
Gain on sale of equipment	1,300
Loss on sale of land	2,500

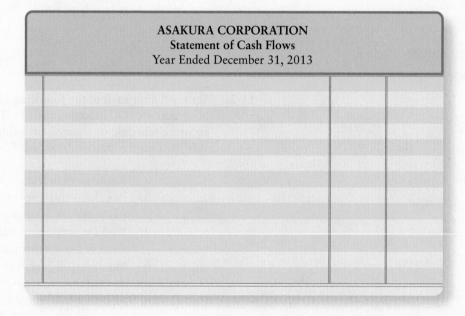

ASAKURA CORPORATION
Statement of Cash Flows
Year Ended December 31, 2013

14-4. For each of the following events, determine if it should be classified as an operating activity (O), investing activity (I), or financing activity (F). Then determine the increase or decrease to the Cash account using the indirect method.

Transaction description	Type of activity	Cash inflow (outflow)
a. Sales on account for the current period amount to $200,000. The January 1 balance in Accounts receivable was $95,000; the December 31 balance was $106,000.	_____	_____
b. Salary expense on the income statement for the current year is $171,500. The Salary payable balance on January 1 was $20,300; the December 31 balance was $17,800.	_____	_____
c. Interest income on the income statement for the current period is $30,000. Interest receivable on January 1 was $2,700; the December 31 balance was $2,250.	_____	_____
d. Sold 1,000 shares of $1 par common stock for cash at $17.	_____	_____
e. Purchased equipment for $35,000 cash down and a $180,000 loan.	_____	_____
f. Declared cash dividends of $23,000 during the current period. Dividends payable on January 1 were $1,500; the December 31 balance was $2,300.	_____	_____
g. Issued $1,500,000, 5-year, 4% bonds at 102.	_____	_____

14-5A. Chief Inc., gathered the following data from its accounting records for the year ended December 31, 2013:

Depreciation expense	$ 18,900
Payment of income taxes	24,500
Collections of accounts receivable	166,700
Prepayment of insurance (for next 2 years)	40,000
Declaration of stock split	65,000
Loss on sale of equipment	8,400
Collection of interest revenue	13,800
Payments of salaries and wages	83,600
Cash sales	102,900
Net income	231,200
Payment of cash dividends	3,500
Payment of dividends	19,400
Dividends received on investments	3,100
Issuance of bonds payable	800,000
Increase in accounts payable	20,300
Payments to suppliers	170,300
Acquisition of machinery by issuing long-term note payable	20,000

Requirements

1. Prepare the operating activities section of the statement of cash flows using the direct method.

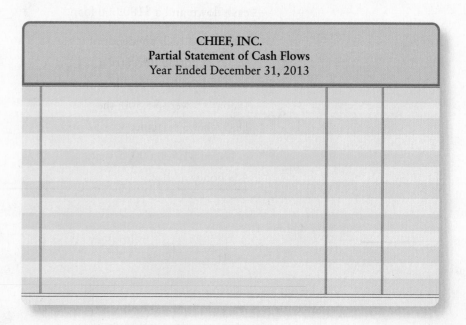

CHIEF, INC.
Partial Statement of Cash Flows
Year Ended December 31, 2013

2A. If Chief plans similar activity for 2014, what is expected free cash flow?

Do It Yourself! Question 1

Indirect Method

Clean, Co., had the following information at December 31, 2013:

CLEAN, CO.
Balance Sheet
December 31, 2013

Assets	2013	2012	Change	Liabilities	2013	2012	Change
Current:				Current:			
Cash	$ 460	$ 320	$140	Accounts payable	$ 800	$ 540	$260
Accounts receivable	510	420	90				
Inventory	710	750	(40)	Long-term notes payable	600	900	
Prepaid rent	170	250	(80)	Total liabilities	$1,400	$1,440	
Equipment	1,350	1,500		**Stockholders' Equity**			
Less acc. depn.	(400)	(650)		Common stock (no par)	$ 200	$ 150	
Net	950	850		Retained earnings	1,200	1,000	
Total assets	$2,800	$2,590		Total equity	$1,400	$1,150	
				Total liabilities and equity	$2,800	$2,590	

CLEAN, CO.
Income Statement
Year Ended December 31, 2013

Sales revenue	$1,800
Less cost of goods sold	(960)
Gross margin	$ 840
Depreciation expense	$ (90)
Rent expense	(140)
Other operating expenses	(195)
Loss on sale of equipment	(55)
Net income	$ 360

Other Information

- Every year, Clean declares and pays cash dividends.
- During 2013, Clean sold old equipment for cash. Clean also bought new equipment for $120 cash and a $140 note payable.
- During 2013, Clean repaid $600 of notes payable in cash and borrowed new long-term notes payable for cash.
- During 2013, new common stock was issued. No stock was retired.

Requirement

2 Distinguish among operating, investing, and financing cash flows

3 Prepare the statement of cash flows by the indirect method

1. Prepare Clean's statement of cash flows for the year ended December 31, 2013, using the indirect method.

Do It Yourself! Question 2

Direct Method

Use the information for Clean, Co., in the previous question.

Requirement

2 Distinguish among operating, investing, and financing cash flows

6 Prepare the statement of cash flows by the direct method (Appendix 14A)

1. Prepare the operating activities section of Clean's statement of cash flows using the direct method.

Quick Practice Solutions

True/False

_T_ 1. The statement of cash flows helps to inform the reader about all of the differences between net income and cash flows from operations. (p. 662)

_T_ 2. A company may have net income but still have a net cash outflow. (p. 662)

_F_ 3. Cash payments for interest expense would be classified as a financing activity.

    False—Cash payments for interest expense would be classified as an *operating* activity. (p. 666)

_T_ 4. Free cash flow is a measure of cash adequacy that focuses on the amount of cash available from operations after paying for planned investments in long-term assets. (p. 676)

_F_ 5. Purchases of plant assets for cash would be classified as a financing activity.

    False—Purchases of plant assets for cash would be classified as an *investing* activity. (p. 670)

_F_ 6. Under the indirect method, depreciation expense would be subtracted from net income in the operating activities.

    False—Under the indirect method, depreciation expense would be *added* to net income under the operating activities. (p. 668)

_F_ 7. The majority of U.S. corporations use the direct method in preparing the statement of cash flows.

    False—The majority of U.S. corporations use the *indirect* method in preparing the statement of cash flows. (p. 664)

_F_ 8. Under the indirect method, the acquisition of land through the issuance of common stock would be an investing activity on the statement of cash flows.

    False—Under the indirect method, the acquisition of land through the issuance of common stock would be a *noncash investing and financing* activity. (p. 674)

_T_ 9. When using the indirect method, a loss on sale of equipment is added to net income under the operating activities. (p. 668)

_F_ 10. Interest received on a bond investment would be shown as an investing cash inflow.

    False—Interest received on a bond investment would be shown as an *operating* cash inflow. (p. 666)

Multiple Choice

1. **Which of the following statements is incorrect?** (p. 662)
    a. A statement of cash flows is a basic financial statement required by GAAP.
    b. A statement of cash flows is dated for a period of time as opposed to a point in time.
    c. One purpose of a statement of cash flows is to predict future cash flows.
    d. The statement of cash flows may be combined with the stockholders' equity section of the balance sheet.

2. **The operating activities section has a relationship with which part of the balance sheet?** (p. 664)
    a. Current assets and current liabilities
    b. Long-term assets
    c. Stockholders' Equity and all liabilities
    d. Stockholders' Equity and long-term liabilities

3. **Dividend payments would be included in which section of the statement of cash flows?** (p. 665)
    a. Operating activities
    b. Financing activities
    c. Investing activities
    d. Dividend payments are not included on the statement of cash flows.

4. **Cash dividends received would be included in which section of the statement of cash flows?** (p. 666)
    a. Operating activities
    b. Financing activities
    c. Investing activities
    d. Cash dividends received are not included on the statement of cash flows.

5. **The purchase of treasury stock would be included in which section of the statement of cash flows?** (p. 665)
    a. Operating activities
    b. Financing activities
    c. Investing activities
    d. The purchase of treasury stock is not included on the statement of cash flows.

6. **Activities that create revenues and expenses are included in which section of the statement of cash flows?** (p. 666)
    a. Investing activities
    b. Operating activities
    c. Financing activities
    d. Noncash investing and financing activities

7. **Where are noncash investing and financing activities reported?** (p. 675)
    a. The financing activities section of the statement of cash flows
    b. The investing activities section of the statement of cash flows
    c. Both (a) and (b) are correct.
    d. An accompanying schedule to the statement of cash flows

8. Where is the gain resulting from the sale of equipment shown under the indirect method? (p. 665)
   a. In the operating activities section as a deduction
   b. In the operating activities section as an addition
   c. In the investing activities section as an addition
   d. In the financing activities section as a deduction

9. Wilson Company's 2013 income statement reports depreciation expense of $25,000. How would depreciation be shown on the statement of cash flows using the direct method for 2013? (p. 705)
   a. As an addition under financing activities
   b. As a deduction under operating activities
   c. As an addition under operating activities
   d. It would not be reported.

10. Which of the following would be shown as a deduction to net income under the operating activities section using the indirect method? (p. 665)
    a. Depletion expense
    b. Increase in Accounts Payable account balance for the period
    c. Increase in Inventory Balance for the period
    d. Decrease in Accounts Receivable account balance for the period

Quick Exercises

14-1.   Your best friend just lost his job because the company he was working for went bankrupt. He was complaining to you that even though the company had been profitable for three years in a row, it still went out of business. He asks you how this can happen. (p. 662)

Requirements

1. Explain the most likely reason for the company's declaring bankruptcy. Could your friend have seen it coming? How?

A profitable company is one in which revenues exceed expenses on an accrual basis. This does not necessarily mean that the company is generating enough cash to pay its bills. The most likely reason your friend's company went bankrupt is the lack of cash. If your friend had access to the statement of cash flows, the cash flow problems would have likely been evident.

2. Discuss the four purposes of the statement of cash flows.

The four purposes of the statement of cash flows are as follows:

1. To help predict future cash flows
2. To evaluate management decisions
3. To determine the company's ability to pay dividends to stockholders and interest and principal to creditors
4. To show the relationship of net income to changes in the business's cash

14-2. State whether each of the following events should be classified as an operating activity (O), investing activity (I), financing activity (F), shown in a separate schedule of noncash investing and financing activities (N), or not disclosed on the statement of cash flows (NA). (pp. 665–666)

I	a.	Received cash from sale of equipment
O	b.	Paid for a three-year insurance policy on property
O	c.	Paid cash for salaries
O	d.	Paid for supplies purchased on account
NA	e.	Received stock dividends
I	f.	Purchased delivery vehicles for cash
N	g.	Retired notes payable by issuing common stock
O	h.	Received cash interest
F	i.	Issued common stock for cash
N	j.	Issued preferred stock in exchange for land

14-3. Using the following data, prepare the operating activities section of a statement of cash flows for Asakura Corporation for the year ended December 31, 2013. Assume the indirect method is used. (pp. 665–674)

Decrease in salary payable	$ 1,500
Increase in accounts payable	2,000
Decrease in accounts receivable	3,500
Net income	108,000
Increase in inventory	5,800
Decrease in prepaid expenses	1,200
Depreciation expense—Equipment	5,000
Depreciation expense—Buildings	7,500
Gain on sale of equipment	1,300
Loss on sale of land	2,500

ASAKURA CORPORATION
Statement of Cash Flows
Year Ended December 31, 2013

Cash flows from operating activities:		
Net income		$108,000
Adjustments to reconcile net income to net cash provided by operating activities:		
Depreciation on equipment	$5,000	
Depreciation on buildings	7,500	
Loss on sale of land	2,500	
Gain on sale of equipment	(1,300)	
Decrease in accounts receivable	3,500	
Decrease in prepaid expenses	1,200	
Increase in inventory	(5,800)	
Decrease in salary payable	(1,500)	
Increase in accounts payable	2,000	13,100
Net cash inflow from operating activities		$121,100

14-4. For each of the following events, determine if it should be classified as an operating activity (O), investing activity (I), or financing activity (F). Then determine the cash inflow or (outflow). (pp. 665–674)

Transaction description	Type of activity	Cash inflow (outflow)
a. Sales on account for the current period amount to $200,000. The January 1 balance in Accounts receivable was $95,000; the December 31 balance was $106,000.	O	$ 189,000
b. Salary expense on the income statement for the current year is $171,500. The Salary payable balance on January 1 was $20,300; the December 31 balance was $17,800.	O	$ (174,000)
c. Interest income on the income statement for the current period is $30,000. Interest receivable on January 1 was $2,700; the December 31 balance was $2,250.	O	$ 30,450
d. Sold 1,000 shares of $1 par common stock for cash at $17.	F	$ 17,000
e. Purchased equipment for $35,000 cash down and a $180,000 loan.	I	$ (35,000)
f. Declared cash dividends of $23,000 during the current period. Dividends payable on January 1 were $1,500; the December 31 balance was $2,300.	F	$ (22,200)
g. Issued $1,500,000, 5-year, 4% bonds at 102.	F	$1,530,000

14-5A. Chief, Inc., gathered the following data from its accounting records for the year ended December 31, 2013: (pp. 676, 701–706)

Depreciation expense	$ 18,900
Payment of income taxes	24,500
Collections of accounts receivable	166,700
Prepayment of insurance (for next 2 years)	40,000
Declaration of stock split	65,000
Loss on sale of equipment	8,400
Collection of interest revenue	13,800
Payments of salaries and wages	83,600
Cash sales	102,900
Net income	231,200
Payment of cash dividends	3,500
Payment of dividends	19,400
Dividends received on investments	3,100
Issuance of bonds payable	800,000
Increase in accounts payable	20,300
Payments to suppliers	170,300
Acquisition of machinery by issuing long-term note payable	20,000

Requirements

1. Prepare the operating activities section of the statement of cash flows using the direct method.

CHIEF, INC.
Partial Statement of Cash Flows
Year Ended December 31, 2013

Cash flows from operating activities:		
Receipts:		
Collections from customers	$ 269,600*	
Dividends received	3,100	
Interest received	13,800	
Total cash receipts		$286,500
Payments:		
To suppliers	$(170,300)	
To employees	(83,600)	
For insurance	(40,000)	
For income tax	(24,500)	
Total cash payments		(318,400)
Net cash outflow from operating activities		$ (31,900)

*($166,700 + $102,900 = $269,600)

2A. If Chief plans similar activity for 2014, what is expected free cash flow?

Free cash flow = Net cash provided by operating activities – Cash payments planned for investments in long-term assets – Cash dividends

Free cash flow = 31,900 – 20,000 – 3,500 = 8,400

Do It Yourself! Question 1 Solutions

Requirement

1. Prepare Clean's statement of cash flows for the year ended December 31, 2013, using the indirect method.

Calculations: Investing Activities

The $140 note payable is a <u>noncash transaction</u>.

Equipment (net)

Bal 12/31/12	850		
Cash purchases	120		
Noncash purchases	140		
		NBV equipment sold	X
		Depreciation expense	90
Bal 12/31/13	950		

X = NBV of equipment sold = $70
Loss = – $55 = Cash received – $70
Cash received on sale of equipment = $15

Calculations: Financing Activities

Notes payable

		Bal 12/31/12	900
Note repayments	600		
		New cash notes	X
		New noncash notes	140
		Bal 12/31/13	600

New cash notes = X = $160

Common stock

		Bal 12/31/12	150
Retirements	0		
		New stock issued	X
		Bal 12/31/13	200

New stock issued = X = $50

Retained earnings

		Bal 12/31/12	1,000
Cash dividends paid	X		
		Net income	360
		Bal 12/31/13	1,200

Cash dividends paid = X = $160

CLEAN, CO.
Statement of Cash Flows
Year Ended December 31, 2013

Operating activities	
Net income	$ 360
+ Depreciation expense	90
+ Loss on sale of equipment	55
– Increase in accounts receivable	(90)
+ Decrease in inventory	40
+ Decrease in prepaid rent	80
+ Increase in accounts payable	260
Total cash flow provided by operating activities	$ 795
Investing activities	
Cash paid to purchase new equipment	$(120)
Cash proceeds from sale of equipment	15
Total cash flow provided by investing activities	$(105)
Financing activities	
Cash proceeds from new notes	$ 160
Cash repayment of old notes	(600)
Cash proceeds from new stock issue	50
Cash dividends paid	(160)
Total cash flow provided by financing activities	$(550)
Total cash flow (change in Cash during year)	$ 140
Cash, December 31, 2012	$ 320
Cash, December 31, 2013	$ 460
Noncash investing and financing activities	
Purchase of equipment with note payable	$ 140

Do It Yourself! Question 2 Solutions

Requirement

1. Prepare the operating activities section of Clean's statement of cash flows using the direct method.

Accounts receivable			
Bal 12/31/12	420		
Sales revenue	1,800		
		Cash collected	X
Bal 12/31/13	510		

$$X = \text{Cash collected from customers} = \$1{,}710$$
$$\text{COGS} = \$960 = \$750 + \text{purchases} - \$710$$
$$\text{Purchases} = \$920$$

Accounts payable			
		Bal 12/31/12	540
Cash payments	X		
		Inventory purchases	920
		Bal 12/31/13	800

$$X = \text{Cash payments to suppliers} = \$660$$

Prepaid rent			
Bal 12/31/12	250		
Cash payments	X		
		Rent expense	140
Bal 12/31/13	170		

$$X = \text{Cash paid as rent} = \$60$$

Operating activities	
Cash collected from customers	$1,710
Cash paid to suppliers	(660)
Cash paid for rent	(60)
Other cash expenses	(195)
Cash flow from operating activities	$ 795

The Power of Practice

For more practice using the skills learned in this chapter, visit MyAccountingLab. There you will find algorithmically generated questions that are based on these Demo Docs and your main textbook's Review and Assess Your Progress sections.

Go to MyAccountingLab and follow these steps:

1. Direct your URL to www.myaccountinglab.com.
2. Log in using your name and password.
3. Click the MyAccountingLab link.
4. Click Study Plan in the left navigation bar.
5. From the table of contents, select Chapter 14, The Statement of Cash Flows.
6. Click a link to work tutorial exercises.

15 Financial Statement Analysis

For years now, you have been a student and have taken many exams. You probably already know that there may be typical responses you have upon receiving your grade. Your first reaction may be the level of satisfaction you have with your grade compared to your previous grades received in that class and the established grading norms for your institution. You may then ask your friends what grade they received so that you can compare your results to them. The instructor may announce the average exam results and you could then determine if you performed better or worse than the average. Students often like to assess their performance by comparing their grade to a standard, their peers, and the average. Businesses often do the same thing. In this chapter, you study various techniques and ratios that a business will use to assess its performance using comparisons to previous results, competitors, and the industry average.

Learning Objectives/Success Keys

1   Perform a horizontal analysis of financial statements.

Horizontal analysis provides comparisons of financial information over time. To analyze a line item in the financial statements, the difference between the current and earlier time period amounts is computed. The dollar amount change of the line item between the periods is useful, but it is more informative to determine the percentage change by dividing the dollar change (current period amount, or this year's balance minus earlier period amount, or last year's balance) by the earlier period amount. *Review the horizontal analysis of the income statement and the balance sheet in Exhibits 15-2 and 15-3 (p. 725).*

2   Perform a vertical analysis of financial statements.

Vertical analysis provides comparisons of individual items on a financial statement to a relative base. The base, which serves as the denominator, is usually net sales for the income statement and total assets for the balance sheet. The vertical analysis percentage is calculated by dividing each financial statement item amount by the relevant base of net sales *or* total assets.

The vertical analysis percentage is shown next to the item amount on the financial statement. *Review the vertical analysis of the income statement and the balance sheet in Exhibits 15-4 and 15-5 (pp. 727–728).*

3 **Prepare and use common-size financial statements.**

A **common-size statement** is similar to the vertical analysis but shows only the vertical analysis percentages of each item in the financial statement. This presentation permits ready comparisons between companies of various sizes. *Review the common-size comparison of SmartTouch versus Learning Tree in Exhibit 15-6 (p. 729).*

4 **Compute the standard financial ratios.**

Financial ratios are helpful to assess a company's performance and financial position. Trends can be determined and comparisons to competing companies can be made. Various ratios are presented to evaluate the following:

- Ability to pay current liabilities

- Ability to sell inventory and collect receivables

- Ability to pay long-term debt

- Profitability

- Stock as investments

Review "Using Ratios to Make Decisions" in the main text for descriptions and formulas for the financial ratios.

Demo Doc 1

Financial Statement Analysis

Learning Objectives 1–4

MeMe Co. had the following information at December 31, 2013:

MEME CO. Balance Sheet December 31, 2013 and 2012		
	2013	**2012**
Assets		
Cash	$150	$130
Accounts receivable	80	145
Inventory	130	190
Total assets	$360	$465
Liabilities		
Accounts payable	90	140
Loans payable	140	220
Total liabilities	$230	$360
Stockholders' Equity		
Common stock	20	10
Retained earnings	110	95
Total stockholders' equity	$130	$105
Total liabilities and equity	$360	$465

MEME CO. Income Statement Years Ended December 31, 2013 and 2012		
	2013	**2012**
Sales revenue	$650	$580
Less cost of goods sold	430	350
Gross profit	$220	$230
Salary expense	120	140
Rent expense	70	80
Net income	$ 30	$ 10

At December 31, 2011, MeMe's inventory was $160 and total equity was $95.

Requirements

1. Prepare horizontal and vertical analyses for MeMe's financial statements.

2. Calculate MeMe's inventory turnover and rate of return on stockholders' equity ratios for both years.

Demo Doc 1 Solutions

Requirement 1

1 Perform a horizontal analysis of financial statements

Prepare horizontal and vertical analyses for MeMe's financial statements.

Part 1	Part 2	Part 3	Demo Doc Complete

Horizontal Analysis

As its name implies, horizontal analysis goes *across* the rows of the financial statements, looking at *one* account and how it has changed.

For *each* number on the balance sheet and income statement, we calculate the dollar change and the percent change.

$$\text{Dollar change} = \text{This year's balance} - \text{Last year's balance}$$

So in the dollar change of Accounts Receivable and Sales Revenue:

$$
\begin{aligned}
\text{Accounts receivable} &= \$80 \ - \ \$145 \\
&= \$(65) \text{ change} \\
\text{Sales revenue} &= \$650 \ - \ \$580 \\
&= \$70 \text{ change}
\end{aligned}
$$

Notice that the negative value on the change in Accounts Receivable indicates that this account has decreased, whereas the positive value on the change in Sales Revenue indicates that this account has increased.

Extra care must be taken when using this calculation on expenses (because they are presented as subtracted/negative numbers on the income statement). The *absolute value* of the expense (that is, ignoring the fact that it is already a negative number) must be used to calculate dollar change. In the dollar change of COGS and Rent Expense:

$$
\begin{aligned}
\text{COGS} &= \$430 \ - \ \$350 \\
&= \$80 \text{ change} \\
\text{Rent expense} &= \$70 \ - \ \$80 \\
&= \$(70) \text{ change}
\end{aligned}
$$

Again, the positive value indicates that COGS increased and the negative value indicates that Rent Expense decreased.

$$\text{Percent change} = \frac{\text{Dollar change}}{\text{Last year's balance}}$$

So in the percent change of Accounts Receivable and Sales Revenue:

$$\text{Accounts receivable} = \frac{\$(65)}{\$145} \text{ change}$$

$$= (44.8)\% \text{ change}$$

$$\text{Sales revenue} = \frac{\$70}{\$580}$$

$$= 12.1\% \text{ change}$$

Again, the percent change numbers are negative for Accounts Receivable (which decreased in 2013) and positive for Sales Revenue (which increased in 2013). The percent change is calculated the same way for expenses, again using the *absolute value* of the expenses. In the percent change of COGS and Rent Expense:

$$\text{COGS} = \frac{\$80}{\$350}$$

$$= 22.9\% \text{ change}$$

$$\text{Rent expense} = \frac{-\$10}{\$80}$$

$$= (12.5)\% \text{ change}$$

MEME CO.
Horizontal Analysis of Balance Sheet
Years Ended December 31, 2013 and 2012

	2013	2012	Increase (Decrease) Amount	Percent
Assets				
Cash	$150	$130	$ 20	15.4%
Accounts receivable	80	145	(65)	(44.8)
Inventory	130	190	(60)	(31.6)
Total assets	$360	$465	$(105)	(22.6)
Liabilities				
Accounts payable	90	140	(50)	(35.7)%
Loans payable	140	220	(80)	(36.4)
Total liabilities	$230	$360	$(130)	(36.1)
Stockholders' Equity				
Common stock	20	10	10	100.0%
Retained earnings	110	95	15	15.8
Total stockholders' equity	$130	$105	$ 25	23.8%
Total liabilities and equity	$360	$465	$(105)	(22.6)%

MEME CO. Horizontal Analysis of Comparative Income Statement Years Ended December 31, 2013 and 2012			Increase (Decrease)	
	2013	**2012**	Amount	Percent
Sales revenue	$650	$580	$ 70	12.1%
Less cost of goods sold	430	350	80	22.9
Gross profit	$220	$230	(10)	(4.3)
Salary expense	120	140	(20)	(14.3)
Rent expense	70	80	(10)	(12.5)
Net income	$ 30	$ 10	$ 20	200.0%

Vertical Analysis

Part 1	**Part 2**	Part 3	Demo Doc Complete

As its name implies, vertical analysis takes *each* number on the financial statements and compares it to others in the same year (that is, *down* the columns of the financial statements). Vertical analysis is sometimes called common-size analysis because it allows two companies of different sizes to be compared (through the use of percentages).

Balance Sheet Vertical Analysis

On the **balance sheet,** each number, whether it is before an asset, a liability, or an equity account is calculated as a percentage of **total assets.**

$$\text{Vertical analysis percent (balance sheet)} = \frac{\text{Account balance}}{\text{Total assets}}$$

So in the case of Accounts Receivable:

$$\text{Vertical analysis percent (2013 Accounts receivable)} = \frac{\$80}{\$360}$$
$$= 22.2\%$$

In other words, about 22% of all the assets in 2013 are in Accounts Receivable.

Income Statement Vertical Analysis

On the **income statement,** each number is calculated as a percentage of **net** *sales revenues.*

$$\text{Vertical analysis percent (income statement)} = \frac{\text{Account balance}}{\text{Net sales revenues}}$$

So in the case of Gross Profit:

$$\text{Vertical analysis percent (2013 Gross profit)} = \frac{\$220}{\$650}$$
$$= \textbf{33.8\%}$$

This means that for every dollar in sales revenues, $0.338 went to Gross Profit. For expenses, the calculation is the same. So in the cases of COGS and Rent Expense:

$$\text{Vertical analysis percent (2013 COGS)} = \frac{\$430}{\$650}$$
$$= \textbf{66.2\%}$$

$$\text{Vertical analysis percent (2013 Rent expense)} = \frac{\$70}{\$650}$$
$$= \textbf{10.8\%}$$

MEME CO.
Vertical Analysis of Balance Sheet
December 31, 2013 and 2012

	2013	2013 %	2012	2012 %
Assets				
Cash	$150	41.7%	$130	28.0%
Accounts receivable	80	22.2	145	31.1 *
Inventory	130	36.1	190	40.9
Total assets	$360	100.0%	$465	100.0%
Liabilities				
Accounts payable	$ 90	25.0%	$140	30.1%
Loans payable	140	38.9	220	47.3
Total liabilities	$230	63.9%	$360	77.4%
Stockholders' Equity				
Common stock	$ 20	5.5 *%	$ 10	2.2%
Retained earnings	110	30.6	95	20.4
Total stockholders' equity	$130	36.1%	$105	22.6%
Total liabilities and equity	$360	100.0%	$465	100.0%

*Rounded down to balance.

MEME CO.
Vertical Analysis of Comparative Income Statement
Years Ended December 31, 2013 and 2012

	2013	2013 %	2012	2012 %
Net sales revenue	$650	100.0%	$580	100.0%
Less cost of goods sold	430	66.2	350	60.3
Gross profit	$220	33.8%	$230	39.7%
Salary expense	120	18.4 *	140	24.1
Rent expense	70	10.8	80	13.8
Net income	$ 30	4.6%	$ 10	1.7%

*Rounded to balance.

Requirement 2

4 Compute the standard financial ratios

Calculate MeMe's inventory turnover and rate of return on stockholders' equity ratios for both years.

Part 1	Part 2	**Part 3**	Demo Doc Complete

$$\text{Inventory turnover} = \frac{\text{COGS}}{\text{Average inventory}}$$

Remember that "average" (when used in a financial ratio) generally means the beginning balance plus the ending balance divided by two.

$$\text{2013 Inventory turnover} = \frac{\$430}{[\frac{1}{2}(190 + 130)]}$$

$$= 2.7 \text{ times}$$

$$\text{2012 Inventory turnover} = \frac{\$350}{[\frac{1}{2}(160 + 190)]}$$

$$= 2 \text{ times}$$

$$\text{Rate of return on stockholders' equity} = \frac{\text{Net income} - \text{Preferred dividends}}{\text{Average common stockholders' equity}}$$

$$\text{2013 Rate of return on stockholders' equity} = \frac{[\$30 - \$0]}{\frac{1}{2}(\$105 + \$130)}$$

$$= 25.5\%$$

$$\text{2012 Rate of return on stockholders' equity} = \frac{[\$10 - \$0]}{\frac{1}{2}(\$95 + \$105)}$$

$$= 10\%$$

Part 1	Part 2	Part 3	**Demo Doc Complete**

Quick Practice Questions

True/False

_____ 1. It is generally considered more useful to know the percentage change in financial statement amounts from year to year than to know the absolute dollar amount of their change.

_____ 2. Benchmarking may be done against an industry average or against a key competitor.

_____ 3. Vertical analysis of financial statements reveals changes in items on the financial statements over time.

_____ 4. Inventory turnover is the ratio of average inventory to cost of goods sold.

_____ 5. Book value per share of common stock has no relationship to market value.

_____ 6. A high current ratio means that a company's current assets represent a relatively large portion (or ratio) of total liabilities.

_____ 7. The debt ratio measures the ability to pay current liabilities.

_____ 8. The acid-test (quick) ratio includes the sum of Cash, Net Accounts Receivable, and Inventory in the numerator

_____ 9. Earnings per share indicates the net income earned for each share of common and preferred stock.

_____ 10. A signal of financial trouble may include cash flow from operations being lower than net income from period to period.

Multiple Choice

1. **Horizontal analysis can be described as which of the following?**
   a. Percentage changes in various financial statement amounts from year to year
   b. The changes in individual financial statement amounts as a percentage of some related total
   c. The change in key financial statement ratios over a certain time frame or horizon
   d. None of the above

2. **Trend percentages can be considered a form of which of the following?**
   a. Ratio analysis
   b. Vertical analysis
   c. Profitability analysis
   d. Horizontal analysis

3. In 2012, net sales were $1,600,000 and in 2013, net sales were $1,750,000. How is the percent change calculated?
   a. Divide $1,600,000 by $1,750,000
   b. Divide $1,750,000 by $1,600,000
   c. Divide $150,000 by $1,750,000
   d. Divide $150,000 by $1,600,000

4. Vertical analysis can be described as which of the following?
   a. Percentage changes in the balances shown in comparative financial statements
   b. The change in key financial statement ratios over a specified period of time
   c. The dollar amount of the change in various financial statement amounts from year to year
   d. Individual financial statement items expressed as a percentage of a base (which represents 100%)

5. What is the base that is used when performing vertical analysis on an income statement?
   a. Net sales
   b. Gross sales
   c. Gross profit
   d. Total expenses

6. What is the base that is used when performing vertical analysis on a balance sheet?
   a. Total assets
   b. Stockholders' equity
   c. Total liabilities
   d. Net assets

7. Which ratio measures the ability to pay long-term debt?
   a. Rate of return on net sales
   b. Earnings per share
   c. Times-interest-earned ratio
   d. Acid-test (quick) ratio

8. Which of the following would be most helpful in the comparison of different-sized companies?
   a. Performing horizontal analysis
   b. Looking at the amount of income earned by each company
   c. Comparing working capital balances
   d. Preparing common-size financial statements

9. Which ratio(s) help(s) in the analysis of working capital?
   a. Current ratio
   b. Acid-test ratio
   c. Debt ratio
   d. Both a and b are correct.

10. Assume that collections from customers on account are being received faster. Which of the following would be true?
    a. The accounts receivable turnover would be higher.
    b. The days' sales in receivables would be higher.
    c. The current ratio would be higher.
    d. None of the above

Quick Exercises

15-1. Selected items from the balance sheet and income statement follow for Susan Company for 2012 and 2013.

Requirement

1. Calculate the amount of the change and the percentage of change for each item.

	2013	2012	$ Change	% Change
Cash	$141,000	$100,000	_____	_____
Accounts receivable	113,000	125,000	_____	_____
Merchandise inventory	70,000	85,000	_____	_____
Accounts payable	63,500	50,000	_____	_____
Sales	150,000	135,000	_____	_____
Cost of goods sold	94,000	87,500	_____	_____

15-2. The income statement for Snack Corporation for the year ended December 31, 2013, follows:

SNACK CORPORATION Income Statement Year Ended December 31, 2013		
Net sales		$750,000
Expenses:		
Cost of goods sold	$268,500	
Selling expenses	45,000	
Depreciation expense	49,300	
Salary expense	35,000	
Rent expense	30,000	
Total expenses		427,800
Net income		$322,200

Requirements

1. Prepare a vertical analysis of the income statement showing appropriate percentages for each item listed.

SNACK CORPORATION
Vertical Analysis of Income Statement
Year Ended December 31, 2013

2. What additional information would you need to determine whether these percentages are good or bad?

15-3. Using the following data for Luminous Corporation for 2013, calculate the ratios that follow:

Market price per share of common stock at 12/31/13	$ 9.00
Net income	65,000
Number of common shares outstanding	25,000
Dividend per share of common stock	$ 1.10

a. earnings per share of common stock

b. price/earnings ratio

c. dividend yield

15-4. Match the function with the appropriate ratio.

Functions:

a. Gives the amount of net income earned for each share of the company's common stock

b. Measures the number of times operating income can cover interest expense

c. Shows ability to pay all current liabilities if they come due immediately

d. Shows the percentage of a stock's market value returned to stockholders as dividends each period

e. Measures ability to collect cash from credit customers

f. Measures ability to pay current liabilities with current assets

g. Indicates the market price of $1 of earnings

h. Measures the difference between current assets and current liabilities

i. Indicates percentage of assets financed with debt

j. Shows the percentage of each sales dollar earned as net income

Ratios:

1. _____ Debt ratio

2. _____ Times-interest-earned ratio

3. _____ Rate of return on net sales

4. _____ Working capital

5. _____ Price/earnings ratio

6. _____ Acid-test ratio

7. _____ Earnings per share of common stock

8. _____ Current ratio

9. _____ Dividend yield

10. _____ Accounts receivable turnover

15-5. Following are selected data from the comparative income statement and balance sheet for Hontwal Corporation for the years ended December 31, 2013 and 2012:

	2013	2012
Net sales (all on credit)	$107,600	$83,000
Cost of goods sold	53,500	52,500
Gross profit	44,700	40,500
Income from operations	16,300	15,000
Interest expense	3,100	3,500
Net income	9,800	9,000
Cash	8,800	8,500
Accounts receivable, net	10,700	12,500
Inventory	20,000	26,000
Prepaid expenses	1,000	900
Total current assets	39,400	46,900
Total long-term assets	50,000	67,000
Total current liabilities	32,000	44,500
Total long-term liabilities	11,000	39,800
Common stock, no par*	10,000	10,000
Retained earnings	25,400	19,600

*NOTE: Two thousand shares of common stock have been issued and outstanding since the company started operations. During the entire fiscal year ended December 31, 2013, the stock was selling for $52 per share.

Requirement

1. Calculate the following ratios at December 31, 2013:

    a. Acid-test ratio

    b. Inventory turnover

    c. Days' sales in receivables

    d. Book value per share of common stock

    e. Earnings per share

    f. Rate of return on total assets

    g. Times-interest-earned ratio

    h. Current ratio

    i. Debt ratio

j. Days in inventory

k. Gross profit percentage

l. Accounts receivable turnover

m. Debt to equity ratio

n. Rate of return on net sales

o. Asset turnover ratio

p. Rate of return on common stockholders' equity

q. Price/earnings ratio

Do It Yourself! Question 1

Tykes, Inc., had the following information at December 31, 2013:

TYKES, INC.
Balance Sheet
December 31, 2013 and 2012

	2013	2012
Assets		
Cash	$400	$300
Accounts receivable	290	350
Inventory	150	220
Total assets	$840	$870
Liabilities		
Accounts payable	140	75
Loans payable	450	600
Total liabilities	590	675
Stockholders' Equity		
Common stock	40	40
Retained earnings	210	155
Total stockholders' equity	250	195
Total liabilities and equity	$840	$870

TYKES, INC.
Income Statement
Years Ended December 31, 2013 and 2012

	2013	2012
Sales revenue	$1,200	$1,000
Less cost of goods sold	800	600
Gross profit	400	400
Insurance expense	200	190
Interest expense	60	80
Net income	$ 140	$ 130

At December 31, 2011, Tykes's inventory was $200 million and total equity was $165 million.

Requirements

1. Prepare a horizontal analysis of Tykes's financial statements.

<table>
<tr><td colspan="5" align="center">TYKES, INC.
Horizontal Analysis of Balance Sheet
December 31, 2013 and 2012</td></tr>
<tr><td></td><td>2013</td><td>2012</td><td colspan="2">Increase (Decrease)</td></tr>
<tr><td></td><td></td><td></td><td>Amount</td><td>Percent</td></tr>
<tr><td align="center">Assets</td><td></td><td></td><td></td><td></td></tr>
<tr><td>Cash</td><td>$400</td><td>$300</td><td></td><td></td></tr>
<tr><td>Accounts receivable</td><td>290</td><td>350</td><td></td><td></td></tr>
<tr><td>Inventory</td><td>150</td><td>220</td><td></td><td></td></tr>
<tr><td>Total assets</td><td>$840</td><td>$870</td><td></td><td></td></tr>
<tr><td align="center">Liabilities</td><td></td><td></td><td></td><td></td></tr>
<tr><td>Accounts payable</td><td>140</td><td>75</td><td></td><td></td></tr>
<tr><td>Loans payable</td><td>450</td><td>600</td><td></td><td></td></tr>
<tr><td>Total liabilities</td><td>590</td><td>675</td><td></td><td></td></tr>
<tr><td align="center">Stockholders' Equity</td><td></td><td></td><td></td><td></td></tr>
<tr><td>Common stock</td><td>40</td><td>40</td><td></td><td></td></tr>
<tr><td>Retained earnings</td><td>210</td><td>155</td><td></td><td></td></tr>
<tr><td>Total stockholders' equity</td><td>250</td><td>195</td><td></td><td></td></tr>
<tr><td>Total liabilities and equity</td><td>$840</td><td>$870</td><td></td><td></td></tr>
</table>

<table>
<tr><td colspan="5" align="center">TYKES, INC.
Horizontal Analysis of Comparative Income Statement
Years Ended December 31, 2013 and 2012</td></tr>
<tr><td></td><td>2013</td><td>2012</td><td colspan="2">Increase (Decrease)</td></tr>
<tr><td></td><td></td><td></td><td>Amount</td><td>Percent</td></tr>
<tr><td>Sales revenue</td><td>$1,200</td><td>$1,000</td><td></td><td></td></tr>
<tr><td>Less cost of goods sold</td><td>800</td><td>600</td><td></td><td></td></tr>
<tr><td>Gross profit</td><td>400</td><td>400</td><td></td><td></td></tr>
<tr><td>Insurance expense</td><td>200</td><td>190</td><td></td><td></td></tr>
<tr><td>Interest expense</td><td>60</td><td>80</td><td></td><td></td></tr>
<tr><td>Net income</td><td>$ 140</td><td>$ 130</td><td></td><td></td></tr>
</table>

2 Perform a vertical analysis of financial statements

3 Prepare and use common-size financial statements

2. Prepare a vertical analysis of Tykes's financial statements.

TYKES, INC.
Vertical Analysis of Balance Sheet
December 31, 2013 and 2012

	2013	2013 %	2012	2012 %
Assets				
Cash	$400		$300	
Accounts receivable	290		350	
Inventory	150		220	
Total assets	$840		$870	
Liabilities				
Accounts payable	140		75	
Loans payable	450		600	
Total liabilities	590		675	
Stockholders' Equity				
Common stock	40		40	
Retained earnings	210		155	
Total stockholders' equity	250		195	
Total liabilities and equity	$840		$870	

TYKES, INC.
Vertical Analysis of Comparative Income Statement
Years Ended December 31, 2013 and 2012

	2013	2013 %	2012	2012 %
Net sales revenue	$1,200		$1,000	
Less cost of goods sold	800		600	
Gross profit	400		400	
Insurance expense	200		190	
Interest expense	60		80	
Net income	$ 140		$ 130	

4 Compute the standard financial ratios

3. Calculate Tykes's inventory turnover and rate of return on stockholders' equity ratios for both years.

Quick Practice Solutions

True/False

<u> T </u> 1. It is generally considered more useful to know the percentage change in financial statement amounts from year to year than to know the absolute dollar amount of their change. (p. 723)

<u> T </u> 2. Benchmarking may be done against an industry average or against a key competitor. (p. 730)

<u> F </u> 3. Vertical analysis of financial statements reveals changes in items on the financial statements over time.

        False—*Horizontal* analysis of financial statements reveals changes in items on the financial statements over time. (p. 727)

<u> F </u> 4. Inventory turnover is the ratio of average inventory to cost of goods sold.

        False—Inventory turnover is the ratio of cost of goods sold to average inventory. (p. 735)

<u> T </u> 5. Book value per share of common stock has no relationship to market value. (p. 743)

<u> F </u> 6. A high current ratio means that a company's current assets represent a relatively large portion (or ratio) of total liabilities.

        False—A high current ratio means that a company's current assets represent a relatively large portion (or ratio) of total *current liabilities*. (p. 733)

<u> F </u> 7. The debt ratio measures the ability to pay current liabilities.

        False—The debt ratio measures the ability to pay *long-term debt*. (p. 737)

<u> F </u> 8. The acid-test (quick) ratio includes the sum of Cash, Net Accounts Receivable, and Inventory in the numerator.

        False—The acid-test (quick) ratio includes the sum of Cash, Short-Term Investments, and Net Receivables. (p. 734)

<u> F </u> 9. Earnings per share indicates the net income earned for each share of common and preferred stock.

        False—Earnings per share indicates the net income earned for each share of the company's *common* stock. (p. 741)

<u> T </u> 10. A signal of financial trouble may include cash flow from operations being lower than net income from period to period. (p. 744)

Multiple Choice

1. Horizontal analysis can be described as which of the following? (p. 723)
   a. Percentage changes in various financial statement amounts from year to year
   b. The changes in individual financial statement amounts as a percentage of some related total
   c. The change in key financial statement ratios over a certain time frame or horizon
   d. None of the above

2. Trend percentages can be considered a form of which of the following? (p. 726)
   a. Ratio analysis
   b. Vertical analysis
   c. Profitability analysis
   d. Horizontal analysis

3. In 2012, net sales were $1,600,000 and in 2013, net sales were $1,750,000. How is the percent change calculated? (p. 724)
   a. Divide $1,600,000 by $1,750,000
   b. Divide $1,750,000 by $1,600,000
   c. Divide $150,000 by $1,750,000
   d. Divide $150,000 by $1,600,000

4. Vertical analysis can be described as which of the following? (p. 737)
   a. Percentage changes in the balances shown in comparative financial statements
   b. The change in key financial statement ratios over a specified period of time
   c. The dollar amount of the change in various financial statement amounts from year to year
   d. Individual financial statement items expressed as a percentage of a base (which represents 100%)

5. What is the base that is used when performing vertical analysis on an income statement? (p. 727)
   a. Net sales
   b. Gross sales
   c. Gross profit
   d. Total expenses

6. What is the base that is used when performing vertical analysis on a balance sheet? (p. 728)
   a. Total assets
   b. Stockholders' equity
   c. Total liabilities
   d. Net assets

7. Which ratio measures the ability to pay long-term debt? (p. 738)
   a. Rate of return on net sales
   b. Earnings per share
   c. Times-interest-earned ratio
   d. Acid-test (quick) ratio

8. Which of the following would be most helpful in the comparison of different-sized companies? (p. 729)
a. Performing horizontal analysis
b. Looking at the amount of income earned by each company
c. Comparing working capital balances
d. Preparing common-size financial statements

9. Which ratio(s) help(s) in the analysis of working capital? (p. 733)
a. Current ratio
b. Acid-test ratio
c. Debt ratio
d. Both a and b are correct.

10. Assume that collections from customers on account are being received faster. Which of the following would be true? (p. 737)
a. The accounts receivable turnover would be higher.
b. The days' sales in receivables would be higher.
c. The current ratio would be higher.
d. None of the above

Quick Exercises

15-1. Selected items from the balance sheet and income statement follow for Susan Company for 2012 and 2013. (p. 724)

Requirement

1. Calculate the amount of the change and the percentage of change for each item.

	2013	2012	$ Change	% Change
Cash	$141,000	$100,000	$41,000	41.0%
Accounts receivable	113,000	125,000	(12,000)	(9.6)
Merchandise inventory	70,000	85,000	(15,000)	(17.6)
Accounts payable	63,500	50,000	13,500	27.0
Sales	150,000	135,000	15,000	11.1
Cost of goods sold	94,000	87,500	6,500	9.6

15-2. The income statement for Snack Corporation for the year ended December 31, 2013, follows: (p. 727)

SNACK CORPORATION
Income Statement
Year Ended December 31, 2013

Net sales		$750,000
Expenses:		
Cost of goods sold	$268,500	
Selling expenses	45,000	
Depreciation expense	49,300	
Salary expense	35,000	
Rent expense	30,000	
Total expenses		427,800
Net income		$233,200

Requirements

1. Prepare a vertical analysis of the income statement showing appropriate percentages for each item listed.

SNACK CORPORATION
Vertical Analysis of Income Statement
Year Ended December 31, 2013

	Amount	Percentage
Net sales	$750,000	100.0%
Expenses		
Cost of goods sold	268,500	35.8
Selling expenses	45,000	6.0
Depreciation expense	49,300	6.6
Salary expense	35,000	4.7
Rent expense	30,000	4.0
Total expenses	427,800	57.1
Net income	$322,200	42.9%

2. What additional information would you need to determine whether these percentages are good or bad?

Additional information to determine whether these percentages are good or bad might include:
- industry averages to compare to Snack Corporation
- the change in each line item percentage over a relevant period of time

15-3. Using the following data for Luminous Corporation for 2013, calculate the ratios that follow: (pp. 733–743)

Market price per share of common stock at 12/31/13	$ 9.00
Net income	65,000
Number of common shares outstanding	25,000
Dividend per share of common stock	1.10

a. earnings per share of common stock

$$\$65,000/25,000 = \$2.60$$

b. price/earnings ratio

$$\$9.00/\$2.60 = 3.5$$

c. dividend yield

$$\$1.10/\$9.00 = 0.12$$

15-4. Match the function with the appropriate ratio. (pp. 733–746)

Functions:

a. Gives the amount of net income earned for each share of the company's common stock
b. Measures the number of times operating income can cover interest expense
c. Shows ability to pay all current liabilities if they come due immediately
d. Shows the percentage of a stock's market value returned to stockholders as dividends for each period
e. Measures ability to collect cash from credit customers
f. Measures ability to pay current liabilities with current assets
g. Indicates the market price of $1 of earnings
h. Measures the difference between current assets and current liabilities
i. Indicates percentage of assets financed with debt
j. Shows the percentage of each sales dollar earned as net income

Ratios:

1. _i_ Debt ratio
2. _b_ Times-interest-earned ratio
3. _j_ Rate of return on net sales
4. _h_ Working capital
5. _g_ Price/earnings ratio

6. __c__ Acid-test ratio
7. __a__ Earnings per share of common stock
8. __f__ Current ratio
9. __d__ Dividend yield
10. __e__ Accounts receivable turnover

15-5.   Following are selected data from the comparative income statement and balance sheet for Hontwal Corporation for the years ended December 31, 2013 and 2012: (pp. 733–743)

	2013	2012
Net sales (all on credit)	$107,600	$83,000
Cost of goods sold	53,500	52,500
Gross profit	44,700	40,500
Income from operations	16,300	15,000
Interest expense	3,100	3,500
Net income	9,800	9,000
Cash	8,800	8,500
Accounts receivable, net	10,700	12,500
Inventory	20,000	26,000
Prepaid expenses	1,000	900
Total current assets	39,400	46,900
Total long-term assets	50,000	67,000
Total current liabilities	32,000	44,500
Total long-term liabilities	11,000	39,800
Common stock, no par*	10,000	10,000
Retained earnings	25,400	19,600

*NOTE: Two thousand shares of common stock have been issued and outstanding since the company started operations. During the entire fiscal year ended December 31, 2013, the stock was selling for $52 per share.

Requirement

1. Calculate the following ratios at December 31, 2013:

   a.   Acid-test ratio

   ($8,800 + $10,700)/$32,000 = 0.61

b. Inventory turnover

$$\frac{\$53,500}{(\$20,000 + \$26,000)/2} = 2.33$$

c. Days' sales in receivables

$$\frac{(\$10,700 + \$12,500)/2}{\$107,600/365} = 39.3 \text{ days}$$

d. Book value per share of common stock

$$\frac{\$10,000 + \$25,400}{2,000} = \$17.70$$

e. Earnings per share

$$\$9,800/2,000 = \$4.90 \text{ per share}$$

f. Rate of return on total assets

$$\frac{\$9,800 + \$3,100}{(\$39,400 + \$50,000 + \$46,900 + \$67,000)/2} = 0.13$$

g. Times-interest-earned ratio

$$\frac{\$16,300}{\$3,100} = 5.26 \text{ times}$$

h. Current ratio

$$\frac{\$39,400}{\$32,000} = 1.23$$

i. Debt ratio

$$\frac{\$32,000 + \$11,000}{\$39,400 + \$50,000} = 0.48$$

j. Days in inventory

$$\frac{365}{2.33} = 156.65$$

k. Gross profit percentage

$$\frac{\$44,700}{\$107,600} = 41.5\%$$

l. Accounts receivable turnover

$$\frac{\$107,600}{(\$12,500 + \$10,700)/2} = 9.28$$

m. Debt to equity ratio

$$\frac{(\$32,000 + \$11,000)}{(\$10,000 + \$25,400)} = 1.21$$

n. Rate of return on net sales

$$\frac{\$9,800}{\$107,600} = 9.1\%$$

o. Asset turnover ratio

$$\frac{\$107,600}{(\$39,400 + \$50,000 + \$46,900 + \$67,000)/2} = 1.06$$

p. Rate of return on common stockholders' equity

$$\frac{\$9,800}{[(\$10,000 + \$25,400) + \$10,000 + \$19,600]/2} = 30.2\%$$

q. Price/earnings ratio

$$\frac{\$52}{(\$9,800/2,000)} = \$10.61$$

Do It Yourself! Question 1 Solutions

Requirements

1. Prepare a horizontal analysis for Tykes's financial statements.

TYKES, INC.
Horizontal Analysis of Balance Sheet
December 31, 2013 and 2012

	2013	2012	Increase Amount	(Decrease) Percent
Assets				
Cash	$400	$300	$100	33.3%
Accounts receivable	290	350	(60)	(17.1)
Inventory	150	220	(70)	(31.8)
Total assets	$840	$870	$ (30)	(3.4)
Liabilities				
Accounts payable	140	75	65	86.7
Loans payable	450	600	(150)	(25.0)
Total liabilities	$590	$675	(85)	(12.6)
Stockholders' Equity				
Common stock	40	40	0	0.0
Retained earnings	210	155	55	35.5
Total stockholders' equity	$250	$195	55	28.2
Total liabilities and equity	$840	$870	$ (30)	(3.4)%

TYKES, INC.
Horizontal Analysis of Comparative Income Statement
Years Ended December 31, 2013 and 2012

	2013	2012	Increase Amount	(Decrease) Percent
Sales revenue	$1,200	$1,000	$200	20.0%
Less cost of goods sold	800	600	$200	33.3
Gross profit	400	400	0	0.0
Insurance expense	200	190	(10)	5.3
Interest expense	60	80	(20)	(25.0)
Net income	$ 140	$ 130	$ 10	7.7%

2. Prepare a vertical analysis for Tykes's financial statements.

TYKES, INC.
Vertical Analysis of Balance Sheet
December 31, 2013 and 2012

	2013	2013 %	2012	2012 %
Assets				
Cash	$400	47.6%	$300	34.5%
Accounts receivable	290	34.5	350	40.2
Inventory	150	17.9	220	25.3
Total assets	$840	100.0%	$870	100.0%
Liabilities				
Accounts payable	140	16.7%	75	8.6%
Loans payable	450	53.5	600	69.0
Total liabilities	590	70.2	675	77.6
Stockholders' Equity				
Common stock	40	4.8	40	4.6
Retained earnings	210	25.0	155	17.8
Total stockholders' equity	250	29.8	195	22.4
Total liabilities and equity	$840	100.0%	$870	100.0%

TYKES, INC.
Vertical Analysis of Comparative Income Statement
Years Ended December 31, 2013 and 2012

	2013	2013 %	2012	2012 %
Net sales revenue	$1,200	100.0%	$1,000	100.0%
Less cost of goods sold	800	66.7	600	60.0
Gross profit	400	33.3	400	40.0
Insurance expense	200	16.6	190	19.0
Interest expense	60	5.0	80	8.0
Net income	$ 140	11.7%	$ 130	13.0%

3. Calculate Tykes's inventory turnover and rate of return on stockholders' equity ratios for both years.

$$2013 \text{ Inventory turnover} = \frac{\$800}{\frac{1}{2}(220 + 150)}$$

$$= 4.3 \text{ times}$$

$$2012 \text{ Inventory turnover} = \frac{\$600}{\frac{1}{2}(200 + 220)}$$

$$= 2.9 \text{ times}$$

$$2013 \text{ Rate of return on stockholders' equity} = \frac{\$140 - \$0}{\frac{1}{2}(\$195 + \$250)}$$

$$= 62.9\%$$

$$2012 \text{ Rate of return on stockholders' equity} = \frac{\$130 - \$0}{\frac{1}{2}(\$165 + \$195)}$$

$$= 72.2\%$$

The Power of Practice

For more practice using the skills learned in this chapter, visit MyAccountingLab. There you will find algorithmically generated questions that are based on these Demo Docs and your main textbook's Review and Assess Your Progress sections.

Go to MyAccountingLab and follow these steps:

1. Direct your URL to www.myaccountinglab.com.
2. Log in using your name and password.
3. Click the MyAccountingLab link.
4. Click Study Plan in the left navigation bar.
5. From the table of contents, select Chapter 15, Financial Statement Analysis.
6. Click a link to work tutorial exercises.

16 Introduction to Management Accounting

WHAT YOU PROBABLY ALREADY KNOW

If you have ever baked a cake, you probably already know that there are ingredients that are required to produce the desired result. You may use a mix that only requires eggs and water, or you may follow a recipe where you must add in all of the ingredients separately. Whichever it may be, you know that the more ingredients necessary to make the cake, the more costly it is. Assume you ask your sister to apply the icing because you're short on time and offer to pay her $5. The amount paid for her services (labor) adds to the cost of the cake. It is certain that without utilities to run the mixer and the oven, you could not make the cake. In business, this would be referred to as overhead. So, it seems that there is a cost of materials, labor, and overhead to make the cake. In this chapter, we will study these three components of cost for manufacturers.

Learning Objectives/Success Keys

1 Distinguish management accounting from financial accounting.

Management accounting provides financial and nonfinancial information to managers and other internal users of information. The data help management plan and control the operations of the business. **Financial accounting** provides financial information to users outside of the business such as creditors, investors, and governmental agencies. *Review Financial Accounting versus Managerial Accounting in Exhibit 16-2 (p. 776).*

2 Identify trends in the business environment and the role of management accountability.

Some of the changes that have taken place over recent years include an increasing shift toward a service economy, global competition, and increasing opportunities for worldwide expansion, time-based competition (including ERP, e-commerce, and JIT management), and an increased focus on promoting continuous improvement in the quality of goods and services produced (total quality management). *Review the section called Today's Business Environment in the main text, as well as management's accountability to stakeholders in Exhibit 16-1 (p. 774).*

3 Apply ethical standards to decision making.

It is more important than ever to be mindful of making ethical judgments. Professional accounting associations have standards of ethical conduct, as do most other professions. In addition, employees are often provided with a code of ethics from their employer. Management accountants are required to maintain their professional competence, preserve the confidentiality of the information they handle, and act with integrity and objectivity. *Review the excerpt of the Institute of Management Accountants' Standards of ethical conduct in Exhibit 16-3 (p. 778).*

4 Classify costs and prepare an income statement for a service company.

All of the costs of a service company are considered period costs. **Period costs** include selling, general, and administrative costs that are included as expenses on the income statement in the period incurred. There is no inventory for a service company and therefore none of the costs incurred are inventoriable. Similarly, there is no cost of goods sold on the income statement. *Review the income statement for a service company in Exhibit 16-4 (p. 779).*

5 Classify costs and prepare an income statement for a merchandising company.

Some costs are **inventoriable product costs**, which are included in the cost of inventory on the balance sheet, until sold. These costs include the total cost of purchasing the inventory, plus the freight that may be required to obtain the goods. When the inventory is sold, it becomes cost of goods sold, one of the largest expenses on the income statement for a merchandising company. Recall from Chapter 5 the calculation of cost of goods sold for a periodic inventory system is to add beginning inventory, purchases, and freight in and subtract ending inventory. *Review the income statement for a merchandising company in Exhibit 16-5 (p. 781).*

6 Classify costs and prepare an income statement and statement of cost of goods manufactured for a manufacturing company.

Manufacturers have three stages and accounts for inventory: raw materials (including the components, ingredients, or parts used in manufacturing), work in process (including raw materials that have some degree of work done but are not completed), and finished goods (completed and ready for sale). The inventoriable product costs in finished goods for a manufacturing company include the elements of cost required to make the goods, including direct materials, direct labor, and manufacturing overhead.

As described under Objective 4, merchandisers consider the cost of purchases and freight in to determine the cost of goods sold. Because manufacturers don't purchase their inventory, the cost of the goods manufactured must be considered to calculate the cost of goods sold for manufacturers. The approach, similar to that used to calculate the cost of goods sold for a merchandiser, is to start with beginning inventory, add direct materials, labor, and manufacturing overhead, and subtract ending inventory. *Review the inventoriable product and period costs analysis in Exhibit 16-8 (p. 786). Also, review the income statement for a manufacturing company in Exhibit 16-7 (p. 786) and carefully study the schedule of cost of goods manufactured, which can be particularly troublesome, in Exhibit 16-10 (p. 788).*

Demo Doc 1

Introduction to Management Accounting

Learning Objectives 1–4

Dark Spray Tanning has hired you as their new management accountant. Data for the month ended April 30, 2013, are as follows:

Wages expense	$ 8,000
Supply expense	3,000
Utility expense	2,000
Rent expense	1,000
Service revenue	17,000

Requirements

1. Your new boss has heard of the term *management accountability*, but doesn't really understand what it means. Explain the concept of management accountability.

2. Explain to your boss the scope of information you can produce as a management accountant.

3. Prepare an income statement for Dark Spray Tanning for the month ended April 30, 2013.

4. In the month of May, Dark Spray decided to sell tanning spray. Based on the following data, prepare Dark Spray's income statement for the month ended May 31, 2013.

Wages expense	$11,000
Supply expense	3,000
Utility expense	2,000
Rent expense	1,000
Sales revenue	30,000*
Purchases	15,000
Ending inventory	6,000

* Assume that 100% of sales revenue is from selling tanning spray.

5. Suppose Dark Spray sold 900 bottles of tanning spray in the month of May. What is its cost per bottle?

Demo Doc 1 Solutions

Requirement 1

1 Distinguish management accounting from financial accounting

Your new boss has heard of the term management accountability, but doesn't really understand what it means. Explain the concept of management accountability.

Part 1	Part 2	Part 3	Part 4	Part 5	Demo Doc Complete

Management accountability is the idea that the manager is responsible for managing the resources of the organization. There are many groups and individuals, called stakeholders, who have an interest in an organization (that is, owners, creditors, customers, suppliers, and the various government organizations). To satisfy the needs of these stakeholders, managers are required to provide information that communicates the decisions made and the results obtained from these decisions.

Management accountability requires two forms of accounting:

- financial accounting for external reporting, and
- management accounting for internal planning, controlling, and decision making.

Remember, planning means choosing goals and deciding how to achieve them. Controlling means evaluating the results of business operations by comparing the actual results to the plan.

Requirement 2

2 Identify trends in the business environment and the role of management accountability

Explain to your boss the scope of information you can produce as a management accountant.

Part 1	Part 2	Part 3	Part 4	Part 5	Demo Doc Complete

Management accounting provides more detailed and timely information than financial accounting does. Managers use this information to

- identify ways to cut costs.
- set prices that will be competitive and yet yield profits.
- identify the most profitable products and customers so the sales force can focus on key profit makers.
- evaluate employees' job performance.

Requirement 3

4 Classify costs and prepare an income statement for a service company

Prepare an income statement for Dark Spray Tanning for the month ended April 30, 2013.

Part 1	Part 2	**Part 3**	Part 4	Part 5	Demo Doc Complete

As you recall from earlier chapters, an income statement reports the organization's revenues and expenses for a period of time.

Dark Spray is a service company, so all of its costs are period costs and it doesn't carry an inventory of product, so there is no cost of goods sold on its income statement. Period costs are costs incurred and expensed in the current accounting period.

Dark Spray's period costs include all expenses for the month of April (wages, supplies, utilities, and rent). Dark Spray's period costs are $8,000 + $3,000 + $2,000 + $1,000 = $14,000 for the month of April 2010.

Here is the income statement for Dark Spray for the month of April 2013.

DARK SPRAY TANNING Income Statement Month Ended April 30, 2013			
Service revenue		$17,000	100%
Expenses:			
Wages expense	$8,000		
Supply expense	3,000		
Utility expense	2,000		
Rent expense	1,000		
Total expenses		14,000	82%
Operating income		$ 3,000	18%

Notice that Dark Spray has no cost of goods sold because it is a service company. Its largest expense on the income statement is for employee salaries. Dark Spray also had an 18% profit margin for the month of April.

Requirement 4

In the month of May, Dark Spray decided to sell tanning spray. Based on the following data, prepare Dark Spray's income statement for the month ended May 31, 2013.

Wages expense	$11,000
Supply expense	3,000
Utility expense	2,000
Rent expense	1,000
Sales revenue	30,000*
Purchases	15,000
Ending inventory	6,000

* Assume that 100% of sales revenue is from selling tanning spray.

Part 1	Part 2	Part 3	**Part 4**	Part 5	Demo Doc Complete

5 Classify costs and prepare an income statement for a merchandising company

Because Dark Spray has purchased products from a supplier that they now resell, Dark Spray is now a merchandiser (retailer). Dark Spray now maintains an inventory.

Dark Spray's income statement will now have cost of goods sold as a major expense. Any product that is not sold in one period will be shown as an asset called merchandise inventory. Merchandise inventory is NOT an expense until it is sold—then the expense becomes cost of goods sold.

The goods available for sale are computed by adding purchases during the period to beginning inventory. Ending inventory is subtracted from cost of goods available for sale to get cost of goods sold. Cost of goods sold is subtracted from sales revenue to get gross profit. Consider the following formula:

	Beginning inventory
+	Purchases
	Goods available for Sale
−	Ending inventory
	Cost of goods sold

So in the case of Dark Spray

	Beginning inventory	$ 0
+	Purchases	15,000
	Goods available for sale	15,000
−	Ending inventory	6,000
	Cost of goods sold	$ 9,000

Subtract $9,000 from sales revenue of $30,000 for a gross profit of $21,000.

Here is Dark Spray's income statement for the month ended May 31, 2013:

DARK SPRAY TANNING
Income Statement
Month Ended May 31, 2013

Sales revenue		$30,000	100%
Cost of goods sold:			
Beginning inventory	$ 0		
Purchases	15,000		
Cost of goods available for sale	15,000		
Ending inventory	(6,000)		
Cost of goods sold		9,000	30%
Gross profit		21,000	70%
Operating expenses:			
Wages expense	11,000		
Supply expense	3,000		
Utility expense	2,000		
Rent expense	1,000	17,000	57%
Operating income		$ 4,000	13%

Gross profit is what remains from sales after the cost of goods sold is subtracted from sales revenue. Gross profit is then used to cover operating expenses and yield a profit (or loss). Managers want to keep an eye on the gross profit percentage, which is a measure of profitability, to make sure that it doesn't fluctuate too much from period to period.

In this case, Dark Spray had a gross profit percentage of 70% and a 13% profit margin. These are calculated as follows:

$$\text{Gross profit percentage} = \frac{\text{Gross profit}}{\text{Sales revenue}}$$

$$\text{Dark Sprays' Gross profit percentage} = \frac{\$21,000}{\$30,000}$$

$$= 70\%$$

$$\text{Profit margin} = \frac{\text{Operating income}}{\text{Sales revenue}}$$

$$\text{Dark Sprays' profit margin} = \frac{\$4,000}{\$30,000}$$

$$= 13\%$$

What this means is that Dark Spray generates $0.70 from each dollar of revenue for the period, which is used to cover its operating expenses and then generate operating income.

Profit margin represents the percentage of revenue that the company keeps as earnings. In this case, Dark Spray generates $0.13 from every revenue dollar as income. Managers watch this as well to make sure that it doesn't drop from period to period. Even if overall earnings increase, it's still possible for a company's profit margin to diminish if, for example, costs increase at a rate greater than sales. This would raise a flag to managers that they may need to exhibit greater control over costs.

Requirement 5

Suppose Dark Spray sold 900 bottles of tanning spray in the month of May. What is its cost per bottle?

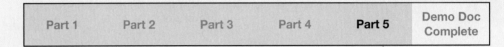

Part 1	Part 2	Part 3	Part 4	**Part 5**	Demo Doc Complete

Cost per unit is determined by dividing total cost by the number of units. Knowing the costs the company incurs per unit it sells helps managers make pricing decisions. They obviously want to make sure they are charging their customers enough to cover their own costs and generate a profit. To calculate the cost per unit

$$\text{Cost per unit} = \frac{\text{Total cost of goods sold}}{\text{Total number of units sold}}$$

Dark Spray wants to know its cost for each bottle of tanning spray it sells. In this case, the total cost of selling 900 bottles is $9,000. So

$$\text{Cost per bottle} = \frac{\$9,000}{900 \text{ bottles}}$$
$$= \$10 \text{ per bottle}$$

Managers will use the per-unit cost information to help them make better decisions. Knowing that their per-unit cost is $10, Dark Spray managers may decide they need to adjust their price.

Part 1	Part 2	Part 3	Part 4	Part 5	**Demo Doc Complete**

Demo Doc 2

Manufacturing Companies

Learning Objectives 5, 6

Chase Toys produces toys for dogs. The following information was available for the month ended November 30, 2013 (assume no beginning or ending raw materials inventory):

Sales revenue	$106,500
Direct materials used	32,000
Direct labor	16,000
Manufacturing overhead*	17,000
Beginning work in process	8,000
Ending work in process	6,000
Operating expenses	32,000
Finished goods, Nov 1, 2013	4,000
Finished goods, Nov 30, 2013	7,200

* All indirect production costs are included in manufacturing overhead.

Requirements

1. Prepare a schedule of cost of goods manufactured for the month ended November 30, 2013.

2. Prepare an income statement for the month ended November 30, 2013.

3. At an internal Chase Toys meeting, you learned that Chase Toys has developed a new product that is expected to produce record profits. Before Chase Toys went public with this product, you advised your girlfriend to invest in Chase Toys. Which standard of ethical conduct for management accountants did you violate? Explain.

Demo Doc 2 Solutions

Requirement 1

6 Classify costs and prepare an income statement and statement of cost of goods manufactured for a manufacturing company

Prepare a schedule of cost of goods manufactured for the month ended November 30, 2013.

Part 1	Part 2	Part 3	Demo Doc Complete

The cost of goods manufactured summarizes the manufacturing activities that took place for the month of November 2010.

The three manufacturing costs—direct materials, direct labor, and manufacturing overhead—are added together to get the total manufacturing costs incurred during November ($32,000 + $16,000 + $17,000 = $65,000). These are added to beginning inventory to yield the total accountable manufacturing costs. Ending inventory is then subtracted from total accountable manufacturing costs to get cost of goods manufactured. Consider the following formula:

Beginning work in process

+ Direct materials used

+ Direct labor used

+ Factory / Manufacturing overhead applied

Current manufacturing costs

− Ending work in process

Cost of goods manufactured

So for Chase Toys

Beginning work in process	$ 8,000
+ Direct materials used	32,000
+ Direct labor used	16,000
+ Factory / Manufacturing overhead applied	17,000
Current manufacturing costs	73,000
− Ending work in process	6,000
Cost of goods manufactured	$67,000

Here is Chase Toys' schedule of cost of goods manufactured for the month ended November 30, 2013:

CHASE TOYS
Schedule of Cost of Goods Manufactured
Month Ended November 30, 2013

Beginning work in process inventory		$ 8,000
Add: Direct materials used	$32,000	
Direct labor	16,000	
Manufacturing overhead	17,000	
Total manufacturing costs incurred during the period		65,000
Total accountable manufacturing costs		73,000
Less: Ending work in process		(6,000)
Cost of goods manufactured		$67,000

Notice the similarity between calculating cost of goods manufactured and calculating cost of goods sold for a merchandiser: Start with the beginning inventory balance, increase it for the additions during the period, and subtract the ending inventory balance.

The cost of goods manufactured becomes part of the finished goods inventory, which will be shown as an asset until the period in which it is sold, when it flows to cost of goods sold.

Note that the inventoriable product costs in Finished Goods for a manufacturing company include the elements of cost required to make the goods. These include the following:

- **Direct materials**—Physical components required to manufacture the product and that can be traced directly to the finished good.
- **Direct labor**—Labor of employees who work directly on the finished product.
- **Manufacturing overhead**—Includes all of the manufacturing costs other than direct materials and direct labor. These typically include factory costs such as insurance, depreciation, and utilities. Overhead also includes **indirect materials** (low value materials that cannot be traced directly to a finished product) and **indirect labor** (supportive factory labor of janitors, managers, and equipment operators that cannot be traced directly to a finished product).

Requirement 2

Prepare an income statement for the month ended November 30, 2013.

Part 1	**Part 2**	Part 3	Demo Doc Complete

6 Classify costs and prepare an income statement and statement of cost of goods manufactured for a manufacturing company

The Cost of Goods Manufactured account summarizes the activities that take place in a manufacturing plant over a period of time. It represents the manufacturing cost of goods that Chase Toys finished during November.

Cost of goods sold is computed as follows:

Beginning inventory	$ 4,000
+ Cost of goods manufactured	67,000
Cost of goods available for sale	71,000
− Ending inventory	7,200
Cost of goods sold	$63,800

Following is Chase Toys' income statement for the month of November:

CHASE TOYS
Income Statement
Month Ended November 30, 2013

Sales revenue		$106,500	100%
Cost of goods sold:			
Beginning finished goods inventory	$ 4,000		
Cost of goods manufactured	67,000		
Cost of goods available for sale	71,000		
Ending finished goods inventory	(7,200)		
Cost of goods sold		63,800	60%
Gross profit		42,700	40%
Operating expenses		32,000	30%
Operating income		$ 10,700	10%

Notice how the cost of goods manufactured amount computed on the schedule in requirement 1 is part of finished goods here—the only inventory that is ready to sell. It becomes part of cost of goods sold on the income statement.

Note that Finished Goods for a manufacturer is like the Inventory account for a merchandiser. In both cases, these accounts represent the inventory that is complete and available to be sold.

Requirement 3

3 Apply ethical standards to decision making

At an internal Chase Toys meeting, you learned that Chase Toys has developed a new product that is expected to produce record profits. Before Chase Toys went public with this product, you advised your girlfriend to invest in Chase Toys. Which standard of ethical conduct for management accountants did you violate? Explain.

Part 1	Part 2	**Part 3**	Demo Doc Complete

Providing confidential company information to your girlfriend is a clear violation of the **confidentiality standard**. Employees must refrain from disclosing confidential information acquired in the course of work except when authorized, unless legally obligated to do so.

Part 1	Part 2	Part 3	**Demo Doc Complete**

Quick Practice Questions

True/False

_____ 1. A system that integrates all of a company's worldwide functions, departments, and data is called supply-chain management.

_____ 2. A budget is a quantitative expression of a plan that helps managers coordinate and implement the plan.

_____ 3. Goods that are partway through the manufacturing process, but not yet complete, are referred to as materials inventory.

_____ 4. Manufacturers use labor, plants, and equipment to convert raw materials into new finished products.

_____ 5. Period costs are operating costs that are expensed in the period in which the goods are sold.

_____ 6. Indirect labor and indirect materials are part of manufacturing overhead.

_____ 7. Trends in the modern business environment include the shift to a service economy and the rise of the global marketplace.

_____ 8. Management has a responsibility to meet regulatory obligations to federal and local government agencies.

_____ 9. Total quality management applies only to manufacturers and promotes the creation of superior products.

_____ 10. The cost of goods manufactured is equal to the sum of direct materials used, direct labor, and manufacturing overhead.

Multiple Choice

1. The primary goal of financial accounting is to provide information to which of the following?
   a. Investors
   b. Creditors
   c. Company managers
   d. Both a and b

2. Which of the following is true about management accounting?
   a. Management accounting provides information to customers.
   b. Management accounting provides information that is required to be audited by certified public accountants.
   c. Management accounting primarily focuses on reporting on the company as a whole on a quarterly or annual basis.
   d. Management accounting is not restricted by GAAP.

3. **Manufacturers may have which accounts on their balance sheet?**
   a. Materials, Work in Process, and Finished Goods
   b. Merchandise, Materials, and Finished Goods
   c. Direct Materials, Direct Labor, and Manufacturing Overhead
   d. Work in Process, Materials, and Manufacturing Overhead

4. **In which category would glue or fasteners to manufacture a table be included?**
   a. Direct materials
   b. Manufacturing overhead
   c. Period costs
   d. Indirect labor

5. **Inventoriable product costs include which of the following?**
   a. Marketing costs
   b. Costs of direct materials, direct labor, and manufacturing overhead used to produce a product
   c. Costs of direct materials and direct labor used to produce a product
   d. Period costs, overhead, and direct labor

6. **When do inventoriable costs become expenses?**
   a. When the manufacturing process begins
   b. When the manufacturing process is completed
   c. When the direct materials are purchased
   d. When the units in inventory are sold

7. **In which category would selling and administrative costs be included?**
   a. Direct materials
   b. Manufacturing overhead
   c. Period costs
   d. Work in process

8. **All *except* which of the following are manufacturing overhead costs?**
   a. Materials used directly in the manufacturing process of the product
   b. Insurance on factory equipment
   c. Salaries of production supervisors
   d. Property tax on factory building

9. **Cost of goods sold for a manufacturer equals cost of goods manufactured plus which of the following?**
   a. Beginning work in process inventory less ending work in process inventory
   b. Ending work in process inventory less beginning work in process inventory
   c. Beginning finished goods inventory less ending finished goods inventory
   d. Ending finished goods inventory less beginning finished goods inventory

10. **At the beginning of 2013, the Taylor Company's Work in Process Inventory account had a balance of $30,000. During 2013, $68,000 of direct materials were used in production, and $66,000 of direct labor costs were incurred. Manufacturing overhead in 2013 amounted to $90,000. The cost of goods manufactured was $220,000 in 2013. What is the balance in the work in process inventory on December 31, 2013?**
    a. $34,000
    b. $24,000
    c. $66,000
    d. $6,000

Quick Exercises

16-1. Use the correct number to categorize each item that follows:

1. Direct materials
2. Selling and general expenses
3. Manufacturing overhead
4. Direct labor

a. _____ wages of assembly line personnel

b. _____ advertising expense

c. _____ rent expense on factory building

d. _____ cost of primary material used to make product

e. _____ rent on office facilities

f. _____ factory supplies used

g. _____ depreciation on office equipment

h. _____ taxes paid on factory building

i. _____ indirect materials used

j. _____ utilities incurred in the office

k. _____ sales supplies used

l. _____ insurance expired on factory equipment

16-2. Venetia Company reports the following information for 2013:

Sales	$83,000
Depreciation on factory equipment	3,600
Direct labor	13,500
Direct materials used	9,100
Factory rent	4,800
Factory utilities	1,600
Indirect labor	4,800
Indirect materials	1,700
Office salary expense	9,800
Sales salary expense	14,100

Compute the following:

a. Inventoriable product costs

b. Period costs

16-3. Indicate whether each of the following costs is a product cost or a period cost:

a. _____ indirect materials used
b. _____ depreciation on factory machinery
c. _____ direct materials used
d. _____ depreciation on store equipment
e. _____ advertising expense
f. _____ plant insurance expired
g. _____ salespersons' commissions
h. _____ indirect labor incurred
i. _____ office supplies used
j. _____ plant manager's salary
k. _____ factory machinery repairs and maintenance
l. _____ factory utilities
m. _____ direct labor incurred

16-4. Inderia Company financial information for the year ended December 31, 2013, follows:

Depreciation	$ 6,700
Direct labor incurred	35,000
Direct materials used	82,000
Indirect labor	4,900
Indirect materials used	2,700
Maintenance	2,800
Property taxes	5,800
Supplies	2,300
Utilities	3,400

There was no beginning or ending finished goods inventory, but work in process inventory began the year with a $5,500 balance and ended the year with a $7,500 balance.

Requirement

1. Prepare a schedule of cost of goods manufactured for Inderia Company for the year ending December 31, 2013.

INDERIA COMPANY
Schedule of Cost of Goods Manufactured
Year Ended December 31, 2013

Do It Yourself! Question 1

Introduction to Management Accounting

Stay Fit Exercise Company has hired you as their new management accountant. Data for the month ended February 28, 2013, is as follows:

Wages expense	$22,000
Supply expense	3,000
Utility expense	1,000
Rent expense	4,500
Service expense	32,000

Requirements

1 Distinguish management accounting from financial accounting

1. Your new boss has heard of the term *total quality management*, but doesn't really understand what it means. Explain the concept of total quality management.

4 Classify costs and prepare an income statement for a service company

2. Prepare an income statement for Stay Fit for the month ended February 28, 2013.

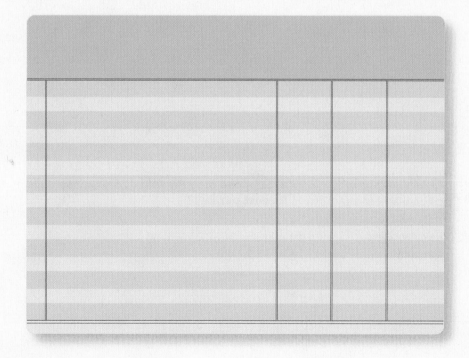

Classify costs and prepare an income statement for a merchandising company

3. In the month of March, Stay Fit decided to sell exercise balls. Based on the following data, prepare Stay Fit's income statement for the month ended March 31, 2013. Calculate Stay Fit's gross profit percentage and profit margin (round to the nearest percentage point).

Wages expense	$24,000
Supply expense	3,000
Utility expense	1,000
Rent expense	4,500
Sales revenue	42,000*
Purchases	8,000
Ending inventory	2,000

* Assume that 100% of sales revenue is from selling exercise balls.

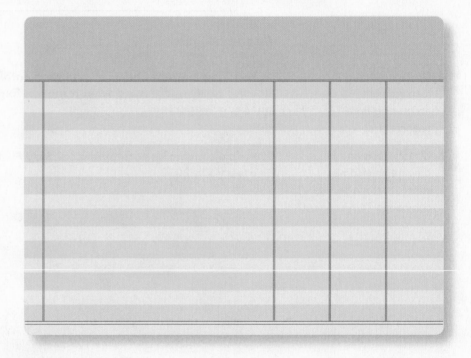

5

Classify costs and prepare an income statement for a merchandising company

4. Suppose Stay Fit sold 375 exercise balls in the month of March. What is its cost per ball?

Do It Yourself! Question 2

Manufacturing Companies

Theme Cans Company produces metal popcorn cans. The following information was available for the month ended August 31, 2013:

Sales revenue	$104,250
Direct materials used	36,000
Direct labor	25,000
Manufacturing overhead	12,000
Beginning work in process	5,000
Ending work in process	3,000
Operating expenses	28,400
Finished goods, Nov 1, 2010	2,500
Finished goods, Nov 30, 2010	5,200

Requirements

6 Classify costs and prepare an income statement and statement of cost of goods manufactured for a manufacturing company

1. Prepare a schedule of cost of goods manufactured for the month ended August 31, 2013.

6 Classify costs and prepare an income statement and statement of cost of goods manufactured for a manufacturing company

2. Prepare Theme Cans' income statement for the month ended August 31, 2013.

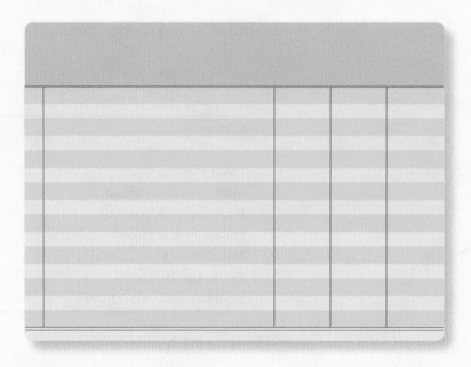

3 Apply ethical standards to decision making

3. As the management accountant for Theme Cans, you are in the process of purchasing new software for the company. One of the suppliers of software gave you a brand new set of expensive golf clubs. Was the acceptance of the golf clubs a violation of any management accountant standard of ethical conduct? Explain.

Quick Practice Solutions

True/False

__F__ 1. A system that integrates all of a company's worldwide functions, departments, and data is called supply-chain management.

      False—A system that integrates all of a company's worldwide functions, departments, and data is called *enterprise resource planning*. (p. 776)

__T__ 2. A budget is a quantitative expression of a plan that helps managers coordinate and implement the plan. (p. 775)

__F__ 3. Goods that are partway through the manufacturing process, but not yet complete, are referred to as materials inventory.

      False—Goods that are partway through the manufacturing process, but not yet complete, are referred to as *work in process*. (p. 783)

__T__ 4. Manufacturers use labor, plants, and equipment to convert raw materials into new finished products. (p. 783)

__F__ 5. Period costs are operating costs that are expensed in the period in which the goods are sold.

      False—Period costs are operating costs that are expensed in the *period incurred*. (p. 779)

__T__ 6. Indirect labor and indirect materials are part of manufacturing overhead. (p. 785)

__T__ 7. Trends in the modern business environment include the shift to a service economy and the rise of the global marketplace. (pp. 776–777)

__T__ 8. Management has a responsibility to meet regulatory obligations to federal and local government agencies. (p. 774)

__F__ 9. Total quality management applies only to manufacturers and promotes the creation of superior products.

      False—Total quality management promotes the creation of *superior products and services*. It applies to entities other than manufacturers. (p. 777)

__F__ 10. The cost of goods manufactured is equal to the sum of direct materials used, direct labor, and manufacturing overhead.

      False—The cost of goods manufactured is equal to the sum of direct materials used, direct labor, and manufacturing overhead *plus* beginning work in process inventory *minus* ending work in process inventory. (p. 787)

Multiple Choice

1. The primary goal of financial accounting is to provide information to which of the following? (p. 774)
   a. Investors
   b. Creditors
   c. Company managers
   d. Both a and b

2. Which of the following is true about management accounting? (pp. 775–776)
   a. Management accounting provides information to customers.
   b. Management accounting provides information that is required to be audited by certified public accountants.
   c. Management accounting primarily focuses on reporting on the company as a whole on a quarterly or annual basis.
   d. Management accounting is not restricted by GAAP.

3. Manufacturers may have which accounts on their balance sheet? (p. 783)
   a. Materials, Work in Process, and Finished Goods
   b. Merchandise, Materials, and Finished Goods
   c. Direct Materials, Direct Labor, and Manufacturing Overhead
   d. Work in Process, Materials, and Manufacturing Overhead

4. In which category would glue or fasteners to manufacture a table be included? (p. 784)
   a. Direct materials
   b. Manufacturing overhead
   c. Period costs
   d. Indirect labor

5. Inventoriable product costs include which of the following? (p. 784)
   a. Marketing costs
   b. Costs of direct materials, direct labor, and manufacturing overhead used to produce a product
   c. Costs of direct materials and direct labor used to produce a product
   d. Period costs, overhead, and direct labor

6. When do inventoriable costs become expenses? (p. 784)
   a. When the manufacturing process begins
   b. When the manufacturing process is completed
   c. When the direct materials are purchased
   d. When the units in inventory are sold

7. In which category would selling and administrative costs be included? (p. 785)
   a. Direct materials
   b. Manufacturing overhead
   c. Period costs
   d. Work in process

8. All *except* which of the following are manufacturing overhead costs? (p. 785)
   a. Materials used directly in the manufacturing process of the product
   b. Insurance on factory equipment
   c. Salaries of production supervisors
   d. Property tax on factory building

9. Cost of goods sold for a manufacturer equals cost of goods manufactured plus which of the following? (p. 787)
   a. Beginning work in process inventory less ending work in process inventory
   b. Ending work in process inventory less beginning work in process inventory
   c. Beginning finished goods inventory less ending finished goods inventory
   d. Ending finished goods inventory less beginning finished goods inventory

10. At the beginning of 2013, the Taylor Company's Work in Process Inventory account had a balance of $30,000. During 2013, $68,000 of direct materials were used in production, and $66,000 of direct labor costs were incurred. Manufacturing Overhead in 2013 amounted to $90,000. The cost of goods manufactured was $220,000 in 2013. What is the balance in the work in process inventory on December 31, 2013? (p. 789)
    a. $34,000
    b. $24,000
    c. $66,000
    d. $6,000

Quick Exercises

16-1.   Use the correct number to categorize each item that follows: (p. 789)

1. Direct materials

2. Selling and general expenses

3. Manufacturing overhead

4. Direct labor

a. _4_ wages of assembly line personnel

b. _2_ advertising expense

c. _3_ rent expense on factory building

d. _1_ cost of primary material used to make productd

e. _2_ rent on office facilities

f. _3_ factory supplies used

g. _2_ depreciation on office equipment

h. _3_ taxes paid on factory building

i. _3_ indirect materials used

j. _2_ utilities incurred in the office

k. _2_ sales supplies used

l. _2_ insurance expired on factory equipment

16-2. Venetia Company reports the following information for 2013:

Sales	$83,000
Depreciation on factory equipment	3,600
Direct labor	13,500
Direct materials used	9,100
Factory rent	4,800
Factory utilities	1,600
Indirect labor	4,800
Indirect materials	1,700
Office salary expense	9,800
Sales salary expense	14,100

Compute the following: (p. 789)

a. Inventoriable product costs

$9,100 + $3,600 + $4,800 + $13,500 + $4,800 + $1,600 + $1,700 = $39,100

b. Period costs

$14,100 + $9,800 = $23,900

16-3. Indicate whether each of the following costs is a product cost or a period cost: (p. 786)

a. _product_ indirect materials used

b. _product_ depreciation on factory machinery

c. _product_ direct materials used

d. _period_ depreciation on store equipment

e. _period_ advertising expense

f. _product_ plant insurance expired

g. _period_ salespersons' commissions

h. _product_ indirect labor incurred

i. _period_ office supplies used

j. _product_ plant manager's salary

k. _product_ factory machinery repairs and maintenance

l. _product_ factory utilities

m. _product_ direct labor incurred

16-4. Inderia Company financial information for the year ended
December 31, 2013, follows:

Depreciation	$ 6,700
Direct labor incurred	35,000
Direct materials used	82,000
Indirect labor	4,900
Indirect materials used	2,700
Maintenance	2,800
Property taxes	5,800
Supplies	2,300
Utilities	3,400

There was no beginning or ending finished goods inventory, but work in process inventory began the year with a $5,500 balance and ended the year with a $7,500 balance. (p. 788)

Requirement

1. Prepare a schedule of cost of goods manufactured for Inderia Company for the year ending December 31, 2013.

INDERIA COMPANY
Schedule of Cost of Goods Manufactured
Year Ended December 31, 2013

Beginning work in process inventory			$ 5,500
Add:			
Direct labor		$82,000	
Direct materials		35,000	
Manufacturing overhead:			
Indirect labor	$4,900		
Indirect materials	2,700		
Depreciation	6,700		
Maintenance	2,800		
Property taxes	5,800		
Supplies	2,300		
Utilities	3,400	28,600	
Total manufacturing costs incurred			
during the year			145,600
Total manufacturing costs to account for			151,100
Less: Ending work in process inventory			(7,500)
Cost of goods manufactured			$143,600

Do It Yourself! Question 1 Solutions

Requirements

1. Your new boss has heard of the term total quality management, but doesn't really understand what it means. Explain the concept of total quality management.

Total quality management is a management philosophy that promotes the goal of providing customers with superior products and services. Companies achieve this goal by continuously improving quality and reducing or eliminating defects and waste. Companies design and build quality into their products and services rather than depending on finding and fixing defects later.

2. Prepare an income statement for Stay Fit for the month ended February 28, 2013.

STAY FIT EXERCISE COMPANY Income Statement Month Ended February 28, 2013			
Service revenue		$32,000	100%
Expenses:			
Wages expense	$22,000		
Rent expense	4,500		
Supply expense	3,000		
Utility expense	1,000		
Total expenses		30,500	95%
Operating income		$ 1,500	5%

3. In the month of March, Stay Fit decided to sell exercise balls. Based on the following data, prepare Stay Fit's income statement for the month ended March 31, 2013. Calculate Stay Fit's gross profit percentage and profit margin (round to the nearest percentage point).

Wages expense	$24,000
Supply expense	3,000
Utility expense	1,000
Rent expense	4,500
Sales revenue	42,000*
Purchases	8,000
Ending inventory	2,000

* Assume that 100% of sales revenue is from selling exercise balls.

STAY FIT EXERCISE COMPANY
Income Statement
Month Ended March 31, 2013

Sales revenue			$42,000	100%
Cost of goods sold:				
Beginning inventory		$ 0		
Purchases		8,000		
Cost of goods available for sale		8,000		
Ending inventory		(2,000)		
Cost of goods sold			6,000	14%
Gross profit			36,000	86%
Operating expenses:				
Wages expense		24,000		
Rent expense		4,500		
Supply expense		3,000		
Utility expense		1,000	32,500	77%
Operating income			$ 3,500	8%

Gross profit percentage	=	$\dfrac{\text{Gross profit}}{\text{Sales revenue}}$
Stay Fit's gross profit percentage	=	$\dfrac{\$36,000}{42,000}$
	= 86%	

Profit margin	=	$\dfrac{\text{Operating income}}{\text{Sales revenue}}$
Stay Fit's profit margin	=	$\dfrac{\$3,500}{42,000}$
	= 8%	

4. Suppose Stay Fit sold 375 exercise balls in the month of March. What is its cost per ball?

$$\text{Cost per unit} = \frac{\text{Total cost of goods sold}}{\text{Total number of units sold}}$$

$$\text{Cost per ball} = \frac{\$6{,}000}{375 \text{ balls}}$$

$$= \$16 \text{ per ball}$$

Do It Yourself! Question 2 Solutions

Requirements

1. Prepare a schedule of cost of goods manufactured for the month ended August 31, 2013.

THEME CANS COMPANY
Schedule of Cost of Goods Manufactured
Month Ended August 31, 2013

Beginning work in process inventory		$ 5,000
Add: Direct materials used	$36,000	
Direct labor	25,000	
Manufacturing overhead	12,000	
Total manufacturing costs incurred during the period		73,000
Total accountable manufacturing costs		78,000
Less: Ending work in process		(3,000)
Cost of goods manufactured		$75,000

2. Prepare Theme Cans' income statement for the month ended August 31, 2013.

THEME CANS COMPANY
Income Statement
Month Ended August 31, 2013

Sales revenue		$104,250	100%
Cost of goods sold:			
Beginning finished goods inventory	$ 2,500		
Cost of goods manufactured	75,000		
Cost of goods available for sale	77,500		
Ending finished goods inventory	(5,200)		
Cost of goods sold		72,300	69%
Gross profit		31,950	31%
Operating expenses		28,400	27%
Operating income		$ 3,550	3%

3. As the management accountant for Theme Cans, you are in the process of purchasing new software for the company. One of the suppliers of software gave you a brand new set of expensive golf clubs. Was the acceptance of the golf clubs a violation of any management accountant standard of ethical conduct? Explain.

The **integrity standard** indicates that the accountant must refuse any gift, favor, or hospitality that would influence *or would appear to influence* actions. The acceptance of a new set of golf clubs is a gift that would appear to influence actions.

The Power of Practice

For more practice using the skills learned in this chapter, visit MyAccountingLab. There you will find algorithmically generated questions that are based on these Demo Docs and your main textbook's Review and Assess Your Progress sections.

Go to MyAccountingLab and follow these steps:

1. Direct your URL to www.myaccountinglab.com.
2. Log in using your name and password.
3. Click the MyAccountingLab link.
4. Click Study Plan in the left navigation bar.
5. From the table of contents, select Chapter 16, Introduction to Management Accounting.
6. Click a link to work tutorial exercises.

17 Job Order and Process Costing

WHAT YOU PROBABLY ALREADY KNOW

If you own a car, you may have already had the unpleasant task of taking your car to a repair shop. Then you probably already know that before work is performed, a cost estimate is usually stated as a certain amount for parts and an hourly amount for labor. The hourly labor charge is much higher than the employees are paid. The charge must be sufficient to cover such overhead costs of running the shop as rent, utilities, maintenance, and supplies. An additional amount is added on top of the costs to create a profit. It is very important to be able to accurately identify all of the projected costs and estimated hours of work that will take place to calculate the cost per hour. In this chapter, we will study how an overhead rate is calculated and allocated to jobs performed.

Now assume that the car repair shop began working on three automobiles. By the end of the day, the mechanics were approximately 2/3 done repairing each of them at the end of the week. If the mechanics were asked how many cars they had finished repairing, they would have to say none. But that would not indicate the amount of time spent during the day working. The mechanics performed 2/3 of the repairs on each of the 3 cars. This is equivalent to performing 2 complete sets of repairs (2/3 × 3 = 2) over the course of the day. Using an *equivalent* number of cars accurately quantifies the amount of work completed during the day. In the appendix to this chapter, we will study the computation of inventory costs. To determine the cost of work in process, we will use this concept of equivalent units for those inventory items that are partially complete.

Learning Objectives/Success Keys

1 Distinguish between job order costing and process costing.

Job order costing accumulates costs for each unique job, assignment, or batch. A construction company, photographer, and law firm may use job order costing because the required work may vary among customers and clients. Other companies operate by performing a similar set of production steps or processes. These companies would use a **process costing** system, which accumulates the costs for each process or department. A cereal manufacturer, bank, and automotive manufacturer might all use process costing.

2 Record materials and labor in a job order costing system.

A **job cost record** is created when the job is started. All of the costs of production will be recorded on this record: direct materials used, direct labor used, and manufacturing overhead. In Demo Doc 1, you will see how materials and labor transactions are recorded in a manufacturer's job order costing system.

3 Record overhead in a job order costing system.

Overhead can include factory depreciation, repairs, insurance, utilities, and other factory costs. The accumulation of these costs is debited to Manufacturing Overhead and credited to the appropriate accounts, as you will see in Demo Doc 2.

4 Record completion and sales of finished goods and adjustment for under- or overallocated overhead.

As goods continue to be worked on and completed, the costs will transfer from the Work in Process Inventory account to the Finished Goods Inventory account. The inventory costs remain in the Finished Goods Asset account until they are sold. When the goods are sold, two entries are required under the perpetual inventory system, as we learned in Chapter 5. One entry is made to record the sale on account or for cash. The other entry removes the cost of inventory and charges Cost of Goods Sold. Manufacturing Overhead is debited for the actual overhead costs and credited for the assigned overhead costs. At year-end, as you will see in Demo Doc 2, the balance in Manufacturing Overhead should be transferred into Cost of Goods Sold.

5 Calculate unit costs for a service company.

The costs for service companies include the labor component and the other indirect office costs. The hourly cost per employee can be calculated as follows:

$$\text{Hourly labor cost} = \frac{\text{Salary and fringe benefits}}{\text{Total number of hours worked}}$$

Other indirect office costs may include rent, utilities, taxes, and support salaries. An hourly cost for indirect costs can be calculated as follows:

$$\text{Predetermined indirect cost allocation rate} = \frac{\text{Total expected indirect costs}}{\text{Total direct labor hours}}$$

To determine the cost of a job, the actual number of hours applied to the job should be multiplied by the hourly labor cost and the predetermined indirect cost allocation rate.

6 Allocate costs using a process costing system - weighted average method (see Appendix 17A).

Instead of job order costing, some companies use a series of steps (called processes) to make large quantities of similar products. These systems are called process costing systems.

Demo Doc 1

Job Order Costing for Manufacturers _____

Learning Objectives 1, 2

Clarence Douglas manufactures specialized art for his customers. Suppose Douglas has the following transactions during the month of March:

a. Purchased raw materials on account, $67,000.

b. Materials costing $45,000 were requisitioned for production. Of this total, $5,000 were indirect materials.

c. Labor time records show that direct labor of $30,000 and indirect labor of $2,000 were incurred, but not yet paid.

Requirements

1. Why would Douglas use the job order costing system?

2. What document would Douglas use to accumulate direct materials, direct labor, and manufacturing overhead costs assigned to each individual job? How do managers use this document to direct and control operations?

3. Prepare summary journal entries for each transaction.

Demo Doc 1 Solutions

Requirement 1

1 Distinguish between job order costing and process costing

Why would Douglas use the job order costing system?

| Part 1 | Part 2 | Part 3 | Demo Doc Complete |

Companies that manufacture batches of unique or specialized products would use a job order costing system to accumulate costs for each job or batch. Because Douglas manufactures specialized art for his customers and the required work may vary from customer to customer, Douglas would use the job order costing system. You will learn about the process costing system, which accumulates costs for production processes as opposed to individual jobs, in Chapter 18.

Requirement 2

2 Record materials and labor in a job order costing system

What document would Douglas use to accumulate direct materials, direct labor, and manufacturing overhead costs assigned to each individual job? How do managers use this document to direct and control operations?

| Part 1 | Part 2 | Part 3 | Demo Doc Complete |

Douglas would use a job cost record to accumulate direct materials, direct labor, and manufacturing overhead costs assigned to each individual job. Managers use job cost records to determine how much each job (and each unit in the job) costs to produce. Managers use cost information to help them set prices and control costs. Cost data help managers identify their most profitable products so that marketing can concentrate on selling these products. Managers also use cost data to make outsourcing decisions and to prepare the company's financial statements.

Managers also use the job cost record to see how they can use materials and labor more efficiently. For example, if a job's costs exceed its budget, managers must do a better job controlling costs on future jobs, or raise the sale price on similar jobs, to be sure that the company remains profitable.

Similarly, managers use labor time records to control labor costs. Together, labor time records and job cost records help managers determine whether employees are working efficiently. If they spend longer than expected on a job, it may not yield a profit.

Managers also use the materials inventory subsidiary ledger to control inventory levels.

Requirement 3

Record materials and labor in a job order costing system

Prepare summary journal entries for each transaction.

Part 1	Part 2	**Part 3**	Demo Doc Complete

a. Purchased raw materials on account, $67,000.

When materials are purchased on account, you want to record the increase in materials inventory, so you would debit Materials Inventory (an asset) by the cost of the materials, $67,000.

You also want to record the increase in liability, so you would credit Accounts Payable (a liability) by $67,000 because this amount is still payable.

Materials inventory	67,000	
Accounts payable		67,000
To record the purchase of materials on account.		

b. Materials costing $45,000 were requisitioned for production. Of this total, $5,000 were indirect materials.

When materials are requisitioned, it means that they move from materials inventory into production to be used. You want to record this movement in the appropriate accounts.

If the materials can be directly traceable to a job, Work in Process will be debited (increased). If the materials do not represent a major component and cannot be traced directly to a job, they are considered indirect materials and are debited to Manufacturing Overhead (increased).

Because $40,000 ($45,000 total materials less $5,000 indirect materials) of the materials can be traced to specific jobs, this amount goes directly into Work in Process Inventory, increasing that asset by $40,000.

The $5,000 in indirect materials is debited (an increase) to Manufacturing Overhead.

Because we are taking all materials out of the Materials Inventory, we reduce this asset with a credit for the total ($45,000).

Work in process inventory (direct material)	40,000	
Manufacturing overhead (indirect material)	5,000	
Materials inventory		45,000
To record direct and indirect materials used.		

c. Labor time records show that direct labor of $30,000 and indirect labor of $2,000 were incurred, but not yet paid.

First, we debit (increase) Manufacturing wages for the full amount of labor, direct and indirect, to accumulate total labor costs. We then credit Wages payable to show the increased liability to our employees.

Manufacturing wages	32,000	
Wages payable		32,000
To record the direct and indirect labor incurred.		

The manufacturing wages need to be assigned to the appropriate accounts. A *labor time record* is completed by each employee who works directly on a job. Each of the jobs and hours worked are identified on the record.

In this case, some of the labor, $30,000, can be traced to specific jobs. This amount, called direct labor, is assigned as a debit (increase) to the asset Work in Process Inventory. The rest of the labor, $2,000, is for indirect labor such as maintenance and janitorial services, and cannot be traced to specific jobs. Therefore, it is debited to Manufacturing Overhead (increased).

Manufacturing wages is credited for the full amount (a decrease), bringing its balance to zero.

Work in process inventory (direct labor)	30,000	
Manufacturing overhead (indirect labor)	2,000	
Manufacturing wages		32,000
To record direct and indirect labor used.		

Part 1	Part 2	Part 3	**Demo Doc Complete**

Demo Doc 2

Allocating Manufacturing Overhead

Learning Objectives 3, 4

Macho Mike's Machine Shop manufactures specialized metal products per its customer's specifications. Macho Mike's uses direct labor cost to allocate its manufacturing overhead. Macho Mike's expects to incur $160,000 of manufacturing overhead costs and to use $400,000 of direct labor cost during 2013.

During November 2013, Macho Mike's Machine Shop had the following selected transactions:

a. **Actual indirect manufacturing labor incurred was $4,200.**

b. **Actual indirect materials used, $3,000.**

c. **Other manufacturing overhead incurred, $2,800 (credit accounts payable).**

d. **Allocated overhead for November (the machine shop incurred $36,000 of direct labor cost during the month).**

e. **Finished jobs that totaled $6,500 on their job cost records.**

f. **Sold inventory for $70,000 (on account) that cost $42,000 to produce.**

Requirements

1. Compute the predetermined manufacturing overhead rate for Macho Mike's.

2. Journalize the transactions.

3. Prepare the journal entry to close the ending balance of manufacturing overhead.

Demo Doc 2 Solutions

Requirement 1

3 Record overhead in a job order costing system

Compute the predetermined manufacturing overhead rate for Macho Mike s.

Part 1	Part 2	Part 3	Demo Doc Complete

Because Macho Mike's uses direct labor cost to allocate overhead to jobs, the predetermined manufacturing overhead rate is computed as follows:

$$\frac{\text{Total estimated manufacturing overhead costs}}{\text{Total estimated direct labor cost}}$$

In this case, the estimated manufacturing overhead cost equals $160,000/estimated direct labor cost of $400,000 = 0.40, or a predetermined manufacturing overhead rate = 40% of *actual* direct labor cost. Another way to think of this is for every $1 spent on direct labor, we incur $0.40 of manufacturing overhead.

It's important to remember that this rate is determined at the beginning of the period, *before* any production has started. This is because actual overhead costs and the actual quantity of the allocation base are not known until the end of the period, so managers need this estimate to make decisions and allocate overhead to individual jobs throughout the period.

Because the allocation base used may be direct labor hours, direct labor cost, machine hours, and other bases, it's important to label this rate accordingly. The predetermined manufacturing overhead rate is multiplied by the allocation base activity to determine the amount of overhead applied to each of the jobs.

Requirement 2

3 Record overhead in a job order costing system

4 Record completion and sales of finished goods and the adjustment for under- or overallocated overhead

Journalize the transactions.

Part 1	Part 2	Part 3	Demo Doc Complete

a. **Actual indirect manufacturing labor incurred was $4,200.**

b. **Actual indirect materials used, $3,000.**

c. **Other manufacturing overhead incurred, $2,800 (credit accounts payable).**

In this case, all actual manufacturing overhead costs incurred during the period are debited to Manufacturing overhead because they cannot be traced to any specific job (that is, they are indirect costs). So Manufacturing Overhead is debited (increased) by

$$\$4,200 + \$3,000 + \$2,800 = \$10,000$$

Indirect manufacturing labor results in a decrease of $4,200 to Manufacturing Wages (a credit).

Indirect materials used results in a decrease of $3,000 to Materials Inventory (a credit), because the materials have been used and are therefore removed from materials inventory.

Other manufacturing overhead is credited (an increase) to Accounts Payable, as indicated in the question, $2,800.

Manufacturing overhead	10,000	
Manufacturing wages		4,200
Materials inventory		3,000
Accounts payable		2,800

d. Allocate overhead for November (the machine shop incurred $36,000 of direct labor cost during the month).

To determine the total overhead allocated to jobs in November, multiply the actual direct labor cost ($36,000) by the predetermined allocation rate of 40% (from requirement 1):

$$\underset{\text{(direct labor cost)}}{\$36,000} \times \underset{\text{(predetermined overhead rate)}}{0.40} = \underset{\text{allocated overhead for November}}{\$14,400}$$

Allocate the overhead to work in process by debiting (increasing) Work in Process Inventory and crediting (decreasing) Manufacturing Overhead by $14,400.

Work in process inventory	14,400	
Manufacturing overhead		14,400

e. Finished jobs that totaled $6,500 on their job cost records.

When the goods are completed, they are transferred from Work in Process to Finished Goods. This reflects work in process that leaves the plant floor and is moved into the finished goods storage area. This is accomplished by debiting (increasing) Finished Goods Inventory by $6,500 and crediting (decreasing) Work in Process Inventory by $6,500.

Finished goods inventory	6,500	
Work in process inventory		6,500

f. Sold inventory for $70,000 (on account) that cost $42,000 to produce.

Debit the asset Accounts Receivable to record the increased amount of $70,000 that is owed to Macho Mike's. Credit (increase) the Revenue account, Sales Revenue, by the same amount.

Debit (increase) the expense Cost of goods sold to record the cost of the sale. Because the goods are no longer in the finished goods inventory, we must credit Finished Goods Inventory to reduce that asset account.

Accounts receivable	70,000	
Sales revenue		70,000
Cost of goods sold	42,000	
Finished goods inventory		42,000

Requirement 3

4 Record completion and sales of finished goods and the adjustment for under- or overallocated overhead

Prepare the journal entry to close the ending balance of manufacturing overhead.

Part 1	Part 2	**Part 3**	Demo Doc Complete

The balance of the Manufacturing Overhead account should be zero at the end of the accounting period. To achieve this, if Manufacturing Overhead has a debit balance, then you would credit Manufacturing Overhead and debit Cost of Goods Sold. If Manufacturing overhead has a credit balance, then you would debit Manufacturing Overhead and credit Cost of Goods Sold.

In this case, manufacturing overhead was overallocated, because the overhead allocated to Work in Process Inventory ($14,400 from requirement 2, transaction **d**) is *more* than the amount actually incurred ($4,200 + $3,000 + $2,800 = $10,000— from transactions **a**, **b**, and **c**).

This results in a credit balance of $4,400 to Manufacturing Overhead. To close the ending balance, we then debit Manufacturing Overhead by $4,400 and credit Cost of Goods Sold by $4,400.

Manufacturing overhead	4,400	
Cost of goods sold		4,400

Why? Because Macho Mike's allocated too much manufacturing overhead to each job, resulting in cost of goods sold being too high (meaning the jobs were charged too much overhead during the period). To close the balance in Manufacturing Overhead, Macho Mike's applies a decrease to Cost of Goods Sold.

Part 1	Part 2	Part 3	**Demo Doc Complete**

Demo Doc 3A

Illustrating Process Costing

6 Allocate costs using a process costing system – weighted average method (see Appendix 17A)

Learning Objective 6

Clear Bottled Water produces packaged water. Clear has two production departments: Blending and Packaging. In the Blending Department, materials are added at the beginning of the process. Conversion costs are added throughout the process for blending. Data for the month of April for the Blending Department are as follows:

Blending Department Data for April:	
Units:	
Beginning work in process	0 units
Started in production during April	116,000 units
Completed and transferred out to Packaging in April	98,000 units
Ending work in process inventory (70% completed)	18,000 units
Costs:	
Beginning work in process	$ 0
Costs added during April:	
Direct materials	54,520
Conversion costs	32,074
Total costs added during April	$86,594

Requirement

1. Use the four-step process to calculate (1) the cost of the units completed and transferred out to the Packaging Department, and (2) the total cost of the units in the Blending Department ending work in process inventory.

Demo Doc 3A Solution

6 Allocate costs using a process costing system – weighted average method (see Appendix 17A)

Requirement 1

Use the four-step process to calculate (1) the cost of the units completed and transferred out to the Packaging Department, and (2) the total cost of the units in the Blending Department ending work in process inventory.

Steps 1 and 2: Summarize the flow of physical units and compute output in terms of equivalent units.

Part 1	Part 2	Part 3	Demo Doc Complete

Total units to account for is the equivalent of units completed and transferred out of packaging in April (98,000) plus the ending work in process inventory of April 30 (18,000):

		Step 1	Step 2: Equivalent Units	
		Flow of	Direct	Conversion
Flow of Production		Physical Units	Materials	Costs
CLEAR BOTTLED WATER				
Blending Department				
Month Ended April 30, 2013				
Units to account for:				
Beginning work in process, March 31		0		
Started in production during April		116,000		
Total physical units to account for		116,000		

Materials are added at the beginning of the blending production process, so equivalent units for materials is the same as the total units.

Completed units have 100% of their conversion costs (98,000).

Conversion costs are added evenly throughout the blending process, so the conversion equivalent units for ending work in process inventory are the total units in ending work in process, 18,000, times the percent complete, 70% = 12,600.

Remember, conversion costs include both direct labor and manufacturing overhead.

CLEAR BOTTLED WATER
Blending Department
Month Ended April 30, 2013

Flow of Production	Step 1 Flow of Physical Units	Step 2: Equivalent Units Direct Materials	Conversion Costs
Units to account for:			
Beginning work in process, March 31	0		
Started in production during April	116,000		
Total physical units to account for	116,000		
Units accounted for:			
Completed and transferred out during April	98,000	98,000	98,000
Ending work in process, April 30	18,000	18,000	12,600
Total physical units accounted for	116,000		
Equivalent units		116,000	110,600

From this, we can see that the total units accounted for is 116,000 units, with 98,000 completed units + 18,000 work in process units = 116,000 equivalent units for direct materials, and 98,000 completed units + 12,600 work in process units = 110,600 equivalent units for conversion costs.

Step 3: Compute the cost per equivalent unit.

Part 1	**Part 2**	Part 3	Demo Doc Complete

The cost per equivalent unit is computed by dividing the costs added during the period by the equivalent units:

$$\text{Cost per equivalent unit for direct materials} = \frac{\text{Total direct material cost}}{\text{Equivalent units for direct material cost}}$$

$$\text{Cost per equivalent unit for conversion cost} = \frac{\text{Total conversion cost}}{\text{Equivalent units for conversion cost}}$$

We know from Step 1 that Clear has 116,000 accountable units. From the question, we know that Clear has $54,520 of total accountable direct materials costs in April.

Using the formula for cost per equivalent unit for direct materials, we divide the total direct materials costs of $54,520 by the equivalent units of materials, determined in Step 2 as 116,000 units = $0.47 per equivalent units for direct materials.

By using equivalent units, we are indicating that $32,074 of conversion costs will blend 110,600 units from the start of the blending process to the end of the blending process. To calculate costs per equivalent unit for conversion costs, we must divide the total conversion costs of $32,074 by the number of equivalent units for conversion, determined in Step 2 to be 110,600 = $0.29 per equivalent units for conversion costs.

CLEAR BOTTLED WATER
Blending Department
Month Ended April 30, 2013

	Step 3: Cost per Equivalent Unit	
	Direct Materials	Conversion Costs
Beginning work in process, March 31	$ 0	$ 0
Costs added during April	54,520	32,074
Total costs for April	$ 54,520	$ 32,074
Divide by equivalent units	÷ 116,000	÷ 110,600
Cost per equivalent unit	$ 0.47	$ 0.29

Step 4: Assign costs to units completed and to units in ending work in process inventory.

Part 1	Part 2	**Part 3**	Demo Doc Complete

Because the units completed and transferred out were started and finished in the month of April, their cost is the full unit cost of $0.76. Shown another way

$98,000 \times \$0.47 = \$46,060$ (direct materials) (100%)
$98,000 \times \underline{\$0.29} = \underline{\$28,420}$ (conversion costs) (100%)
$98,000 \times \underline{\$0.76} = \underline{\$74,480}$

The ending work in process is complete regarding materials because they are added in their entirety at the beginning of the mixing process.

The conversion costs in ending work in process are only 70% complete because conversion costs occur evenly throughout the mixing process. Multiplying each by their respective per-unit cost

$18,000 \times \$0.47 = \$\ 8,460$ (direct materials) (100%)
$12,600 \times \$0.29 = \underline{\$\ 3,654}$ (conversion costs) (70%)
$\underline{\$12,114}$

The solution to the problem is (1) the $74,480 cost of the goods completed and transferred out of the Blending Department to the Packaging Department during April added to (2) the $12,114 cost of the ending work in process in the Blending Department as of April 30 = total costs accounted for of $86,594.

CLEAR BOTTLED WATER
Blending Department
Month Ended April 30, 2013

		Step 4: Assign Costs		
		Direct Materials	Conversion Costs	Total
Units completed and transferred out to Packaging in April	[98,000 ×	($0.47 +	$0.29)]	= $74,480
Ending work in process, April 30:				
Direct materials	18,000 ×	0.47		= 8,460
Conversion costs	12,600 ×		0.29	= 3,654
Total ending work in process, March 31				**$12,114**
Total costs accounted for				$86,594

Part 1	Part 2	Part 3	**Demo Doc Complete**

Demo Doc 4A

Weighted-Average Process Costing

6 Allocate costs using a process costing system – weighted average method (see Appendix 17A)

Learning Objective 6

Easy Flow produces tubes for toothpaste. Easy has two departments: Molding and Packaging. In the second department, Packaging, conversion costs are incurred evenly throughout the process. Packaging materials are not added until the end of the packaging process. Costs in beginning work in process inventory include transferred in costs of $28,360, direct labor of $12,369, and manufacturing overhead of $10,000. October data from the Packaging Department are as follows:

EASY FLOW Packaging Department Month Ended October 31, 2013		
	Units	**Dollars**
Beginning inventory, Sept. 30 (60% complete)	5,700	$50,729
Production started:		
Transferred in	120,000	575,000
Direct materials		155,100
Conversion costs:		
Direct labor		240,000
Manufacturing overhead		185,000
Total conversion costs		$425,000
Total to account for	125,700	$1,205,829
Transferred out	110,000	$?
Ending inventory (30% complete)	15,700	$?

Easy Flow uses weighted-average process costing.

Requirements

1. Compute Easy Flow's equivalent units for the month of October.

2. Compute the cost per equivalent unit for October.

3. Assign the costs to units completed and transferred out and to ending inventory.

Demo Doc 4A Solutions

6 Allocate costs using a process costing system – weighted average method (see Appendix 17A)

Requirement 1

Compute Easy Flow's equivalent units for the month of October.

Part 1	Part 2	Part 3	Part 4	Demo Doc Complete

The 110,000 units completed and transferred out are 100% completed regarding transferred in, direct materials, and conversion costs. That is why the equivalent units are 100%.

The ending work in process inventory is 100% complete regarding transferred in. In other words, Easy Flow doesn't need to transfer any additional costs from another department to complete the units in ending inventory.

Because direct materials are added at the end of the packaging process, they are zero completed in terms of work in process.

Units in ending inventory are only 30% finished in terms of conversion costs. Another way to think of this is that the conversion costs applied to the ending inventory so far will complete 15,700 units 30% of the way (15,700 x 0.30 = 4,710), or those same conversion costs would complete 4,710 units 100% of the way.

<table>
<tr><td colspan="4" align="center">EASY FLOW
Packaging Department
Month Ended October 31, 2013</td></tr>
<tr><td></td><td colspan="3" align="center">Equivalent Units</td></tr>
<tr><td>Flow of Production</td><td align="center">Transferred In</td><td align="center">Direct Materials</td><td align="center">Conversion Costs</td></tr>
<tr><td>Units accounted for:</td><td></td><td></td><td></td></tr>
<tr><td>Completed and transferred out during October</td><td align="right">110,000</td><td align="right">110,000</td><td align="right">110,000</td></tr>
<tr><td>Ending work in process inventory, October 31</td><td align="right">15,700</td><td align="right">0</td><td align="right">4,710</td></tr>
<tr><td>Equivalent units</td><td align="right">125,700</td><td align="right">110,000</td><td align="right">114,710</td></tr>
</table>

So the total equivalent units for the Packaging Department during October is 125,700 transferred-in units, 110,000 direct material units, and 114,710 conversion costs units.

Requirement 2

Compute the cost per equivalent unit for October.

Part 1	Part 2	Part 3	Part 4	Demo Doc Complete

Determine total costs for each of the three categories. We know from the question that we have beginning inventory of $28,360 transferred-in costs and $22,369 in conversion costs ($12,369 for direct labor and $10,000 manufacturing overhead), for a total of $50,729. The direct materials are zero for beginning work in process because they are added at the end of the packaging process.

EASY FLOW Packaging Department Month Ended October 31, 2013	Equivalent Units			
	Transferred In	Direct Materials	Conversion Costs	Total
Beginning work in process inventory, Sept. 30	$28,360	$ 0	$22,369	$50,729

During October, we saw $575,000 in costs transferred in from the Molding Department, $155,100 in direct materials costs, and $425,000 in conversion costs, for a total of $1,155,100 in costs added during October. As a check, make sure that the sum of the totals of the transferred-in, direct materials, and conversion costs equals the sum of the total beginning work in process and the total of costs added during October.

EASY FLOW Packaging Department Month Ended October 31, 2013	Equivalent Units			
	Transferred In	Direct Materials	Conversion Costs	Total
Beginning work in process inventory, Sept. 30	$ 28,360	$ 0	$ 22,369	$ 50,729
Costs added during October	575,000	155,100	425,000	1,155,100
Total costs	$603,360	$155,100	$447,369	$1,205,829

Now that we have our total costs, we must divide total costs for each of the categories by the equivalent units for each respective category (as determined in requirement 1) to determine the cost per equivalent unit.

From this, we determine that the transferred-in costs are

$$\frac{\$603,360}{125,700 \text{ units}} = \$4.80 \text{ per unit}$$

Direct materials costs are

$$\frac{\$155,100}{110,000 \text{ units}} = \$1.41 \text{ per unit}$$

Conversion costs are

$$\frac{\$447,369}{114,710 \text{ units}} = \$3.90 \text{ per unit}$$

EASY FLOW
Packaging Department
Month Ended October 31, 2013

	Equivalent Units			
	Transferred In	Direct Materials	Conversion Costs	Total
Beginning work in process inventory, Sept. 30	$ 28,360	$ 0	$ 22,369	$ 50,729
Costs added during October	575,000	155,100	425,000	1,155,100
Total costs	$603,360	$155,100	$447,369	
Divide by equivalent units	÷ 125,700	÷ 110,000	÷ 114,710	
Cost per equivalent unit	$ 4.80	$ 1.41	$ 3.90	
Total costs to account for				$1,205,829

We will use this to assign total costs for October in the Packaging Department to units completed and to units in ending work in process inventory.

Requirement 3

Assign the costs to units completed and transferred out and to ending inventory.

Part 1	Part 2	**Part 3**	Part 4	Demo Doc Complete

Completed and Transferred Out

Finished Goods Inventory consists of all three cost categories, so Easy Flow multiplies the total units transferred out by the sum of the three costs.

In this case, 110,000 units have been completed and transferred out during October. We know from requirement 2 that cost per transferred-in unit is $4.80, cost per unit for direct materials is $1.41, and the per-unit conversion cost is $3.90. The 110,000 completed units receive 100% of their transferred-in, direct material, and conversion costs. Shown another way

$$110,000 \times \$\ 4.80 = \$\ \ 528,000 \text{ (transferred in)}$$
$$110,000 \times \$\ 1.41 = \$\ \ 155,100 \text{ (direct materials)}$$
$$110,000 \times \$\ 3.90 = \$\ \ 429,000 \text{ (conversion costs)}$$
$$110,000 \times \$10.11 = \$1,112,100 \text{ Total transferred}$$

The $1,112,100 will be transferred out to finished goods because the Packaging Department is the last process in Easy Flow production (debit Finished Goods, credit Work in Process).

		Assign Costs			
EASY FLOW **Packaging Department** Month Ended October 31, 2013					
		Transferred In	Direct Materials	Conversion Costs	Total
Units completed and transferred out to					
Finished goods inventory	110,000 ×	($4,80 +	$1.41 +	$3.90)	= $1,112,100

Ending Inventory

Part 1	Part 2	Part 3	**Part 4**	Demo Doc Complete

Because direct materials are added at the end of the packaging process, they have not yet been added to the units in ending work in process.

We know from requirement 1 that the ending work in process inventory is 15,700 transferred-in units, 0 direct materials, and 4,710 conversion cost equivalent units. Shown another way

$$15,700 \times \$4.80 = \$75,360 \text{ (transferred in)}$$
$$0 \times \$1.41 = \$\qquad 0 \text{ (direct materials)}$$
$$4,710 \times \$3.90 = \underline{\$18,369} \text{ (conversion costs)}$$
$$\$93,729$$

The $93,729 ending work in process inventory will be listed as an asset on Easy Flow's balance sheet (both Work in Process and Finished Goods are inventory and, therefore, assets).

EASY FLOW
Packaging Department
Month Ended October 31, 2013

		Assign Costs			
		Transferred In	Direct Materials	Conversion Costs	Total
Units completed and transferred out to					
Finished goods inventory	110,000 ×	($4.80 +	$1.41 +	$3.90)	= **$1,112,000**
Ending work in process inventory, Oct. 31:					
Transferred-in costs	15,700 ×	4.80	0		= 75,360
Direct materials			0		0
Conversion costs	4,710 ×			3.90	= 18,369
Total ending work in process inventory, Oct. 31					$ 93,729
Total costs accounted for					$1,205,829

Make sure the total costs to account for, $1,112,100 + $93,729 = $1,205,829, matches with the total costs from requirement 2.

Part 1	Part 2	Part 3	Part 4	**Demo Doc Complete**

Quick Practice Questions

True/False

_____ 1. Process costing is used by companies that produce large numbers of identical units in a continuous fashion.

_____ 2. A food and beverage company would most likely use a job order costing system.

_____ 3. A job cost record is a document that accumulates direct materials, direct labor, and manufacturing overhead costs assigned to each individual job.

_____ 4. For jobs that the company has started but not yet finished, the job cost records form the subsidiary ledger for the general ledger account Work in Process Inventory.

_____ 5. When materials are requisitioned for a job, the Materials Inventory account is debited.

_____ 6. A labor time record identifies the employee, the amount of time spent ona particular job, and the labor cost charged to the job.

_____ 7. Manufacturing overhead is credited for actual manufacturing overhead costs incurred throughout the year.

_____ 8. The allocation base is a common denominator that links indirect manufacturing overhead costs to the cost objects.

_____ 9. Work in process inventory is credited for the cost of direct labor in a job order costing system.

_____ 10. The required adjustment for an underallocation of manufacturing overhead results in a credit to Cost of Goods Sold.

_____ 11A. In a process costing system, a separate Work in Process Inventory account is maintained for each process.

_____ 12A. In a process costing system, costs flow into Finished Goods Inventory only from the Work in Process Inventory of the last manufacturing process.

_____ 13A. Wong Corporation had 25,000 units completed and transferred out and 8,000 units that were 35% complete. The equivalent units total 33,000.

_____ 14A. The entry to transfer goods in process from Department A to Department B includes a debit to Work in process—Department A.

_____ 15A. The cost per equivalent unit must be computed for direct materials, conversion, and transferred-in costs in a subsequent department.

_____ 16A. The number of equivalent units may be greater than the number of accountable physical units.

_____ 17A. The cost per equivalent unit is calculated separately for each of the three components of cost—direct materials, direct labor, and manufacturing overhead.

_____ 18A. Unique or custom-made goods would be accounted for by using a process costing system.

_____ 19A. Conversion costs are generally added evenly throughout the process.

_____ 20A. If a department has beginning inventory of 2,000 units, 23,000 units are started into production, and ending inventory is 1,500 units, then 22,500 units are completed.

Multiple Choice

1. What are the two basic types of costing systems?
   a. Job order costing and process costing
   b. Periodic costing and perpetual costing
   c. Product costing and materials inventory costing
   d. Periodic costing and process costing

2. Which type of business can use a job order costing system?
   a. Service and manufacturing businesses
   b. Manufacturing and merchandising businesses
   c. Service and merchandising businesses
   d. Service, merchandising, and manufacturing businesses

3. Which of the following industries is most likely to use a process costing system?
   a. Paint
   b. Aircraft
   c. Construction
   d. Unique furniture accessories

4. Which of the following companies is most likely to use job order costing?
   a. Kellogg's Cereal Company
   b. Elizabeth's Custom Furniture Company
   c. ExxonMobil Oil Refinery
   d. DuPont Chemical Company

5. Which of the following would be necessary to record the purchase of materials on account using a job order costing system?
   a. Credit to Work in Process Inventory
   b. Debit to Accounts Payable
   c. Debit to Materials Inventory
   d. Debit to Work in Process Inventory

6. Which of the following would be debited to record the direct materials used?
   a. Finished Goods Inventory
   b. Materials Inventory
   c. Work in Process Inventory
   d. Cost of Goods Manufactured

7. Which of the following would be debited to assign direct labor costs actually incurred?
   a. Finished Goods Inventory
   b. Manufacturing Overhead
   c. Wages Payable
   d. Work in Process Inventory

8. Which of the following would be debited to assign the costs of indirect labor?
   a. Manufacturing Overhead
   b. Work in Process Inventory
   c. Finished Goods Inventory
   d. Wages Payable

9. What is the document that is prepared by manufacturing personnel to request materials for the production process?
   a. Materials requisition
   b. Cost ticket
   c. Job order card
   d. Manufacturing ticket

10. Opaque Corporation uses a job order costing system. The Work in Process Inventory balance on December 31, 2013, consists of Job No. 120, which has a balance of $19,000. Job No. 120 has been charged with manufacturing overhead of $5,100. Opaque allocates manufacturing overhead at a predetermined rate of 85% of direct labor cost. What is the amount of direct materials charged to Job No. 120?
    a. $7,565
    b. $5,900
    c. $7,000
    d. $7,900

11A. In a process costing system, the number of Work in Process Inventory accounts is equal to what amount?
    a. The number of products produced
    b. The number of Production Departments
    c. The number used in a job order costing system
    d. Cannot be determined without additional information

12A. In a process costing system, the entry to record the use of direct materials in production would include which of the following?
    a. Debit to Work in Process Inventory
    b. Debit to Materials Inventory
    c. Debit to Finished Goods Inventory
    d. Credit to Finished Goods Inventory

13A. The entry to record a $24,000 transfer from the Assembly Department to the Finishing Department would include which of the following?
    a. Debit to Work in Process Inventory—Assembly
    b. Debit to Finished Goods Inventory
    c. Credit to Work in Process Inventory—Assembly
    d. Credit to Materials Inventory

14A. During the period, 50,000 units were completed, and 3,600 units were on hand at the end of the period. If the ending work in process inventory was 75% complete as to direct materials and 25% complete as to conversion costs, the equivalent units for direct materials under the weighted-average method would be what amount?

a. 45,900
b. 47,700
c. 48,000
d. 52,700

15A. Beginning work in process is 900 units, units completed and transferred out in October are 3,200 units, and ending work in process is 500 units. Under weighted-average costing, what are units started into production in October?

a. 2,300
b. 2,800
c. 3,200
d. 3,600

16A. Conversions costs consist of which of the following?

a. Direct materials and direct labor
b. Direct labor and manufacturing overhead
c. Direct materials and manufacturing overhead
d. Product costs and period costs

17A. The Lloyd Company uses a process costing system. There were no units in beginning work in process, 1,400 were started, and 1,000 units were completed and transferred out. The units at the end of the period were 60% complete regarding materials and 40% complete regarding conversion. The cost of materials added during the current period amounted to $31,944; the cost of conversion added during the current period amounted to $30,016. What are the equivalent units for materials?

a. 1,200
b. 1,240
c. 1,320
d. 1,400

18A. Refer to Question 17A. What are equivalent units for conversion costs?

a. 1,160
b. 1,280
c. 1,300
d. 1,320

19A. Refer to Question 17A. What is the cost per equivalent unit for materials?

a. $22.50
b. $22.82
c. $24.20
d. $25.76

20A. Refer to Question 17A. What is the cost per equivalent unit for conversion?

a. $22.74
b. $23.45
c. $25.01
d. $25.88

Quick Exercises

17-1. State whether each the following companies would be more likely to use a job order costing system or a process costing system:

a. home builder ————————————————————————
b. custom furniture manufacturer ————————————————
c. custom jewelry manufacturer ————————————————
d. carpet manufacturer ————————————————————
e. soft drink bottler ————————————————————
f. concrete manufacturer ————————————————————
g. paint manufacturer ————————————————————

17-2. Inspector Company has two departments, Alpha and Beta. Manufacturing overhead is allocated based on direct labor cost in Department Alpha and direct labor hours in Department Beta. The following additional information is available:

	Estimated Amounts	
	Department Alpha	**Department Beta**
Direct labor costs	$289,600	$457,500
Direct labor hours	27,900	34,200
Manufacturing overhead costs	279,000	242,000
Actual data for completed Job No. 732 is as follows:		
Direct materials requisitioned	$28,700	$44,600
Direct labor cost	32,400	40,800
Direct labor hours	4,600	3,600

Requirements

1. Compute the predetermined manufacturing overhead rate for Department Alpha.

2. Compute the predetermined manufacturing overhead rate for Department Beta.

3. What is the total manufacturing overhead cost for Job No. 732?

4. If Job No. 732 consists of 350 units of product, what is the average unit cost of this job?

17-3. Robin Corporation uses a job order costing system.

Journalize the following transactions in Robin's general journal for the current month:

a. Purchased materials on account, $94,000.

	General Journal			
Date	Accounts		Debit	Credit

b. Requisitioned $49,700 of direct materials and $4,500 of indirect materials for use in production.

	General Journal			
Date	Accounts		Debit	Credit

c. Factory payroll incurred and due to employees, $85,000.

	General Journal			
Date	Accounts		Debit	Credit

d. Allocated factory payroll, 80% direct labor, 20% indirect labor.

	General Journal			
Date	Accounts		Debit	Credit

e. Recorded depreciation on factory equipment of $11,000 and other manufacturing overhead of $52,000 (credit accounts payable).

	General Journal			
Date	Accounts		Debit	Credit

f. Allocated manufacturing overhead based on 120% of direct labor cost.

	General Journal			
Date	Accounts		Debit	Credit

g. Cost of completed production for the current month, $175,000.

General Journal			
Date	Accounts	Debit	Credit

h. Cost of finished goods sold, $166,000; selling price, $210,000 (all sales on account).

General Journal			
Date	Accounts	Debit	Credit

17-4. The following activities took place in the Work in Process Inventory account for Bergen Manufacturing during August:

General Journal			
Date	Accounts	Debit	Credit

Work in process balance, August 1	$ 25,000
Direct materials used	120,000

Total manufacturing labor incurred in August was $160,000 and 75% of manufacturing labor represents direct labor. The predetermined manufacturing overhead rate is 130% of direct labor cost. Actual manufacturing overhead costs for August amounted to $150,000.

Two jobs were completed with total costs of $140,000 and $80,000, respectively. They were sold on account for $250,000 and $136,000, respectively.

Requirements

1. Compute the balance in Work in Process Inventory on August 31.

2. Journalize the following:

a. Direct materials used in August.

General Journal			
Date	Accounts	Debit	Credit

b. The total manufacturing labor incurred in August.

	General Journal			
Date	Accounts		Debit	Credit

c. The entry to assign manufacturing labor to the appropriate accounts.

	General Journal			
Date	Accounts		Debit	Credit

d. The allocated manufacturing overhead for August.

	General Journal			
Date	Accounts		Debit	Credit

e. The entry to move the completed jobs into finished goods inventory.

	General Journal			
Date	Accounts		Debit	Credit

f. The entry to sell the two completed jobs on account.

	General Journal			
Date	Accounts		Debit	Credit

17-5. The following account balances as of October 1, 2013, were selected from the general ledger of Mackenzie Company:

Work in process inventory	$ 0
Materials inventory	35,000
Finished goods inventory	60,000

Additional data:

a. Cost of direct materials placed in production during October totaled $170,000. There were no indirect material requisitions during October 2013.
b. Actual manufacturing overhead for October amounted to $62,000.
c. Finished Goods Inventory balance on October 31 was $30,000.
d. The predetermined manufacturing overhead rate is based on direct labor cost. The budget for 2013 called for $330,000 of direct labor cost and $349,000 of manufacturing overhead costs.
e. The only job unfinished on October 31, 2013, was Job No. 312, for which total labor charges were $5,600 (800 direct labor hours) and total direct material charges were $12,000.
f. October 31 balance in Materials Inventory was $29,000.
g. Total direct labor cost for October was $48,000.

Requirements

1. Determine the predetermined manufacturing overhead rate.

2. Determine the amount of materials purchased during October.

3. Determine cost of goods manufactured for October.

4. Determine the Work in Process Inventory balance on October 31.

5. Determine cost of goods sold for October.

6. Determine whether manufacturing overhead is overallocated or underallocated. What is the account balance at October 31?

17-6A. Given the following products or services, identify which of the following would use a process costing system.

a.	Cereal	f.	Custom swimming pools
b.	Office buildings	g.	Airplanes
c.	Paint	h.	Cellular telephones
d.	Soft drinks	i.	Personal computers
e.	Custom kitchen cabinets	j.	Surgical operation

17-7A. Department 7 has no beginning work in process inventory. During the current period, 13,500 units were placed into production. At the end of the current period, 12,000 units were transferred to Department 8. The ending units in Department 7 were 82% complete regarding direct materials and 70% complete regarding conversion costs. Compute the equivalent units for direct materials and conversion costs.

17-8A. Journalize the following transactions:

a. Issued $8,800 of direct materials to production in the Painting Department.

General Journal			
Date	Accounts	Debit	Credit

b. Manufacturing labor in the Painting Department amounted to $10,000.

General Journal			
Date	Accounts	Debit	Credit

c. Allocated manufacturing labor to the appropriate accounts: 65% direct labor; 35% indirect labor. The pay rate for all direct labor is $20 per hour.

General Journal			
Date	Accounts	Debit	Credit

d. Allocated manufacturing overhead in the Painting Department at $15 per direct labor hour.

	General Journal		
Date	Accounts	Debit	Credit

e. Transferred $7,600 of product from the Painting Department to finished goods inventory.

	General Journal		
Date	Accounts	Debit	Credit

17-9A. Amerisama Company makes a variety of products. Its Texturing Department reports the following information for September of the current year:

Units:	
Completed and transferred out	7,400
Unfinished units, work in process, September 30	3,500*

*100% complete for direct materials and 40% complete for conversion costs incurred.

Costs:	
Direct materials	$110,000
Direct labor	55,000
Manufacturing overhead	80,000

Requirements

1. Compute the equivalent units for direct materials and conversion costs.

2. Compute the cost per equivalent unit for direct materials and conversion costs.

3. Compute the cost of the goods completed and transferred out.

4. Compute the cost of the work in process at September 30.

17-10A. Southern Corporation manufactures airplane parts. The company uses the weighted-average method of process costing. Information for the Assembly Department for the month of March is as follows:

Units:	
Work in process inventory, March 1 (75% complete for direct materials, 40% complete for conversion costs)	25,000 units
Units transferred in from Finishing dept.	150,000 units
Units completed and transferred out	140,000 units
Work in process inventory, March 31 (55% complete for direct materials, 20% complete for conversion costs)	60,000 units
Costs:	
Direct materials:	
Work in process inventory, March 1	$ 90,000
Added during March	567,000
Conversion costs:	
Work in process inventory, March 1	61,800
Added during March	721,000
Transferred-in costs:	
Work in process inventory, March 1	315,000
Units transferred in from Cutting Dept. during March	1,575,000

Requirements

1. Compute the total cost of units completed and transferred out.

2. Compute the total cost of work in process inventory on March 31.

Do It Yourself! Question 1

Bell Boxers is a customized clothing manufacturer. Bell has the following transactions:

a. **Purchased raw materials on account, $20,000.**

b. **Materials costing $15,000 were requisitioned for production. Of this total, $1,500 worth were indirect materials.**

c. **Labor time records show that direct labor of $24,000 and indirect labor of $3,000 were incurred, but not yet paid.**

Requirements

1. **Why would Bell Boxers use the job order costing system?**

2. **What document would Bell Boxers use to accumulate direct materials, direct labor, and manufacturing overhead costs assigned to each job?**

3. **Journalize each transaction.**

1 Distinguish between job order costing and process costing

2 Record materials and labor in a job order costing system

2 Record materials and labor in a job order costing system

General Journal				
Date	Accounts		Debit	Credit

General Journal				
Date	Accounts		Debit	Credit

General Journal				
Date	Accounts		Debit	Credit

General Journal				
Date	Accounts		Debit	Credit

Do It Yourself! Question 2

Quality Cabinet Maker manufactures specialized cabinets. Because of its unique specialization, Quality Cabinet is labor-intensive, so it uses direct labor cost to allocate its overhead. Quality Cabinet expects to incur $240,000 of manufacturing overhead costs and to use $300,000 of direct labor cost during 2013.

During May 2013, Quality Cabinet actually incurred $22,000 of direct labor cost and recorded the following transactions:

a. **Indirect actual manufacturing labor, $5,100.**

b. **Indirect actual materials used, $6,200.**

c. **Other manufacturing overhead incurred, $7,000 (credit accounts payable).**

d. **Allocated overhead for May.**

e. **Transferred 45,000 of product to finished goods.**

f. **Sold product on account, $60,000; cost of the product, $33,000.**

Requirements

3 Record overhead in a job order costing system

1. **Compute the predetermined manufacturing overhead for Quality.**

3 Record overhead in a job order costing system

2. **Journalize the transactions in the general journal.**

General Journal				
Date	Accounts		Debit	Credit

General Journal				
Date	Accounts		Debit	Credit

General Journal				
Date	Accounts		Debit	Credit

General Journal

Date	Accounts	Debit	Credit

General Journal

Date	Accounts	Debit	Credit

General Journal

Date	Accounts	Debit	Credit

General Journal

Date	Accounts	Debit	Credit

4 Record completion and sales of finished goods and the adjustment for under- or overallocated overhead

3. Prepare the journal entry to close the ending balance of Manufacturing Overhead.

Date	Accounts	Debit	Credit

Do It Yourself! Question 3A

Jiggling Jelly produces packaged jelly. Jiggling has two production departments: Blending and Packaging. In the Blending Department, materials are added at the beginning of the process. Conversion costs are added throughout the process for blending. Data for the month of June for the Blending Department are as follows:

Units:	
Beginning work in process	0 units
Started in production during June	32,500 units
Completed and transferred out to Packaging in June	28,000 units
Ending work in process inventory (20% completed)	4,500 units
Costs:	
Beginning work in process	$ 0
Costs added during June:	
Direct materials	15,925
Conversion costs	24,998
Total costs added during June	$40,923

Requirements

1. Use the four-step process to calculate (1) the cost of the units completed and transferred out to the Packaging Department, and (2) the total cost of the units in the Blending Department ending work in process inventory.

Steps 1 and 2

JIGGLING JELLY
Blending Department
Month Ended June 30, 2013

Step 3

JIGGLING JELLY
Blending Department
Month Ended June 30, 2013

Step 4

JIGGLING JELLY		
Blending Department		
Month Ended June 30, 2013		

Do It Yourself! Question 4A

Quality Chemicals produces a chemical that it sells to hospitals. Quality has two departments: Mixing and Packaging. In the second department, Packaging, conversion costs are incurred evenly throughout the process. Packaging materials are not added until the end of the packaging process. Costs in beginning work in process inventory include transferred-in costs of $88,000, direct labor of $44,000, and manufacturing overhead of $21,000. July data from the Packaging Department are as follows:

<table>
<tr><td colspan="3" align="center">QUALITY CHEMICALS
Packaging Department
Month Ended July 31, 2013</td></tr>
<tr><td></td><td>Units</td><td>Dollars</td></tr>
<tr><td>Beginning inventory, June 30 (80% complete)</td><td>55,000</td><td>$153,000</td></tr>
<tr><td>Production started:</td><td></td><td></td></tr>
<tr><td>   Transferred in</td><td>230,000</td><td>293,900</td></tr>
<tr><td>   Direct materials</td><td></td><td>250,800</td></tr>
<tr><td>   Conversion costs:</td><td></td><td></td></tr>
<tr><td>   Direct labor</td><td></td><td>189,250</td></tr>
<tr><td>   Manufacturing overhead</td><td></td><td>105,000</td></tr>
<tr><td>   Total conversion costs</td><td></td><td>294,250</td></tr>
<tr><td>Total to account for</td><td>285,000</td><td>$991,950</td></tr>
<tr><td>Transferred out</td><td>220,000</td><td>$?</td></tr>
<tr><td>Ending inventory (30% complete)</td><td>65,000</td><td>$?</td></tr>
</table>

Quality uses the weighted-average method for process costing.

Requirements

1. Compute Quality's equivalent units for the month of July.

<table>
<tr><td colspan="4" align="center">QUALITY CHEMICALS
Packaging Department
Month Ended July 31, 2013</td></tr>
<tr><td></td><td></td><td></td><td></td></tr>
<tr><td></td><td></td><td></td><td></td></tr>
<tr><td></td><td></td><td></td><td></td></tr>
<tr><td></td><td></td><td></td><td></td></tr>
<tr><td></td><td></td><td></td><td></td></tr>
</table>

2. Compute the cost per equivalent unit for July.

QUALITY CHEMICALS Packaging Department Month Ended July 31, 2013				

3. Assign the costs to units completed and transferred out and to ending work in process inventory.

QUALITY CHEMICALS Packaging Department Month Ended July 31, 2013				

Quick Practice Solutions

True/False

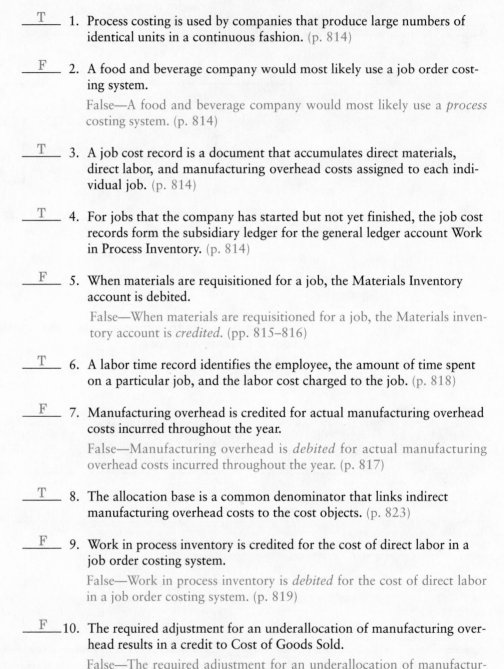

__T__ 1. Process costing is used by companies that produce large numbers of identical units in a continuous fashion. (p. 814)

__F__ 2. A food and beverage company would most likely use a job order costing system.

   False—A food and beverage company would most likely use a *process* costing system. (p. 814)

__T__ 3. A job cost record is a document that accumulates direct materials, direct labor, and manufacturing overhead costs assigned to each individual job. (p. 814)

__T__ 4. For jobs that the company has started but not yet finished, the job cost records form the subsidiary ledger for the general ledger account Work in Process Inventory. (p. 814)

__F__ 5. When materials are requisitioned for a job, the Materials Inventory account is debited.

   False—When materials are requisitioned for a job, the Materials inventory account is *credited*. (pp. 815–816)

__T__ 6. A labor time record identifies the employee, the amount of time spent on a particular job, and the labor cost charged to the job. (p. 818)

__F__ 7. Manufacturing overhead is credited for actual manufacturing overhead costs incurred throughout the year.

   False—Manufacturing overhead is *debited* for actual manufacturing overhead costs incurred throughout the year. (p. 817)

__T__ 8. The allocation base is a common denominator that links indirect manufacturing overhead costs to the cost objects. (p. 823)

__F__ 9. Work in process inventory is credited for the cost of direct labor in a job order costing system.

   False—Work in process inventory is *debited* for the cost of direct labor in a job order costing system. (p. 819)

__F__ 10. The required adjustment for an underallocation of manufacturing overhead results in a credit to Cost of Goods Sold.

   False—The required adjustment for an underallocation of manufacturing overhead results in a *debit* to Cost of goods sold. (p. 827)

_T_ 11A. In a process costing system, a separate Work in Process Inventory account is maintained for each process. (p. 861)

_T_ 12A. In a process costing system, costs flow into Finished Goods Inventory only from the Work in Process Inventory of the last manufacturing process. (p. 857)

_F_ 13A. Wong Corporation had 25,000 units completed and transferred out and 8,000 units that were 35% complete. The equivalent units total 33,000.

False—Equivalent units would be *27,800*; 25,000 + (8,000 × 0.35). (p. 863)

_F_ 14A. The entry to transfer goods in process from Department A to Department B includes a debit to Work in process—Department A.

False—The entry to transfer goods in process from Department A to Department B includes a *credit* to Work in process—Department A. (p. 868)

_T_ 15A. The cost per equivalent unit must be computed for direct materials, conversion, and transferred-in costs in a subsequent department. (pp. 863–865)

_F_ 16A. The number of equivalent units may be greater than the number of accountable physical units.

False—The number of equivalent units *cannot* be greater than the number of accountable physical units. (p. 863)

_F_ 17A. The cost per equivalent unit is calculated separately for each of the three components of cost—direct materials, direct labor, and manufacturing overhead.

False—The cost per equivalent is calculated separately for direct materials, conversion costs, and transferred-in costs *as applicable*. (p. 863)

_F_ 18A. Unique or custom-made goods would be accounted for by using a process costing system.

False—Unique or custom-made goods would be accounted for by using a *job order costing system*. (p. 820)

_T_ 19A. Conversion costs are generally added evenly throughout the process. (p. 863)

_F_ 20A. If a department has beginning inventory of 2,000 units, 23,000 units are started into production, and ending inventory is 1,500 units, then 22,500 units are completed.

False—If a department has beginning inventory of 2,000 units, 23,000 units are started into production, and ending inventory is 1,500 units, then *23,500* (2,000 + 23,000 − 1,500) units are completed. (pp. 859–870)

Multiple Choice

1. **What are the two basic types of costing systems?** (p. 814)
   a. Job order costing and process costing
   b. Periodic costing and perpetual costing
   c. Product costing and materials inventory costing
   d. Periodic costing and process costing

2. **Which type of business can use a job order costing system?** (p. 814)
   a. Service and manufacturing businesses
   b. Manufacturing and merchandising businesses
   c. Service and merchandising businesses
   d. Service, merchandising, and manufacturing businesses

3. **Which of the following industries is most likely to use a process costing system?** (p. 856)
   a. Paint
   b. Aircraft
   c. Construction
   d. Unique furniture accessories

4. **Which of the following companies is most likely to use job order costing?** (p. 814)
   a. Kellogg's Cereal Company
   b. Elizabeth's Custom Furniture Company
   c. Exxon Mobil Oil Refinery
   d. DuPont Chemical Company

5. **Which of the following would be necessary to record the purchase of materials on account using a job order costing system?** (p. 816)
   a. Credit to Work in Process Inventory
   b. Debit to Accounts Payable
   c. Debit to Materials Inventory
   d. Debit to Work in Process Inventory

6. **Which of the following would be debited to record the direct materials used?** (p. 817)
   a. Finished Goods Inventory
   b. Materials Inventory
   c. Work in Process Inventory
   d. Cost of Goods Manufactured

7. **Which of the following would be debited to assign direct labor costs actually incurred?** (p. 819)
   a. Finished Goods Inventory
   b. Manufacturing Overhead
   c. Wages Payable
   d. Work in Process Inventory

8. **Which of the following would be debited to assign the costs of indirect labor?** (p. 822)
   a. Manufacturing Overhead
   b. Work in Process Inventory
   c. Finished Goods Inventory
   d. Wages Payable

9. What is the document that is prepared by manufacturing personnel to request materials for the production process? (p. 817)
   a. Materials requisition
   b. Cost ticket
   c. Job order card
   d. Manufacturing ticket

10. Opaque Corporation uses a job order costing system. The Work in Process Inventory balance on December 31, 2013, consists of Job No. 120, which has a balance of $19,000. Job No. 120 has been charged with manufacturing overhead of $5,100. Opaque allocates manufacturing overhead at a predetermined rate of 85% of direct labor cost. What is the amount of direct materials charged to Job No. 120? (p. 817)
    a. $7,565
    b. $5,900
    c. $7,000
    d. $7,900

11A. In a process costing system, the number of Work in Process Inventory accounts is equal to what amount? (p. 857)
    a. The number of products produced
    b. The number of Production Departments
    c. The number used in a job order costing system
    d. Cannot be determined without additional information

12A. In a process costing system, the entry to record the use of direct materials in production would include which of the following? (p. 865)
    a. Debit to Work in Process Inventory
    b. Debit to Materials Inventory
    c. Debit to Finished Goods inventory
    d. Credit to Finished Goods inventory

13A. The entry to record a $24,000 transfer from the Assembly Department to the Finishing Department would include which of the following? (p. 868)
    a. Debit to Work in Process Inventory—Assembly
    b. Debit to Finished Goods Inventory
    c. Credit to Work in Process Inventory—Assembly
    d. Credit to Materials Inventory

14A. During the period, 50,000 units were completed, and 3,600 units were on hand at the end of the period. If the ending work in process inventory was 75% complete as to direct materials and 25% complete as to conversion costs, the equivalent units for direct materials under the weighted-average method would be what amount? (pp. 863–870)
    a. 45,900
    b. 47,700
    c. 48,000
    d. 52,700

15A. Beginning work in process is 900 units, units completed and transferred out in October are 3,200 units, and ending work in process is 500 units. Under weighted-average costing, what are units started into production in October? (pp. 859–870)

a. 2,300
b. 2,800
c. 3,200
d. 3,600

16A. Conversions costs consist of which of the following? (p. 859)

a. Direct materials and direct labor
b. Direct labor and manufacturing overhead
c. Direct materials and manufacturing overhead
d. Product costs and period costs

17A. The Lloyd Company uses a process costing system. There were no units in beginning work in process, 1,400 were started, and 1,000 units were completed and transferred out. The units at the end of the period were 60% complete regarding materials and 40% complete regarding conversion. The cost of materials added during the current period amounted to $31,944; the cost of conversion added during the current period amounted to $30,016. What are the equivalent units for materials? (pp. 859–862)

a. 1,200
b. 1,240
c. 1,320
d. 1,400

18A. Refer to Question 17A. What are equivalent units for conversion costs? (pp. 863–870)

a. 1,160
b. 1,280
c. 1,300
d. 1,320

19A. Refer to Question 17A. What is the cost per equivalent unit for materials? (pp. 863–870)

a. $22.50
b. $22.82
c. $24.20
d. $25.76

20A. Refer to Question 17A. What is the cost per equivalent unit for conversion? (pp. 863–870)

a. $22.74
b. $23.45
c. $25.01
d. $25.88

Quick Exercises

17-1. State whether each of the following companies would be more likely to use a job order costing system or a process costing system: (p. 814)

a. home builder	job order costing
b. custom furniture manufacturer	job order costing
c. custom jewelry manufacturer	job order costing
d. carpet manufacturer	process costing
e. soft drink bottler	process costing
f. concrete manufacturer	process costing
g. paint manufacturer	process costing

17-2. Inspector Company has two departments, Alpha and Beta. Manufacturing overhead is allocated based on direct labor cost in Department Alpha and direct labor hours in Department Beta. The following additional information is available: (p. 824)

Estimated Amounts		
	Department Alpha	Department Beta
Direct labor costs	$289,600	$457,500
Direct labor hours	27,900	34,200
Manufacturing overhead costs	279,000	242,000

Actual data for completed Job No. 732 is as follows:		
Direct materials requisitioned	$28,700	$44,600
Direct labor cost	32,400	40,800
Direct labor hours	4,600	3,600

Requirements

1. Compute the predetermined manufacturing overhead rate for Department Alpha.

$279,000/$289,600 = 96.3% of direct labor cost

2. Compute the predetermined manufacturing overhead rate for Department Beta.

$242,000/34,200 hours = $7.08 per direct labor hour

3. What is the total manufacturing overhead cost for Job No.732?

Dept. Alpha ($32,400 ☐ 96.3%) $31,201
Dept. Beta   ($7.08 ☐ 3,600)   25,488
                                 $56,689

4. If Job No. 732 consists of 350 units of product, what is the average unit cost of this job?

$28,700 + $32,400 + $31,201 + $44,600 + $40,800 + $25,488 = $203,189
$203,189/350 units = $580.54

17-3. Robin Corporation uses a job order costing system. (pp. 815–827)

Journalize the following transactions in Robin's general journal for the current month:

a. **Purchased materials on account, $94,000.**

b. **Requisitioned $49,700 of direct materials and $4,500 of indirect materials for use in production.**

c. **Factory payroll incurred and due to employees, $85,000.**

d. **Allocated factory payroll, 80% direct labor, 20% indirect labor.**

e. **Recorded depreciation on factory equipment of $11,000 and other manufacturing overhead of $52,000 (credit accounts payable).**

f. **Allocated manufacturing overhead based on 120% of direct labor cost.**

g. **Cost of completed production for the current month, $175,000.**

h. **Cost of finished goods sold, $166,000; selling price, $210,000 (all sales on account).**

General Journal

	Date	Accounts	Debit	Credit
a.		Materials inventory	94,000	
		Accounts payable		94,000

General Journal

	Date	Accounts	Debit	Credit
b.		Work in process inventory	49,700	
		Manufacturing overhead	4,500	
		Materials inventory		54,200

General Journal

	Date	Accounts	Debit	Credit
c.		Manufacturing wages	85,000	
		Wages payable		85,000

General Journal

	Date	Accounts	Debit	Credit
d.		Work in process inventory ($85,000 × 0.80)	68,000	
		Manufacturing overhead ($85,000 × 0.20)	17,000	
		Manufacturing wages		85,000

General Journal

	Date	Accounts	Debit	Credit
e.		Manufacturing overhead	63,000	
		Accumulated dep.—Factory equip.		11,000
		Accounts payable		52,000

General Journal

	Date	Accounts	Debit	Credit
f.		Work in process inventory ($68,000 × 1.20)	81,600	
		Manufacturing overhead		81,600

General Journal

	Date	Accounts	Debit	Credit
g.		Finished goods inventory	175,000	
		Work in process inventory		175,000

General Journal

	Date	Accounts	Debit	Credit
h.		Accounts receivable	210,000	
		Sales revenue		210,000
		Cost of goods sold	166,000	
		Finished goods inevntory		166,000

17-4. The following activities took place in the Work in Process Inventory account for Bergen Manufacturing during August: (pp. 815–819)

Work in process balance, August 1	$ 25,000
Direct materials used	120,000

Total manufacturing labor incurred in August was $160,000 and 75% of manufacturing labor represents direct labor. The predetermined manufacturing overhead rate is 130% of direct labor cost. Actual manufacturing overhead costs for August amounted to $150,000.

Two jobs were completed with total costs of $140,000 and $80,000, respectively. They were sold on account for $250,000 and $136,000, respectively.

Requirements

1. Compute the balance in Work in Process Inventory on August 1.

$25,000 + $120,000 + (75% × $160,000) + (130% × 75% × $160,000) − $140,000 − $80,000 = $201,000

2. Journalize the following:

    a. Direct materials used in August.
    b. The total manufacturing labor incurred in August.
    c. The entry to assign manufacturing labor to the appropriate accounts.
    d. The allocated manufacturing overhead for August.
    e. The entry to move the completed jobs into finished goods inventory.
    f. The entry to sell the two completed jobs on account.

General Journal

	Date	Accounts	Debit	Credit
a.		Work in process inventory	120,000	
		Materials inventory		120,000

General Journal

	Date	Accounts	Debit	Credit
b.		Manufacturing wages	160,000	
		Wages payable		160,000

General Journal

	Date	Accounts	Debit	Credit
c.		Work in process inventory ($160,000 × 75%)	120,000	
		Manufacturing overhead ($160,000 × 25%)	40,000	
		Manufacturing wages		160,000

General Journal

	Date	Accounts	Debit	Credit
d.		Work in process inventory	156,000	
		Manufacturing overhead ($120,000 × 1.30)		156,000

General Journal

	Date	Accounts	Debit	Credit
e.		Finished goods inventory ($140,000 + $80,000)	220,000	
		Work in process inventory		220,000

General Journal

	Date	Accounts	Debit	Credit
f.		Accounts receivable	386,000	
		Sales revenue ($250,000 + $136,000)		386,000
		Cost of goods sold ($140,000 + 80,000)	220,000	
		Finished goods inventory		220,000

17-5. The following account balances as of October 1, 2013, were selected from the general ledger of Mackenzie Company: (pp. 815–827)

Work in process inventory	$	0
Materials inventory		35,000
Finished goods inventory		60,000

Additional data:

a. Cost of direct materials placed in production during October totaled $170,000. There were no indirect material requisitions during October 2013.

b. Actual manufacturing overhead for October amounted to $62,000.

c. Finished goods inventory balance on October 31 was $30,000.

d. The predetermined manufacturing overhead rate is based on direct labor cost. The budget for 2013 called for $330,000 of direct labor cost and $349,000 of manufacturing overhead costs.

e. The only job unfinished on October 31, 2013, was Job No. 312, for which total labor charges were $5,600 (800 direct labor hours) and total direct material charges were $12,000.

f. October 31 balance in Materials Inventory was $29,000.

g. Total direct labor cost for October was $48,000.

Requirements

1. Determine the predetermined manufacturing overhead rate.

$$\$349,000/\$330,000 = 106\% \text{ of direct labor cost}$$

2. Determine the amount of materials purchased during October.

$$\$35,000 + X - \$170,000 = \$29,000$$
$$-\$135,000 + X = \$29,000$$
$$X = \$164,000$$

3. Determine cost of goods manufactured for October.

$$\$48,000 + (106\% \times \$48,000) + \$170,000 - \$5,600 - \$12,000 - (106\% \times \$5,600) = \$245,344$$

4. Determine the Work in Process Inventory balance on October 31.

$$\$5,600 + (106\% \times \$5,600) + \$12,000 = \$23,536$$

5. Determine cost of goods sold for October.

$$\$60,000 + \$245,344 - \$30,000 = \$275,344$$

6. Determine whether manufacturing overhead is overallocated or underallocated. What is the account balance at October 31?

$$\text{Actual manufacturing overhead} = \$62,000:$$
$$\text{Allocated manufacturing overhead} = \$48,000 \times 106\% = \$50,880$$
$$\$62,000 - \$50,800 = \$11,120 \text{ underallocated}$$

17-6 Identify which of the following products or services would use a process costing system. (p. 814)

a.	Cereal	f.	Custom swimming pools
b.	Office buildings	g.	Airplanes
c.	Paint	h.	Cellular telephones
d.	Soft drinks	i.	Personal computers
e.	Custom kitchen cabinets	j.	Surgical operation

17-7A. Department 7 has no beginning work in process inventory. During the current period, 13,500 units were placed into production. At the end of the current period, 12,000 units were transferred to Department 8. The ending units in Department 7 were 82% complete regarding direct materials and 70% complete regarding conversion costs. Compute the equivalent units for direct materials and conversion costs. (pp. 856–862)

Direct materials
$$12,000 + (1,500 \times 0.82) = 13,305$$

Conversion costs
$$12,000 + (1,500 \times 0.70) = 13,050$$

17-8A. Journalize the following transactions. (pp. 856–870)

a. Issued $8,800 of direct materials to production in the Painting Department.
b. Manufacturing labor in the Painting Department amounted to $10,000.
c. Allocated manufacturing labor to the appropriate accounts: 65% direct labor; 35% indirect labor. The pay rate for all direct labor is $20 per hour.
d. Allocated manufacturing overhead in the Painting Department at $15 per direct labor hour.
e. Transferred $7,600 of product from the Painting Department to finished goods inventory.

		General Journal			
	Date	Accounts		Debit	Credit
a.		Work in process inventory—Carving		8,800	
		Materials inventory			8,800

		General Journal			
	Date	Accounts		Debit	Credit
b.		Manufacturing wages		10,000	
		Wages payable			10,000

General Journal

	Date	Accounts	Debit	Credit
c.		Work in process inventory—Painting ($10,000 × 0.65)	6,500	
		Manufacturing overhead ($10,000 × 0.35)	3,500	
		Manufacturing wages		10,000

General Journal

	Date	Accounts	Debit	Credit
d.		Work in process inventory—Painting	7,500	
		Manufacturing overhead ($15 × $10,000/$20)		7,500

General Journal

	Date	Accounts	Debit	Credit
e.		Finished goods inventory	7,600	
		Work in process inventory—Painting		7,600

17-9A. Amerisama Company makes a variety of products. Its Texturing Department reports the following information for September of the current year:
(pp. 863–870)

Units:	
Completed and transferred out	7,400
Unfinished units, work in process, September 30	3,500*

*100% complete for direct materials and 40% complete for conversion costs incurred.

Costs:	
Direct materials	$110,000
Direct labor	55,000
Manufacturing overhead	80,000

Requirements

1. Compute the equivalent units for direct materials and conversion costs.

Equivalent units:

Direct materials
7,400 + 3,500 = 10,900 equivalent units

Conversion costs
7,400 + (3,500 × 0.40) = 8,800

2. Compute the cost per equivalent unit for direct materials and conversion costs.

Cost per equivalent unit:

Direct materials
$110,000/10,900 = $10.09

Conversion costs
($55,000 + $80,000)/8,800 = $15.34

3. Compute the cost of the goods completed and transferred out.

7,400 × ($10.09 + $15.34) = $188,182

4. Compute the cost of the work in process at September 30.

(3,500 × 1.00) × $10.09 = 35,315
(3,500 × 0.40) × $15.34 = 21,476
                          59,791

17-10A. Southern Corporation manufactures airplane parts. The company uses the weighted-average method of process costing. Information for the Assembly Department for the month of March is as follows: (pp. 856–862)

Units:	
Work in process inventory, March 1 (75% complete for direct materials, 40% complete for conversion costs)	25,000 units
Units transferred in from Finishing Dept.	150,000 units
Units completed and transferred out	140,000 units
Work in process inventory, March 31 (55% complete for direct materials, 20% complete for conversion costs)	60,000 units
Costs:	
Direct materials:	
Work in process inventory, March 1	$ 90,000
Added during March	567,000
Conversion costs:	
Work in process inventory, March 1	61,800
Added during March	721,000
Transferred-in costs:	
Work in process inventory, March 1	315,000
Units transferred in from Cutting dept. during March	1,575,000

Requirements

1. Compute the total cost of units completed and transferred out.

Direct materials equivalent units
140,000 + (60,000 × 0.55) = 173,000

Conversion costs equivalent units
140,000 + (60,000 × 0.20) = 152,000

Transferred-in equivalent units
25,000 + 150,000 = 175,000

Cost per equivalent unit:
Direct materials
$657,000/173,000 = $3.80

Conversion costs
$782,800/152,000 = $5.15
Transferred-in
$1,890,000/175,000 = $10.80

Costs of units completed and transferred out
140,000 × ($3.80 + $5.15 + $10.80) = $2,765,000

2. Compute the total cost of work in process inventory on March 31.

Costs of March 31 work in process
(22,000 × $3.80) + (8,000 × $5.15) + (60,000 × $10.80) = $83,600 + $41,200 + $648,000 = $772,800

Do It Yourself! Question 1 Solutions

Requirements

1. Why would Bell Boxers use the job order costing system?

Companies that manufacture batches of unique or specialized products would use a job order costing system to accumulate costs for each job or batch. Because Bell Boxers manufactures specialized clothing for customers and the required work may vary from customer to customer, Bell would use the job order costing system.

2. What document would Bell use to accumulate direct materials, direct labor, and manufacturing overhead costs assigned to each individual job?

Bell would use a job cost record to accumulate direct materials, direct labor, and manufacturing overhead costs assigned to each individual job.

3. Journalize each transaction.

	Date	Accounts	Debit	Credit
		General Journal		
a.		Materials inventory	20,000	
		Accounts payable		20,000

	Date	Accounts	Debit	Credit
		General Journal		
b.		Work in process inventory	13,500	
		Manufacturing overhead	1,500	
		Materials inventory		15,000

	Date	Accounts	Debit	Credit
		General Journal		
c.		Manufacturing wages	27,000	
		Wages payable		27,000
		Work in process inventory	24,000	
		Manufacturing overhead	3,000	
		Manufacturing wages		27,000

Do It Yourself! Question 2 Solutions

Requirements

1. Compute the predetermined manufacturing overhead for Quality.

$240,000/$300,000 = 0.80 or 80% of direct labor cost

2. Journalize the transactions in the general journal.

	Date	Accounts	Debit	Credit
		General Journal		
a.		Manufacturing overhead	5,100	
		Manufacturing wages		5,100

	Date	Accounts	Debit	Credit
		General Journal		
b.		Manufacturing overhead	6,200	
		Materials inventory		6,200

	Date	Accounts	Debit	Credit
		General Journal		
c.		Manufacturing overhead	7,000	
		Accounts payable		7,000

	Date	Accounts	Debit	Credit
		General Journal		
d.		Work in process inventory	17,600	
		Manufacturing overhead		17,600

General Journal

	Date	Accounts	Debit	Credit
e.		Finished goods inventory	45,000	
		Work in process inventory		45,000

General Journal

	Date	Accounts	Debit	Credit
f.		Accounts receivable	60,000	
		Sales revenue		60,000
		Cost of goods sold	33,000	
		Finished goods inventory		33,000

3. Record the journal entry to close the ending balance of manufacturing overhead.

		Accounts	Debit	Credit
		Cost of goods sold	700	
		Manufacturing overhead		700

Do It Yourself! Question 3A Solutions

Requirement

1. Use the four-step process to calculate (1) the cost of the units completed and transferred out to the Packaging Department and (2) the total cost of the units in the Blending Department ending work in process inventory.

Step 1: Summarize the flow of physical units;

Step 2: Compute output in terms of equivalent units.

JIGGLING JELLY
Blending Department
Month Ended June 30, 2013

	Step 1 Flow of Physical Units	Step 2: Equivalent Units Direct Materials	Conversion Costs
Flow of Production			
Units to account for:			
Beginning work in process, May 31	0		
Started in production during June	32,500		
Total physical units to account for	32,500		
Units accounted for:			
Completed and transferred out during June	28,000	28,000	28,000
Ending work in process, June 30	4,500	4,500	900
Total physical units accounted for	32,500		
Equivalent units		32,500	28,900

Step 3: Compute the cost per equivalent unit.

JIGGLING JELLY
Blending Department
Month Ended June 30, 2013

	Step 3: Cost per Equivalent Unit Direct Materials	Conversion Costs
Beginning work in process, May 31	$ 0	$ 0
Costs added during June	15,925	24,998
Total costs for June	$15,925	$24,998
Divide by equivalent units	÷ 32,500	÷ 28,900
Cost per equivalent unit	$ 0.49	$ 0.865

Step 4: Assign costs to units completed and to units in ending work in process inventory.

JIGGLING JELLY
Blending Department
Month Ended June 30, 2013

		Step 4: Assign Costs		
		Direct Materials	Conversion Costs	Total
Units completed and transferred out to Packaging in June	[28,000 ×	($0.49 +	$0.865)	= $37,940
Ending work in process, June 30:				
Direct materials	4,500 ×	0.49		= 2,205
Conversion costs	900 ×		0.865	= 778*
Total ending work in process, June 30				$ 2,983
Total costs accounted for				$40,923

900 × $0.865 = $778.50, rounded to $778

Do It Yourself! Question 4A Solutions

Requirements

1. Compute Quality's equivalent units for the month of July.

QUALITY CHEMICALS
Packaging Department
Month Ended July 31, 2013

	Equivalent Units		
Flow of Production	Transferred In	Direct Materials	Conversion Costs
Units accounted for:			
Completed and transferred out during July	220,000	220,000	220,000
Ending work in process inventory, July 31	65,000	0	19,500
Equivalent units	285,000	220,000	239,500

2. Compute the cost per equivalent unit for July.

QUALITY CHEMICALS
Packaging Department
Month Ended July 31, 2013

	Equivalent Units			
	Transferred In	Direct Materials	Conversion Costs	Total
Beginning work in process inventory, June 30	$ 88,000	$ 0	$ 65,000	$153,000
Costs added during July	293,900	250,800	294,250	838,950
Total costs	$381,900	$250,800	$359,250	
Divide by equivalent units	÷ 285,000	÷ 220,000	÷ 239,500	
Cost per equivalent unit	$ 1.34	$ 1.14	$ 1.50	
Total costs to account for				$991,950

3. Assign the costs to units completed and transferred out and to ending inventory.

QUALITY CHEMICALS
Packaging Department
Month Ended July 31, 2013

		Assign Costs			
		Transferred In	Direct Materials	Conversion Costs	Total
Units completed and transferred out to					
Finished goods inventory	220,000 ×	($1.34 +	$1.41 +	$1.50)	= $875,000
Ending work in process inventory, July 31:					
Transferred-in costs	65,000 ×	1.34			= 87,100
Direct materials			0		0
Conversion costs	19,500 ×			1.50	= 29,250
Total ending work in process inventory, July 31					$116,350
Total costs accounted for					$991,950

The Power of Practice

For more practice using the skills learned in this chapter, visit MyAccountingLab. There you will find algorithmically generated questions that are based on these Demo Docs and your main textbook's Review and Assess Your Progress sections.

Go to MyAccountingLab and follow these steps:

1. Direct your URL to www.myaccountinglab.com.
2. Log in using your name and password.
3. Click the MyAccountingLab link.
4. Click Study Plan in the left navigation bar.
5. From the table of contents, select Chapter 17, Job Order and Process Costing.
6. Click a link to work tutorial exercises.

18 Activity-Based Costing and Other Cost Management Tools

WHAT YOU PROBABLY ALREADY KNOW

WHAT YOU PROBABLY ALREADY KNOW

Many colleges and universities charge a set amount of tuition for full-time students. It does not matter if students take 12 or 18 credits or if they are a philosophy or computer science major. Is it fair that a philosophy major taking 12 credits pays the same tuition as a computer science major taking 18 credits? You probably already know that computer science classes are held in a computer lab, which requires hardware and software and holds fewer students than a philosophy classroom. Certainly more classes that are taken require more costs incurred by the institution for faculty and operating costs. It is clear that the number of credits and classroom support required by the nature of the course generates costs. It would be helpful for the college to know the real costs of each program. It could help the college make decisions to discontinue, reduce, or expand programs; curtail costs by understanding what drives the costs; and possibly even devise a tuition structure intended to pass program costs onto students more equitably. In this chapter, we will learn about activity-based costing (ABC). ABC is a system, as described, that assigns costs to products and services according to the action that causes the resources to be used. There are benefits to all entities to identify accurate costs of the goods and services they provide.

Learning Objectives/Success Keys

 Develop activity-based costs (ABC).

To develop an activity-based cost (ABC) system, the steps outlined in Exhibit 18-4 (p. 883) must be performed. *Review Exhibit 18-3 (p. 882) for examples of activities and cost drivers. An example of implementing the four steps to develop an activity-based cost system is shown in Exhibit 18-4 (p. 883). Be sure to study Exhibit 18-4 carefully to understand each step of the process.*

2 Use activity-based management (ABM) to achieve target costs.

- **Pricing and Product Mix**—ABC more accurately identifies product costs and consequently gross profit. Better decisions can then be made about pricing and the product mix.

- **Cutting Costs**—Identifying the cost drivers and all of the activities that are being used to manufacture the product also provides a clear understanding of what causes costs to be incurred. When companies need to cut costs, they are armed with more information as to how to cut costs or redesign the process to be more efficient.

- **Routine Planning and Control**—Management can use ABC information to create budgets and analyze variances in more detail by activities.

3 Describe a just-in-time (JIT) production system, and record its transactions.

A **JIT production system** obtains the required materials as needed to satisfy customer orders. The goal is to have what you need *when* you need it, a near-zero inventory level. The production takes place in work centers where employees work in a team to complete the manufacturing process.

Under JIT, the manufacturing accounting is somewhat different from job-order and process-costing systems. There is one account for Raw Materials Inventory and Work in Process Inventory called Raw and in Process Inventory. This account is debited for purchases of direct materials. Labor and overhead incurred are also recorded in one account, Conversion Costs. The Raw and in Process Inventory and Conversion Costs accounts are reduced (credited) for the products completed, which is debited to Finished Goods. *Review Exhibits 18-13 and 18-14 (pp. 894–895) for differences between the traditional and just-in-time costing.*

4 Use the four types of quality costs to make decisions.

The four types of quality costs are as follows:

- **Prevention costs**—Costs incurred to avoid inferior quality goods or services

- **Appraisal costs**—Costs incurred to detect inferior quality goods or services

- **Internal failure costs**—Costs incurred to uncover and correct inferior quality goods or services before delivery to customers

- **External failure costs**—Costs incurred due to the lack of uncovering inferior quality goods or services until after they are delivered to customers

Review Exhibit 18-16 (p. 898) for examples of the four types of quality costs.

Demo Doc 1

Activity-Based Costing

Learning Objectives 1, 2

Home Beauty uses activity-based costing to account for its concrete countertop manufacturing process. Company managers have identified three manufacturing activities: mold assembly, mixing, and finishing. The budgeted activity costs for the year and their allocation bases are as follows:

Activity	Total Budgeted cost	Allocation Base
Mold assembly	$14,000	Number of parts
Mixing	$32,000	Number of batches
Finishing	$27,000	Number of direct labor hours

Home Beauty expects to produce 2,500 countertops during the year. The countertops are expected to use 10,000 parts, require 8,000 batches, and use 3,750 finishing hours.

Direct material cost is expected to be $40 per countertop and direct labor cost is expected to be $37.50 per countertop.

Requirements

1. Compute the cost allocation rate for each activity.

2. Compute the indirect manufacturing cost of each countertop.

3. Home Beauty would like to bid on selling 50 countertops to Ben Jones Builder. Assuming that Home Beauty requires a 30% markup on total costs, what bid price should Home Beauty use on the Ben Jones proposal?

Demo Doc 1 Solutions

Requirement 1

1 Develop activity-based costs (ABC)

Compute the cost allocation rate for each activity.

Part 1	Part 2	Part 3	Demo Doc Complete

For Home Beauty, we have the first few steps in developing an ABC system based on the information given in the question:

Home Beauty identifies three manufacturing activities:	Home Beauty estimates the total budgeted cost for each activity:	The allocation base for each activity is the primary cost driver for each. Home Beauty identifies these:	Home Beauty estimates the quantities of each cost driver allocation base:
Mold assembly	$14,000	# of parts	10,000 parts
Mixing	$32,000	# of batches	8,000 batches
Finishing	$27,000	# of direct labor hours	3,750 direct labor hours

To compute the cost allocation rate for each activity, divide the total budgeted cost of each activity by the estimated total quantity of the cost driver's allocation base:

$$\text{Mold assembly cost allocation rate} = \frac{\$14,000}{10,000 \text{ parts}} = \$1.40 \text{ per part}$$

$$\text{Mixing cost allocation rate} = \frac{\$32,000}{8,000 \text{ batches}} = \$4.00 \text{ per batch}$$

$$\text{Finishing cost allocation rate} = \frac{\$27,000}{3,750 \text{ direct labor hours}} = \$7.20 \text{ DL hour}$$

We will use the cost allocation *rate* for each activity to compute the indirect manufacturing cost of each countertop in the next requirement.

Requirement 2

1 Develop activity-based costs (ABC)

Compute the indirect manufacturing cost of each countertop.

Part 1	Part 2	Part 3	Demo Doc Complete

To calculate the indirect cost of manufacturing each countertop, we must calculate the average *quantity* of each cost allocation base used per countertop. The average quantity of each cost allocation base used per countertop is calculated by dividing the expected total used for each base by the number of countertops Home Beauty expects to produce.

We know from the question that Home Beauty expects to produce 2,500 countertops during the year, requiring 10,000 parts, 8,000 mixing batches, and 3,750 direct labor hours per countertop. Calculations are as follows:

$$\text{Parts per countertop} = \frac{10,000}{2,500} = 4 \text{ parts per countertop}$$

$$\text{Batches per countertop} = \frac{8,000}{2,500} = 3.2 \text{ batches per countertop}$$

$$\text{Finishing hours per countertop} = \frac{3,750}{2,500} = 1.5 \text{ DL hours per countertop}$$

To compute the indirect manufacturing cost of each countertop, multiply the average quantity of each activity cost allocation base used per countertop by the cost allocation rate (as determined in requirement 1).

Activity	Actual Quantity of Cost Allocation Base Used per Countertop		Activity Cost Allocation Rate		Standard Activity Cost per Countertop
Mold assembly	4	×	$1.40	=	$ 5.60
Mixing	3.2	×	$4.00	=	$12.80
Finishing	1.5	×	$7.20	=	$10.80
Total indirtect cost per countertop					$29.20

Shown another way, you can also solve this using total costs. We know that:

Total assembly cost	= $14,000
Total mixing cost	= $32,000
Total finishing cost	= $27,000
Total indirect manufacturing cost	= $73,000

You can calculate the indirect manufacturing cost per countertop by summing the total costs and dividing by the number of countertops produced during the year:

Indirect manufacturing cost of each countertop = $73,000/2,500
= $29.20 per countertop

This is also a good way to check your work.

So, Home Beauty estimates that each countertop will incur $29.20 in indirect manufacturing costs. This cost will help us compute the total cost of producing each countertop in the next requirement, which, among other decisions, helps management determine a sales price for each countertop.

Requirement 3

Home Beauty would like to bid on selling 50 countertops to Ben Jones Builder. Assuming that Home Beauty requires a 30% markup on total costs, what bid price should Home Beauty use on the Ben Jones proposal?

Part 1	Part 2	**Part 3**	Demo Doc Complete

To determine the bid price, Home Beauty must first determine the cost of producing one countertop. The cost would be direct materials + direct labor + indirect cost.

We know from the question that direct materials are expected to be $40 per countertop and direct labor is expected to be $37.50 per countertop. In requirement 2, we determined that indirect manufacturing costs amount to $29.20 per countertop. So, Home Beauty's cost of producing one countertop is:

$$\$40 + \$37.50 + \$29.20 = \$106.70 \text{ cost per countertop}$$

Because they require a 30% markup, the price that Home Beauty would charge per countertop is 130% of the cost:

$$\$138.71 \times 50 = \$6,935.50$$

Home Beauty is bidding on a job of 50 countertops, so the total bid price would be as follows:

$$\$138.71 \times 50 = \$6,935.50$$

Again, shown another way, we can reach the same computation using total costs. We know from the question that direct material cost is expected to be $40 per countertop and direct labor cost is expected to be $37.50 per countertop. For 2,500 countertops, direct material costs = 2,500 × $40 = $100,000, and direct labor cost = 2,500 × $37.50 = $93,750. So our total costs are:

Total assembly cost	= $ 14,000
Total mixing cost	= $ 32,000
Total finishing cost	= $ 27,000
Direct material cost	= $100,000
Direct labor cost	= $ 93,750
Total cost	= $266,750

We then determine the cost per unit as total cost divided by the number of units:

$$\text{Cost per unit} = \$266{,}750/2{,}500$$
$$= \$106.70 \text{ cost per countertop}$$

This matches the cost per countertop computed earlier in this requirement. Calculations would continue as before:

Price per countertop	$= \$106.70 \times 130\%$ markup
	$= \$138.71$
Total bid price	$= \$138.71 \times 50$ bids
	$= \$6{,}935.50$

This is also a good way to check your work.

Part 1	Part 2	Part 3	**Demo Doc Complete**

Demo Doc 2

Other Cost Management Tools

Learning Objectives 3, 4

Healthy Heart manufactures a smoothie mix for franchised retail outlets. Healthy Heart uses JIT costing. The standard unit cost of producing a case of smoothie mix is $8: $5 for direct materials and $3 for conversion costs. Direct materials purchased on account during April totaled $120,000. Actual conversion costs totaled $75,900. Healthy Heart completed 25,000 cases of smoothie mix during April and sold 24,000 cases.

Requirements

1. Prepare the April journal entries for the transactions.

2. Make the entry to close the under- or overallocated conversion costs to Cost of Goods Sold.

Demo Doc 2 Solutions

Requirement 1

3 Describe a just-in-time (JIT) production system, and record its transactions

Prepare the April journal entries for the transactions.

Part 1	Part 2	Demo Doc Complete

Companies that use a JIT system do not use a separate Work in Process Inventory account. Instead, they use two inventory accounts: Raw and in Process Inventory and Finished Goods Inventory.

The Raw and in Process Inventory account combines direct materials with work in process.

Purchases of direct materials will require a debit (increase) to the Raw and in Process Inventory account.

In this case, Healthy Heart purchased $120,000 of direct materials on account in April. So the two accounts affected are Raw and in Process Inventory and Accounts Payable.

For the purchase of direct material, Healthy Heart will make the following journal entry:

Raw and in process inventory		120,000	
Accounts payable			120,000

Under the JIT philosophy, workers perform many tasks. Because little labor is directly traceable to individual finished products, most companies using JIT combine labor and manufacturing overhead costs into an account called Conversion Costs.

The Conversion Costs account is a temporary account that works like the Manufacturing Overhead account.

To record the actual conversion costs, Healthy Heart will make the following journal entry:

Conversion costs		75,900	
Various accounts (wages payable, accumulated depreciation, and so forth)			75,900

The Various accounts used as credits will depend on the conversion cost incurred (for example, labor : wages payable, depreciation : accumulated depreciation, utilities : accounts payable).

Goods completed are recorded at the standard cost of completing those goods.

The total cost of the finished goods is calculated by multiplying the total units completed, 25,000, by the standard cost of $8 per unit ($5 for direct materials and $3 for conversion costs) = $200,000.

Raw and in Process Inventory is credited for the standard direct material cost of the units completed:

25,000 units completed × $5 direct materials cost = $125,000

Conversion Costs is credited (increased) for the standard conversion cost of the units completed:

25,000 units completed × $3,000 conversion costs = $75,000

Healthy Heart will make the following journal entry for the 25,000 units completed:

Finished goods inventory (25,000 units × $8)	200,000	
Raw and in process inventory (25,000 × $5)		125,000
Conversion costs (25,000 × $3)		75,000

Goods sold are recorded at the standard cost of completing the goods.

Healthy Heart sold 24,000 units with a standard cost of $8 per unit. The units sold will be recorded at a cost of $192,000:

Cost of goods sold	192,000	
Finished goods inventory		192,000

Remember, this is not recording the sales revenue, but rather Healthy Heart's costs associated with the number of cases of smoothie mix that it sold.

Requirement 2

Make the entry to close the under- or overallocated conversion costs to Cost of Goods Sold.

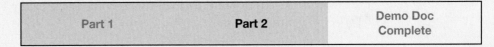

Part 1	**Part 2**	Demo Doc Complete

Just like under- and overallocated manufacturing overhead, under- or overallocated conversion costs are closed to Cost of Goods Sold at the end of the period.

Healthy Heart had actual conversion costs of $75,900 (debit) and standard conversion costs (from requirement 1) of $75,000 (credit), therefore conversion costs were underallocated.

A debit of $75,900 and a credit of $75,000 yields a credit (decrease) of $900. Healthy Heart will make the following journal entry to close the Conversion Costs account:

Cost of goods sold	900	
Conversion costs		900

Part 1	Part 2	**Demo Doc Complete**

Quick Practice Questions

True/False

_____ 1. ABC costing is generally less accurate than traditional cost systems.

_____ 2. ABC systems take more effort to allocate indirect costs to products that caused the costs than do traditional cost systems.

_____ 3. The target price is what manufacturers are willing to pay to produce a product.

_____ 4. Activity-based management refers to using activity-based cost information to make decisions that increase profits while satisfying customers' needs.

_____ 5. Appraisal costs occur when poor-quality goods or services are not detected until after delivery to customers.

_____ 6. Internal failure costs occur to avoid poor-quality goods or services.

_____ 7. The cost allocation rate for each activity is equal to the estimated total indirect costs of the activity divided by the estimated total quantity of cost allocation base.

_____ 8. Overhead costs incurred are recorded in the Conversion Cost account.

_____ 9. Just-in-time costing means systematically evaluating activities in an effort to reduce costs while satisfying customers' needs.

_____ 10. The goal of total quality management is to provide customers with superior products and services.

Multiple Choice

1. The cost of training personnel is an example of which of the following types of cost?
   a. Internal failure cost
   b. External failure cost
   c. Prevention cost
   d. Appraisal cost

2. Which of the following is most likely to be the cost driver for the packaging and shipping activity?
   a. Number of orders
   b. Number of components
   c. Number of setups
   d. Hours of testing

3. **What is the last step in developing an ABC system?**
   a. Identify the activities
   b. Allocate costs to the cost object
   c. Estimate the total quantity of the cost driver
   d. Estimate the total indirect costs of each activity

4. **Which of the following statements regarding activity-based costing systems is false?**
   a. ABC systems can create more accurate product costs.
   b. ABC systems may only be used by service companies.
   c. ABC systems are more complex and costly than traditional systems.
   d. ABC systems are used in both manufacturing and nonmanufacturing companies.

5. **Alpha Company manufactures breadboxes and uses an activity-based costing system. The following information is provided for the month of May:**

Activity	Estimated Indirect Activity Costs	Allocation Base	Estimated Quantity of Allocation Base
Materials handling	$ 3,500	Number of parts	5,000 parts
Assembling	$12,000	Number of parts	5,000 parts
Packaging	$ 5,750	Number of breadboxes	1,250 breadboxes

   Each breadbox consists of four parts and the direct materials cost per breadbox is $7.00.

   What is the cost of materials handling and assembling per breadbox?
   a. $ 4.60
   b. $12.40
   c. $14.40
   d. $17.00

6. **Refer to question 5. What is the total manufacturing cost per breadbox?**
   a. $12.40
   b. $17.40
   c. $24.00
   d. $26.00

7. **The cost of inspection at various stages of production is an example of which of the following?**
   a. Appraisal cost
   b. Prevention cost
   c. Internal failure cost
   d. External failure cost

8. **The process of designing products that achieve cost targets and meet specified standards of quality and performance is referred to as which of the following?**
   a. Value engineering
   b. Developmental engineering
   c. Design engineering
   d. Total engineering

9. Which of the following is true for a JIT production system?
   a. JIT requires longer setup times than a traditional production system.
   b. JIT produces goods in smaller batches than a traditional production system.
   c. JIT has like machines grouped together in the production facility.
   d. JIT requires higher inventory levels.

10. What are the lost profits from the loss of customers called?
    a. Prevention cost
    b. Internal failure cost
    c. Appraisal cost
    d. External failure cost

Quick Exercises

18-1.   Compare and contrast activity-based costing with traditional systems using a single application base for conversion costs.

18-2.   Pandora Servers Company uses activity-based costing to account for its manufacturing process. The following are the four activities identified with the process and their budgeted costs for the month of May.

Activity	Total Budgeted Cost	Allocation Base
Materials handling	$110,000	Number of parts
Machine setup	21,000	Number of setups
Assembling	32,000	Number of parts
Packaging	8,000	Number of finished units

Pandora expects to produce 1,000 units in the month of May. The units are expected to use 25,000 parts and require 15 setups.

Requirements

1. Compute the cost allocation rate for each activity.

2. Compute the average manufacturing cost of each sewing machine assuming direct materials are $195 per machine.

18-3. Music Man Corporation manufactures two models of music players: a standard model and a deluxe model. Using activity-based costing, three activities have been identified as cost drivers. These activities, as well as the estimated total cost associated with them for the month of July, are shown as follows:

	(1) Number of Materials Requisitions	(2) Number of Product Inspections	(3) Number of Orders Shipped
Standard	460	150	167
Deluxe	620	210	129
Estimated total activity cost	$38,000	$15,000	$28,000

Requirement

1. Determine the amount of each cost pool applied for the: (a) standard model, and (b) deluxe model.

18-4. Compare and contrast the major features of a just-in-time production system with a traditional production system.

18-5. Identify each of the following as a prevention cost, an appraisal cost, an internal failure cost, or an external failure cost.

a. Salaries of receiving department employees responsible for inspecting all purchased parts and materials _____
b. Maintenance costs incurred to keep the production machinery operating at full capacity _____
c. Service costs at customer sites _____
d. Salaries of the employees who inspect the final product _____
e. Salaries of the service department personnel who handle repairs under warranty _____
f. Cost of two-week training course for new employees _____
g. Lost profits from customers who did not place an order due to lack of availability of product _____
h. The cost of reworking defective product _____
i. Customer returns due to defective merchandise _____
j. Costs of designing the product _____

Do It Yourself! Question 1

Activity-Based Costing

Grand Slam uses activity-based costing to account for its baseball pitching machine manufacturing process. Company managers have identified three manufacturing activities: purchasing, assembly, and finishing. The budgeted activity costs for the year and their allocation bases are as follows:

Activity	Total Budgeted Cost	Allocation Base
Purchasing	$16,000	Number of purchase orders
Assembly	$40,000	Number of parts
Finishing	$22,000	Number of direct labor hours

Grand Slam expects to produce 1,000 pitching machines during the year. The machines are expected to require a total of 400 purchase orders, 50,000 parts, and 4,000 finishing hours.

Direct material cost is expected to be $160 per machine and direct labor cost is expected to be $80 per machine.

Requirements

Develop activity-based costs (ABC)

1. Compute the cost allocation rate for each activity.

Purchasing cost allocation rate	=	
Assembly cost allocation rate	=	
Finishing cost allocation rate	=	

Develop activity-based costs (ABC)

2. Compute the indirect manufacturing cost of each machine.

Activity	Actual Quantity of Cost Allocation Base Used per Machine	Activity Cost Allocation Rate	Standard Activity Cost per Machine
Purchasing			
Assembly			
Finishing			
Total indirtect cost per machine			

Use activity-based management (ABM) to achieve target costs

3. Grand Slam would like to bid on selling 40 pitching machines to Pirate Family Fun Park. Assuming that Grand Slam requires a 25% markup, what bid price should Grand Slam use on the Pirate proposal?

Do It Yourself! Question 2

Other Cost Management Tools

Back to Life reconditions automobile batteries. Back to Life uses JIT costing. The standard unit cost of reconditioning a battery is $9: $4 for direct materials and $5 for conversion costs. Direct materials purchased on account during November totaled $62,000. Actual conversion costs totaled $78,000. Back to Life reconditioned 15,000 batteries during November and sold 14,000 batteries.

Requirements

3 Describe a just-in-time (JIT) production system, and record its transactions

1. Prepare the November journal entries for the transactions.

Date	Accounts	Debit	Credit

Date	Accounts	Debit	Credit

Date	Accounts	Debit	Credit

Date	Accounts	Debit	Credit

4 Use the four types of quality costs to make decisions

2. Make the entry to close the under- or overallocated Conversion Costs to Cost of Goods Sold.

Date	Accounts	Debit	Credit

Quick Practice Solutions

True/False

F____ 1. ABC costing is generally less accurate than traditional cost systems.

False—ABC costing is generally *more* accurate than traditional cost systems. (p. 885)

T____ 2. ABC systems take more effort to allocate indirect costs to products that caused the costs than do traditional costing systems. (p. 884)

F____ 3. The target price is what manufacturers are willing to pay to produce a procuct.

False—The target price is what *customers are willing to pay* for the products or service. (p. 887)

T____ 4. Activity-based management refers to using activity-based cost information to make decisions that increase profits while satisfying customers' needs. (p. 886)

F____ 5. Appraisal costs occur when poor-quality goods or services are not detected until after delivery to customers.

False—*External failure costs* occur when poor-quality goods or services are not detected until after delivery to customers. (p. 898)

F____ 6. Internal failure costs occur to avoid poor-quality goods or services.

False—*Preventive costs* occur to avoid poor-quality goods or services. (p. 898)

T____ 7. The cost allocation rate for each activity is equal to the estimated total indirect costs of the activity divided by the estimated total quantity of cost allocation base. (p. 883)

T____ 8. Overhead costs incurred are recorded in the Conversion Cost account. (p. 886)

F____ 9. Just-in-time costing means systematically evaluating activities in an effort to reduce costs while satisfying customers' needs.

False—*Value engineering costing* means systematically evaluating activities in an effort to reduce costs while satisfying customers' needs. (p. 893)

T____ 10. The goal of total quality management is to provide customers with superior products and services. (p. 897)

Multiple Choice

1. The cost of training personnel is an example of which of the following types of cost? (p. 898)
   a. Internal failure cost
   b. External failure cost
   c. Prevention cost
   d. Appraisel cost

2. Which of the following is most likely to be the cost driver for the packaging and shipping activity? (pp. 884–886)
   a. Number of orders
   b. Number of components
   c. Number of setups
   d. Hours of testing

3. What is the last step in developing an ABC system? (p. 885)
   a. Identify the activities
   b. Allocate costs to the cost object
   c. Estimate the total quantity of the cost driver
   d. Estimate the total indirect costs of each activity

4. Which of the following statements regarding activity-based costing systems is false? (p. 883)
   a. ABC systems can create more accurate product costs.
   b. ABC systems may only be used by service companies.
   c. ABC systems are more complex and costly than traditional systems.
   d. ABC systems are used in both manufacturing and nonmanufacturing companies.

5. Alpha Company manufactures breadboxes and uses an activity-based costing system. The following information is provided for the month of May:

Activity	Estimated Indirect Activity Costs	Allocation Base	Estimated Quantity of Allocation Base
Materials handling	$ 3,500	Number of parts	5,000 parts
Assembling	$12,000	Number of parts	5,000 parts
Packaging	$ 5,750	Number of breadboxes	1,250 breadboxes

Each breadbox consists of four parts and the direct materials cost per breadbox is $7.00.

What is the cost of materials handling and assembling per breadbox? (p. 883)
   a. $4.60
   b. $12.40
   c. $14.40
   d. $17.00

6. Refer to question 5. What is the total manufacturing cost per breadbox? (p. 889)
   a. $12.40
   b. $17.40
   c. $24.00
   d. $26.00

7. **The cost of inspection at various stages of production is an example of which of the following?** (p. 898)
   a. Appraisal cost
   b. Prevention cost
   c. Internal failure cost
   d. External failure cost

8. **The process of designing products that achieve cost targets and meet specified standards of quality and performance is referred to as which of the following?** (p. 887)
   a. Value engineering
   b. Developmental engineering
   c. Design engineering
   d. Total engineering

9. **Which of the following is true for a JIT production system?** (p. 893)
   a. JIT requires longer setup times than a traditional production system.
   b. JIT produces goods in smaller batches than a traditional production system.
   c. JIT has like machines grouped together in the production facility.
   d. JIT requires higher inventory levels.

10. **What are the lost profits from the loss of customers called?** (p. 898)
    a. Prevention cost
    b. Internal failure cost
    c. Appraisal cost
    d. External failure cost

Quick Exercises

18-1. **Compare and contrast activity-based costing with traditional systems using a single application base for conversion costs.** (pp. 883–886)

Activity-based costing (ABC) is a system that focuses on activities as the fundamental cost objects. The activity costs are the foundation for accumulating the indirect costs of products, services, and customers. ABC systems allocate the indirect costs of manufacturing overhead to the products, services, or customers based on what caused them, the cost drivers. Each cost driver is selected for its causal relationship to an activity. The more precise the relationship, the more accurate the product cost. This method gives managers better information for decision making. In addition, developments in information technology make ABC less costly than before and much more feasible.

Single-rate costing applies indirect costs to products on the basis of a single allocation base, historically direct labor. This method is simpler than ABC and less costly. However, no single factor drives all indirect manufacturing costs. Thus, this method may distort the cost of products.

18-2. Pandora Servers Company uses activity-based costing to account for its manufacturing process. Following are the four activities identified with the process and their budgeted costs for the month of May: (pp. 883–886)

Activity	Total Budgeted Cost	Allocation Base
Materials handling	$110,000	Number of parts
Machine setup	21,000	Number of setups
Assembling	32,000	Number of parts
Packaging	8,000	Number of finished units

Pandora expects to produce 1,000 units in the month of May. The units are expected to use 25,000 parts and require 15 setups.

Requirements

1. Compute the cost allocation rate for each activity.

$110,000 / 25,000 parts = $4.40
$21,000 / 15 setups = $1,400
$32,000 / 25,000 parts = $1.28
$ 8,000 / 1,000 finished units = $8.00

2. Compute the average manufacturing cost of each unit assuming direct materials are $195 per machine.

25,000 / 1,000 = 25 parts × $4.40 = $110
15 / 1,000 = 0.015 setups × $1,400 = $21
25,000 / 1,000 = 25 parts × $1.28 = $32
1,000 / 1,000 = 1 unit × $8.00 = $8
$110 + $21 + $32 + $8 + $195 = $366

18-3. Music Man Corporation manufactures two models of music players: a standard model and a deluxe model. Using activity-based costing, three activities have been identified as cost drivers. These activities, as well as the estimated total cost associated with them for the month of July, are shown below: (pp. 883–886)

	(1) Number of Materials Requisitions	(2) Number of Product Inspections	(3) Number of Orders Shipped
Standard	460	150	167
Deluxe	620	210	129
Estimated total activity cost	$38,000	$15,000	$28,000

Requirement

1. Determine the amount of each cost pool applied for the: (a) standard model, and (b) deluxe model.

Materials requisitions:

(a) 460 + 620 = 1,080
     (460 / 1,080) × $38,000 = $16,185 standard

(b) (620 / 1,080) × $38,000 = $21,815 deluxe

Product inspections:

(a) 150 + 210 = 360
     (150 / 360) × $15,000 = $6,250 standard
(b) (210 / 360) × $15,000 = $8,750 deluxe

Orders shipped:

(a) 167 + 129 = 296
     (167 / 296) × $28,000 = $15,797 standard
(b) (129 / 296) × $28,000 = $12,203 deluxe

18-4. **Compare and contrast the major features of a just-in-time production system with a traditional production system.** (pp. 893–897)

Traditional production systems often produce enormous waste in two specific areas: inventories and manufacturing processes. Inventories are maintained at high levels to guard against poor quality in raw materials, poor quality in production, machine breakdowns, long setup times on production equipment, and stock outs. However, large inventories tie up cash and hide production problems. Manufacturing processes set up machines according to function, causing raw materials and parts to travel long distances back and forth through a factory. Machines are kept busy, resulting in product being pushed through the system, regardless of downstream demand.

Just-in-time production systems have the following characteristics:

1. Production activities are arranged by the sequence of operations, reducing moving time.
2. Machine setup times are reduced through employee training and new technology.
3. Production is scheduled in small batches just in time to satisfy needs.
4. Employees are trained to do more than operate a single machine.

18-5. **Identify each of the following as a prevention cost, an appraisal cost, an internal failure cost, or an external failure cost.** (p. 898)

   a. Salaries of receiving department employees responsible for inspecting all purchased parts and materials
     appraisal cost

   b. Maintenance costs incurred to keep the production machinery operating at full capacity
     prevention cost

   c. Service costs at customer sites
     external failure cost

   d. Salaries of the employees who inspect the final product
     appraisal cost

   e. Salaries of the service department personnel who handle repairs under warranty
     external failure cost

   f. Cost of two-week training course for new employees
     prevention cost

   g. Lost profits from customers who did not place an order due to lack of availability of product
     external failure cost

   h. The cost of reworking defective product
     internal failure cost

   i. Customer returns due to defective merchandise
     external failure cost

   j. Costs of designing the product
     prevention cost

Do It Yourself! Question 1 Solutions

Requirements

1. Compute the cost allocation rate for each activity.

$$\text{Purchasing cost allocation rate} = \frac{\$16,000}{400 \text{ purchase orders}} = \$40.00 \text{ per purchase order}$$

$$\text{Assembly cost allocation rate} = \frac{\$40,000}{50,000 \text{ parts}} = \$0.80 \text{ per part}$$

$$\text{Finishing cost allocation rate} = \frac{\$22,000}{4,000 \text{ direct labor hours}} = \$5.50 \text{ per direct labor hour}$$

2. Compute the indirect manufacturing cost of each machine.

$$\text{Purchasing orders per machine} = \frac{400 \text{ purchase orders}}{1,000 \text{ machines}} = 0.4 \text{ purchase orders per machine}$$

$$\text{Parts per machine} = \frac{50,000 \text{ parts}}{1,000 \text{ machines}} = 50 \text{ parts per machine}$$

$$\text{Finishing hours per machine} = \frac{4,000 \text{ direct labor hours}}{1,000 \text{ machines}} = 4 \text{ direct labor hours per machine}$$

Activity	Actual Quantity of Cost Allocation Base Used per Machine		Activity Cost Allocation Rate		Standard Activity Cost per Machine
Purchasing	0.4	×	$40.00	=	$16
Assembly	50	×	$ 0.80	=	40
Finishing	4	×	$ 5.50	=	22
Total indirect cost per machine					$78

3. Grand Slam would like to bid on selling 40 pitching machines to Pirate Family Fun Park. Assuming that Grand Slam requires a 25% markup, what bid price should Grand Slam use on the Pirate proposal?

Direct materials + Direct labor + Indirect manufacturing cost = Cost per machine
Cost = $160 + $80 + $78
= $318 per machine
Cost per machine × Markup = Sales price per machine
$318 × 125% = $397.50 per machine
Total bid for 40 machines:
$397.50 × 40 machines = $15,900 total bid

Do It Yourself! Question 2 Solutions

Requirements

1. Prepare the November journal entries for the transactions.

Date	Accounts and explanation	Debit	Credit
	Raw and in process inventory	62,000	
	Accounts payable		62,000

Date	Accounts and explanation	Debit	Credit
	Conversion costs	78,000	
	Various accounts (wages payable, accumulated depreciation, and so forth)		78,000

Date	Accounts and explanation	Debit	Credit
	Finished goods inventory	135,000	
	Raw and in process inventory		60,000
	Conversion costs		75,000

Date	Accounts and explanation	Debit	Credit
	Cost of goods sold	126,000	
	Finished goods inventory		126,000

2. Make the entry to close the under- or overallocated Conversion Costs to Cost of Goods Sold.

Date	Accounts and explanation	Debit	Credit
	Cost of goods sold	3,000	
	Conversion costs		3,000

The Power of Practice

For more practice using the skills learned in this chapter, visit MyAccountingLab. There you will find algorithmically generated questions that are based on these Demo Docs and your main textbook's Review and Assess Your Progress sections.

Go to MyAccountingLab and follow these steps:

1. Direct your URL to www.myaccountinglab.com.
2. Log in using your name and password.
3. Click the MyAccountingLab link.
4. Click Study Plan in the left navigation bar.
5. From the table of contents, select Chapter 18, Activity-Based Costing and Other Cost Management Tools.
6. Click a link to work tutorial exercises.

19 Cost-Volume-Profit Analysis

WHAT YOU PROBABLY ALREADY KNOW

If you decide to sign up for cell phone service, you know that there is a choice of providers and plans. Assume that you are debating whether to enroll in one of two plans. The first plan has 450 free anytime minutes, which costs $40 a month plus $0.45/minute beyond 450. The second plan has 900 free anytime minutes, which costs $60 a month plus $0.40/minute beyond 900. Your objective is to minimize your cost. To accomplish this, you are using concepts like fixed and variable costs that we will study in this chapter. The monthly amount of $40 or $60 is fixed; once the plan is selected, you will be charged that monthly amount regardless of the number of minutes you use. In addition, you will be charged a variable cost per minute if you exceed the allowed number of minutes. If you estimate that you will be using about 600 anytime minutes, which plan is cheaper? Plan one would be $40 + [(600 − 450) × $0.45] = $107.50; plan two would be $60 + 0 = $60. The second plan is cheaper.

Learning Objectives/Success Keys

 Identify how changes in volume affect costs.

There are three types of costs—fixed, variable, and mixed. **Fixed costs** are costs that do not change over wide ranges of volume. The range of volume over which fixed costs are constant is called the **relevant range**. Building rent, furniture depreciation, and the salary of an office manager would be examples of fixed costs. If fixed costs are $100,000 and 10,000 units are produced, the fixed cost per unit is $10 ($100,000/10,000). If the volume doubles to 20,000 units, the fixed cost per unit is reduced to $5 per unit. **Variable costs** are costs that increase in total as the volume of activity increases and decrease as the volume of activity decreases. **Total variable costs** change in direct proportion to changes in volume. Direct materials and direct labor are examples of variable costs. If it costs $3 per unit for direct materials, the total variable cost when 10,000 units are produced is $30,000. If the volume doubles to 20,000, the total variable cost is now $60,000, but the variable cost per unit is unchanged at $3 per unit. **Mixed costs** have both variable and fixed components. The **high-low method** is used to separate the mixed cost into the variable and fixed elements. *Review Exhibits 19-1 and 19-2 (pp. 925–926) to see the impact of varying volume amounts on total variable and fixed costs.*

2   Use CVP analysis to compute breakeven points.

The **breakeven point** is the sales level at which operating income is zero. Sales revenue equals total fixed and variable costs. There are three approaches you can use to compute the breakeven point. The **income statement approach** uses the income statement to facilitate the calculation of breakeven units sold (see Demo Doc 1). The contribution margin is the difference between sales revenue and variable costs. The **contribution margin approach** is a shortcut to the income statement approach. The **contribution margin ratio approach** is used when you do not have detailed information on individual products. You will use these three approaches in Demo Doc 1.

Rounding Note: When calculating the breakeven sales units or sales dollars, it is possible to obtain a fractional amount. To be conservative, you should always round up to the next higher unit or dollar.

Review Summary Problem 1 for computations of breakeven sales units and dollars.

3   Use CVP analysis for profit planning, and graph the CVP relations.

As you will also see in Demo Doc 1, you can use the three approaches to compute breakeven to also determine the number of units that must be sold to create a desired net income.

The cost-volume-profit relationship can be graphed using increments of volume within the relevant range as the horizontal axis and dollars as the vertical axis. Total sales revenue is zero at zero volume and would increase linearly $10 for each unit of volume using the example in Summary Problem 1 of the main textbook (p. 935). Total costs would start on the vertical axis at $10,000, the total fixed costs, and would increase linearly $4 for variable costs for each unit of volume. The point at which the total sales revenue line equals total costs is the breakeven point. Drawing a vertical line from that point would indicate the breakeven volume in units. *Review Summary Problem 1 for computations of sales units and dollars to achieve desired results. Review the cost-volume-profit graph in Exhibit 19-5 (p. 934).*

4   Use CVP methods to perform sensitivity analyses.

Sensitivity analysis is a "what if" technique that shows how profits will be affected if sales prices, costs, or underlying assumptions change. Using technology tools with an understanding of the interrelationship between the elements of cost, volume, and profit, it can be determined what the effect may be on net income of making business decisions.

5   Calculate the breakeven point for multiple products or services.

Most companies sell multiple product lines or services. Each product or service may have a different contribution margin. It is necessary to calculate the weighted-average contribution margin of all of the sales using a sales mix, as you will see in Demo Doc 2. **A sales mix** is the combination of products that make up total sales. *Review the Summary Problem 2 in the main textbook (p. 944).*

6 Distinguish between variable costing and absorption costing (see Appendix 19A, located at myaccountinglab.com).

GAAP requires that we assign both variable and fixed manufacturing costs to products. This approach is called absorption costing because products absorb both fixed and variable manufacturing costs.

Demo Doc 1

Use CVP to Plan Profits

Learning Objectives 2, 3

Crew Cut Mowing Service mows residential lawns. The average amount it charges to mow a single lawn is $30. Crew Cut has calculated the average variable cost of mowing a lawn to be about $18. Their monthly fixed cost is $1,200.

Requirements

1. Use the contribution margin approach to calculate how many lawns Crew Cut must mow in a month to break even.

2. Use the contribution margin ratio approach to determine Crew Cut's breakeven point in sales dollars.

3. Use the income statement approach to prove that your solutions to requirements 1 and 2 are correct.

4. The owner of Crew Cut currently works for another lawn service and earns $2,800 per month. He does not want to incur the risk of owning his own business unless he believes that he can have profit of at least the amount he currently earns. Determine the number of lawns Crew Cut must mow in a month to earn a profit of $2,800.

Demo Doc 1 Solutions

Requirement 1

2 Use CVP analysis to compute breakeven points

Use the contribution margin approach to calculate how many lawns Crew Cut must mow in a month to break even.

Part 1	Part 2	Part 3	Part 4	Demo Doc Complete

The contribution margin tells managers how much revenue is left after paying variable costs. That revenue is used for *contributing* toward first covering fixed costs and then generating a profit. The contribution margin is calculated by subtracting variable costs from the sales revenue. Therefore,

Sales price per unit – Variable cost per unit = Contribution margin per unit

Crew Cut's variable cost per lawn (unit) is $18. Therefore, its unit contribution margin is

Sales price per lawn	$30
Variable cost per lawn	(18)
Contribution margin per lawn	$12

That means that after variable costs are covered, Crew Cut has $12 per lawn that it mows, which then contributes toward fixed costs until fixed costs are covered, after which point Crew Cut will begin to generate $12 profit per lawn.

Breakeven is the level of sales at which total operating revenues is equal to total expenses (fixed and variable). In other words, the level at which income is zero. To compute the breakeven using the contribution margin approach:

$$\text{Breakeven} = \frac{\text{Fixed cost}}{\text{Contribution margin per unit}}$$

$$= \frac{\$1,200}{\$12}$$

$$= 100 \text{ lawns}$$

In this case, Crew Cut must be able to mow 100 lawns per month to break even. That is because at 100 lawns, Crew Cut has earned just enough contribution margin to cover total fixed costs. Every lawn mowed after the breakeven point contributes the unit contribution margin to profit. For example, if Crew Cut mows 101 lawns, then it would earn $12 profit.

Requirement 2

2 Use CVP analysis to compute breakeven points

Use the contribution margin ratio approach to determine Crew Cut's breakeven point in sales dollars.

Part 1	Part 2	Part 3	Part 4	Demo Doc Complete

So far, we have seen that computing the breakeven point for a simple business that sells only one product is pretty straightforward. But larger companies that do not have detailed information on individual products use their contribution margin *ratio* to predict profits, rather than using individual unit contribution margins on each of their products.

The contribution margin ratio is the ratio of contribution margin to sales revenue. In other words, these companies compute their breakeven point in terms of sales dollars. This enables managers to do CVP analysis with aggregated information across many products with varied selling prices. We calculate the contribution margin ratio as follows:

$$\text{Contribution margin ratio} = \frac{\text{Contribution margin per unit}}{\text{Sales revenue per unit}}$$

So, in this case the contribution margin ratio is equal to the contribution margin per unit (determined in requirement 1 to be $12 per lawn) divided by the sales revenue per unit ($30 per lawn).

$$\text{Contribution margin ratio} = \frac{\$12}{\$30}$$
$$= \$0.40 \text{ (or } 40\%)$$

This means that each dollar of sales revenue contributes 40% ($0.40) toward fixed costs and profit. To compute breakeven using the contribution margin ratio:

$$\text{Breakeven sales in dollars} = \frac{\text{Fixed cost}}{\text{Contribution margin ratio}}$$

We know that Crew Cut's fixed cost is $1,200 and its contribution margin ratio is 40%, so:

$$\text{Breakeven sales in dollars} = \frac{\$1,200}{40\%}$$
$$= \$3,000$$

Crew Cut must produce revenue of $3,000 per month to cover its fixed costs and variable costs (that is, break even). This is consistent with our previous calculations for breakeven (that is, 100 lawns × $30 per lawn = $3,000).

Requirement 3

Use the income statement approach to prove that your solutions to requirements 1 and 2 are correct.

Part 1	Part 2	**Part 3**	Part 4	Demo Doc Complete

By multiplying Crew Cut's breakeven in units, 100, by what they charge to mow each lawn, $30, we have proven that our answers to requirements 1 and 2 are the same because the result equals the same as what we calculated in requirement 2, $3,000.

2 Use CVP analysis to compute breakeven points

Sales revenue (100 units × $30)	$3,000
Less: Variable cost (100 units × $18)	1,800
Total contribution margin	1,200
Less: Fixed cost	1,200
Operating income	$ 0

After deducting the variable cost of $1,800 for 100 lawns and the fixed cost of $1,200, the income statement illustrates that Crew Cut would produce $0 operating income at a breakeven level of 100 units.

Requirement 4

The owner of Crew Cut currently works for another lawn service and earns $2,800 per month. He does not want to incur the risk of owning his own business unless he believes that he can have profit of at least the amount he currently earns. Determine the number of lawns Crew Cut must mow in a month to earn a profit of $2,800.

| Part 1 | Part 2 | Part 3 | **Part 4** | Demo Doc Complete |

Up until now, we have computed how many lawns (or sales revenue) Crew Cut needs to mow in order to break even. We know that it must mow 100 lawns, or the equivalent of $3,000 in sales, to break even. Anything less would be a loss. Anything more would be profit.

Now, Crew Cut wants to know how many lawns it needs to mow to generate $2,800 in profit. Because Crew Cut wants to know the number of lawns (units), we will use the formula based on the unit contribution margin.

Using the contribution margin approach, utilize the desired profit of $2,800 as fixed cost (in CVP analysis, always think of desired profit as a fixed cost):

$$\text{Desired profit sales level} = \frac{\text{(Fixed cost + Desired profit)}}{\text{Contribution margin per unit}}$$

In this way, it is very similar to calculating breakeven, except now the desired profit is treated as a fixed cost in our calculations (remember, the contribution margin per unit = selling price per unit − variable cost per unit):

$$\text{Desired profit sales level} = \frac{(\$1,200 + \$2,800)}{(\$30 - \$18)}$$
$$= \frac{\$4,000}{\$12}$$
$$= 333.33, \textbf{ rounded to 334 lawns}$$

Once you know your breakeven, another way to think of this is to divide your desired profit by your contribution margin and add the difference to your breakeven:

$$\$2,800/\$12 = 234 \text{ lawns (rounded)}$$
$$234 \text{ lawns} + 100 \text{ breakeven} = 334 \text{ lawns}$$

Use CVP analysis for profit planning, and graph the CVP relations

This analysis shows that Crew Cut must mow 334 lawns to earn a profit of $2,800 (remember, we round up in this case to avoid partial units/lawns). If Crew Cut also wanted to know how much sales revenue it would need to earn $2,800 profit, it could use this figure to do the calculation:

334 lawns × $30 per lawn = $10,020 sales revenue

The desired profit is treated as a fixed cost in our calculations. Using this data of 334 lawns to achieve the desired profit, the owner of Crew Cut can decide if it is worth leaving his current job to focus on Crew Cut. This data can also be used as a management tool to help determine marketing strategy, hiring policy, and aid in other types of decision making.

As before, you can use the income statement approach to prove these figures:

Sales revenue (334 × $30)	$10,020
Less: Total variable costs (334 × $18)	6,012
Total contribution margin (334 × $12)	4,008
Less: Total fixed costs	1,200
Operating income	$ 2,808*

*The $8 operating income results from rounding a lawn [(334 − 333.33) × $12] 5 $8

Whenever rounding must occur in a problem, such as when we rounded up from 333.33 to 334 lawns to avoid a partial unit, there will often be a small difference when proving the numbers in this way.

Part 1	Part 2	Part 3	Part 4	Demo Doc Complete

Demo Doc 2

Using CVP for Sensitivity Analysis

Learning Objectives 2, 4, 5

Hacker Golf has developed a unique swing trainer golf club. It currently has a production company produce the golf club for it at a cost of $22. Other variable costs total $6, whereas monthly fixed costs are $16,000. Hacker currently sells the trainer golf club for $48.

Requirements
NOTE: Solve each requirement as a separate situation.

1. Calculate Hacker's breakeven point in units.

2. Hacker is considering raising its selling price to $49.95. Calculate the new breakeven in units.

3. Hacker has found a new company to produce the golf club at a lower cost of $19 each. Calculate the new breakeven in units.

4. Because many customers have requested a golf glove to go along with the trainer club, Hacker is considering selling gloves. It only expects to sell one glove for every four trainer clubs it sells. Hacker can purchase the gloves for $5 each and sell them for $9 each. Total fixed costs should remain the same at $16,000 per month. Calculate the breakeven point in units for trainer clubs and golf gloves.

5. Use a contribution margin income statement to prove the breakeven point calculated in requirement 4.

Demo Doc 2 Solutions

Requirement 1

 Use CVP analysis to compute breakeven points

Calculate Hacker's breakeven point in units.

Part 1	Part 2	Part 3	Part 4	Part 5	Part 6	Part 7	Demo Doc Complete

To determine how changes in sales prices, costs, or volume affect profits, let us first start by calculating the current breakeven point.

To determine the breakeven point, we first must calculate the contribution margin per unit. The contribution margin per unit is calculated by subtracting variable costs from the sales revenue. Therefore:

> Contribution margin per unit = Sales price per unit – Variable cost per unit

Hacker's variable cost per club (unit) is the price it pays for each club ($22) plus its additional variable costs ($6). Therefore, its unit contribution margin is

Selling price per club	$48
Variable cost per club ($22 + $6)	(28)
Contribution margin per club	$20

The contribution margin represents the amount from each unit sold that is available to recover fixed costs. That means that after variable costs are covered, Hacker earns $20 per club, which then contributes toward fixed costs until fixed costs are covered, after which point Hacker will begin to generate $20 profit per club sold.

Breakeven is the level of sales at which income is zero. To compute breakeven using the contribution margin approach:

$$\text{Breakeven} = \frac{\text{Fixed cost}}{\text{Contribution margin per unit}}$$

$$= \frac{\$16,000}{\$20}$$

$$= 800 \text{ trainer clubs}$$

Requirement 2

Use CVP methods to perform sensitivity analyses

Hacker is considering raising its selling price to $49.95. Calculate the new breakeven in units.

Part 1	**Part 2**	Part 3	Part 4	Part 5	Part 6	Part 7	Demo Doc Complete

In this case, the selling price is changing, but <u>Hacker's</u> variable and fixed costs are staying the same as in the original question ($28 and $16,000, respectively). The new selling price for the club is going to be $1.95 higher than the original price: from $48.00 to $49.95.

Once we update the original data to reflect the changes, the data are then processed with the same calculations. First, calculate the new contribution margin:

Selling price per club	$49.95
Variable cost per club ($221 + 6)	(28.00)
Contribution margin per club	$21.95

Using the contribution margin approach:

$$\text{Breakeven in units} = \frac{\text{Fixed cost}}{\text{Contribution margin per unit}}$$

$$= \frac{\$16,000.00}{\$21.95}$$

$$= 728.93, \textbf{ rounded up to 729 } \text{trainer clubs}$$

Again, we round because Hacker cannot sell a partial unit (the .93 in the actual calculation).

With the increased selling price, breakeven has been reduced from 800 clubs to 729 clubs. The higher price means that each club contributes more to fixed costs.

You can prove this using the income statement approach:

Sales revenue (729 × $49.95)	$36,414
Less: Variable costs (729 × $28)	20,412
Total contribution margin	16,002
Less: Fixed costs	16,000
Operating income	$ 2*

*The $2 profit results from rounding 728.93 clubs to 729 (0.07 × $21.95 = $2)

Remember that as selling prices increase (provided all costs remain the same), the volume required to break even or achieve target profit goals decreases. Conversely, as selling prices decrease, the volume required to break even or achieve target profit goals increases.

Consider the following:

Selling price goes from $50 to $60, variable costs stay at $20, and total fixed costs are $60,000.

Old contribution margin was $50 – $20 = $30.

Old breakeven point in **units** was $60,000 / $30 = 2,000 units.

New contribution margin is $60 – $20 = $40.

New breakeven point in **units** is $60,000 / $40 = 1,500 units.

There is an *inverse* relationship between contribution margin (an increase of $10 in this case) and breakeven in units (a decrease of 500 units in this case).

Requirement 3

4 Use CVP methods to perform sensitivity analyses

Hacker has found a new company to produce the golf club at a lower cost of $19 each. Calculate the new breakeven in units.

Part 1	Part 2	**Part 3**	Part 4	Part 5	Part 6	Part 7	Demo Doc Complete

Once costs begin to change, a new breakeven must be calculated to determine the effects of the changes. In this case, the variable cost is changing, yet fixed costs and the sales price are staying the same as in the original question ($16,000 and $48, respectively).

In this case, we calculate as we normally would, except that our contribution margin will be different:

> Contribution margin per unit = Sales price per unit − Variable cost per unit

Hacker's variable cost per club (unit) is the price it pays for each club (now $19) plus its additional variable costs ($6). Therefore, its unit contribution margin is

Selling price per club	$48
Variable cost per club ($19 + $6)	(25)
Contribution margin per club	$23

Using the contribution margin approach:

$$\text{Breakeven in units} = \frac{\text{Fixed cost}}{\text{Contribution margin per unit}}$$

$$= \frac{\$16,000}{\$23}$$

$$= 695.65, \text{ rounded up to 696 clubs}$$

With the reduced variable cost, Hacker's breakeven in units decreases from 800 clubs to 696 clubs. Using this information, Hacker's management must decide if it is worth the risk to switch to a new producer.

You can also prove this using the income statement approach:

Sales revenue (696 × $48)	$33,408
Less: Variable costs (696 × $25)	17,400
Total contribution margin	16,008
Less: Fixed costs	16,000
Operating income	$ 8*

The $8 profit results from rounding [(696 − 695.65) × $23] = $8

With both fixed and variable costs, remember that as these costs increase, so does the volume needed to break even or achieve target profits. Conversely, as these costs decrease, the volume needed to break even or achieve target profits also decreases.

Requirement 4

5 Calculate the breakeven point for multiple products or services

Because many customers have requested a golf glove to go along with the trainer club, Hacker is considering selling gloves. It only expects to sell one glove for every four trainer clubs it sells. Hacker can purchase the gloves for $5 each and sell them for $9 each. Total fixed costs should remain the same at $16,000 per month. Calculate the breakeven point in units for trainer clubs and golf gloves.

Part 1	Part 2	Part 3	**Part 4**	Part 5	Part 6	Part 7	Demo Doc Complete

Calculating the breakeven point is fairly straightforward when a company is only dealing with one product. But Hacker is now considering selling two products rather than just one. Now breakeven becomes a little more complicated. This is because different products will have different effects on the contribution margins because of different costs and selling prices. So the company needs to consider the sales mix (a combination of products that make up total sales) in figuring CVP relationships.

You can use the same formulas to determine the breakeven point considering the sales mix, but before calculating breakeven, you must calculate the weighted-average contribution margin of all the products first. You saw another weighted-average for process costing in Chapter 19. In this case, the sales mix provides the weights.

Step 1: Calculate the weighted-average contribution margin.

Hacker believes that it can sell one glove for every four trainer clubs that it sells. This would give it a 4:1 sales mix. So it expects that 4/5 (or 80%) of its sales will be trainer clubs, and 1/5 (or 20%) of its sales will be gloves.

Recall that Hacker pays $28 in variable costs for its clubs and sells them for $48, for a contribution margin of $20 per unit. The gloves will cost it $5 per pair and sell for $9, for a contribution margin of $4 per unit:

	Clubs	Gloves	Total
Sales price per unit	$48	$9	
Deduct: variable cost per unit	(28)	(5)	
Contribution margin per unit	$20	$4	

The weighted-average contribution margin is calculated by multiplying the contribution margin per unit by the sales mix expected for each. Once we have a total contribution margin ($80 + $4 = $84, in this case), we divide the total contribution margin by the total sales mix in units (5), as follows:

| | Sales Mix Percentage | | |
	80% Clubs	20% Gloves	Total
Sales price per unit	$48	$9	
Deduct: Variable cost per unit	(28)	(5)	
Contribution margin per unit	$20	$4	
Sales mix in units	4	1	5.00
Contribution margin per product	$80	$4	$84.00
Weighted-average contribution margin ($84/5)			$16.80

Another way to calculate this is to multiply each product's contribution margin by its sales mix percentage:

Clubs: $20 × 80% = $16.00
Gloves $ 4 × 20% = $ 0.80
                   = $16.80

The $16.80 represents an average contribution margin for all the products Hacker sells. The golf clubs are weighted more heavily because Hacker expects to sell four times as many clubs compared to the gloves.

The next step is to calculate the breakeven in units for the bundle of products.

Step 2:   Calculate the breakeven point in units for the total of both products combined.

| Part 1 | Part 2 | Part 3 | Part 4 | **Part 5** | Part 6 | Part 7 | Demo Doc Complete |

This is calculated using the following formula:

$$\frac{\text{Total sales}}{\text{in units}} = \frac{\text{Fixed cost}}{\text{Weighted-average contribution margin per unit}}$$

We know from the question that fixed costs will not be affected, so they should remain at $16,000. The weighted-average contribution margin, as we just calculated, is $16.80 per unit. So we compute as follows:

$$\text{Total sales in unit} = \frac{\$16,000}{\$16.80}$$
$$= 952.38, \textbf{ rounded to 953}$$

Recall that we round up because Hacker cannot sell a partial unit.

Hacker must sell a combined 953 clubs and gloves to break even. Management needs to know how many units of each product must be sold to break even.

The next step is to determine the breakeven point in units for each product.

Step 3: Calculate the breakeven in units for each product line.

Part 1	Part 2	Part 3	Part 4	Part 5	**Part 6**	Part 7	Demo Doc Complete

Because Hacker believes that it will sell four trainer clubs for every one glove, the total breakeven, 953, is multiplied by each product's respective percent of expected total sales:

Breakeven sales of clubs (953 × 80%) = 762.4, **rounded to 763**

Breakeven sales of gloves (953 × 20%) = 190.6, **rounded to 191**
= 954 total units

So from this analysis, we know that Hacker needs to sell 763 trainer clubs and 191 gloves to break even. The breakeven point in sales dollars is:

763 clubs × $48 = $36,624
plus 191 gloves × $ 9 = $ 1,719
for a total = $38,343

Requirement 5

5 Calculate the breakeven point for multiple products or services

Use a contribution margin income statement to prove the breakeven point calculated in requirement 4.

Part 1	Part 2	Part 3	Part 4	Part 5	Part 6	**Part 7**	Demo Doc Complete

To test the calculation of the breakeven point, you would add together the revenue generated from all sales, subtract the variable costs for each of the clubs and gloves, and then subtract the total fixed costs. The result should balance to zero (or close to zero, in cases in which rounding occurs).

HACKER GOLF
Contribution Margin Income Statement

			Clubs	Gloves	Total
Sales revenue:					
	Trainer clubs (763 × $48)		$36,624		
	Gloves (191 × $9)			$1,719	$38,343
Variable costs:					
	Trainer clubs (763 × $28)		21,364		
	Gloves (191 × $5)			955	$22,319
Contribution margin			$15,260	$ 764	$16,024
Fixed costs					(16,000)
Operating income					$ 24

There is a slight $24 profit at the breakeven level because of rounding to whole units.

Part 1	Part 2	Part 3	Part 4	Part 5	Part 6	Part 7	**Demo Doc Complete**

Quick Practice Questions

True/False

_____ 1. Total fixed costs do not change as production levels decrease.

_____ 2. On a CVP graph, the vertical distance between the total expense line and the total sales revenue line equals the operating income or loss.

_____ 3. Sensitivity analysis is a "what if" technique that asks what a result will be if a predicted amount is not achieved or if an underlying assumption changes.

_____ 4. The margin of safety is the excess of breakeven sales over expected sales.

_____ 5. The contribution margin is the band of volume where total fixed costs remain constant and the variable cost _per unit_ remains constant.

_____ 6. Gray Company sells two products, X and Y. For the coming year, Gray predicts the sale of 5,000 units of X and 10,000 units of Y. The contribution margins of the two products are $2 and $3, respectively. The weighted-average contribution margin would be $2.50.

_____ 7. An easy method to separate mixed costs into variable and fixed components is the high-low method.

_____ 8. Sensitivity analysis is the combination of products that make up total sales.

_____ 9. If a mixed cost has a high level of activity of 1,200 hours and a cost of $16,500 and a low level of activity of 800 hours and a cost of 12,500, the variable cost per unit is $5.

_____10. Using the information in Question 9, the fixed cost would be $4,000.

Multiple Choice

1. **A cost whose total amount changes in direct proportion to a change in volume is what type of cost?**
    a. Fixed cost
    b. Variable cost
    c. Mixed cost
    d. Irrelevant cost

2. **Which of the following is a fixed cost?**
    a. Salary of plant manager
    b. Sales commissions
    c. Direct materials
    d. Delivery costs

3. **What is the effect on total variable costs of changes in production?**
    a. Remain the same as production levels change
    b. Decrease as production increases
    c. Decrease as production decreases
    d. Increase as production decreases

4. What is the effect on fixed costs per unit of changes in production?
   a. Increase as production increases
   b. Decrease as production decreases
   c. Increase as production decreases
   d. Remain the same as production levels change

5. What is contribution margin?
   a. Fixed expenses plus variable expenses
   b. Sales revenues minus variable expenses
   c. Fixed expenses minus variable expenses
   d. Sales revenues minus fixed expenses

6. If the sale price per unit is $75, variable expenses per unit are $40, target operating income is $22,000, and total fixed expenses are $20,000, what is the total number of units that must be sold to reach the target operating income?
   a. 571
   b. 629
   c. 1,050
   d. 1,200

7. Canine Company produces and sells dog treats for discriminating pet owners. The unit selling price is $10, unit variable costs are $7, and total fixed costs are $3,300. How many dog treats must Canine Company sell to break even?
   a. 194
   b. 330
   c. 471
   d. 1,100

8. Fixed Company produces a single product selling for $30 per unit. Variable costs are $12 per unit and total fixed costs are $4,000. What is the contribution margin ratio?
   a. 0.40
   b. 0.60
   c. 1.67
   d. 2.50

9. Which of the following will decrease the breakeven point assuming no other changes in the cost-volume-profit relationship?
   a. A decrease in the sale price per unit
   b. An increase in the sale price per unit
   c. An increase in total fixed costs
   d. An increase in the variable costs per unit

10. Gould Enterprises sells computer disks for $1.50 per disk. Unit variable expenses total $0.90. The breakeven sales in units are 3,000 and budgeted sales in units are 4,300. What is the margin of safety?
    a. $ 780
    b. $1,950
    c. $2,580
    d. $4,500

Quick Exercises

19-1. Place an F in the space provided if the cost is typically a fixed cost, a V if it is a variable cost, or an M if it is a mixed cost.

a. _____ Units-of-production depreciation
b. _____ Property taxes
c. _____ Packing materials
d. _____ Building rent ($2,000 plus 5% of sales revenue per month)
e. _____ Sales commissions
f. _____ Delivery expenses
g. _____ Insurance expense
h. _____ Direct materials
i. _____ Photocopying machine rent (X amount per month plus Y amount per copy)
j. _____ Executive salaries

19-2. Calculate the unknowns for the following situations based on the given data.

Actual total sales revenue	$600,000
Total fixed cost	130,000
Unit variable cost	$ 15
Contribution margin ratio	40%

a. Breakeven point in dollars

b. Unit selling price

c. Unit contribution margin

d. Breakeven point in units

e. Margin of safety

19-3. Taylor Company produces handheld games and has gathered the following information:

Total fixed costs	$256,000
Unit variable cost	$ 6
Planned sales in units	48,000

Requirement

1. Assuming breakeven sales in units of 30,000, compute:

a. Sales price per unit

b. Contribution margin ratio

c. Breakeven sales in dollars

19-4. Calculate the unknowns for the following situations based on the given data. All situations are independent of each other.

Total fixed costs	$231,000
Unit sale price	$ 100
Unit variable cost	$ 40

    a. Calculate the breakeven point in units.

    b. Calculate the breakeven point in dollar sales.

    c. Assume the unit sale price increases by 10%. Other data are unchanged. Calculate the breakeven point in units.

    d. Assume the unit variable cost increases by 5%. Other data are unchanged. Calculate the breakeven point in units.

    e. Assume total fixed costs increase by $6,000. Other data are unchanged. Calculate the breakeven point in units.

19-5. Super Fries Company manufactures two different types of frozen french fries, one plain and one with chilli. The following information is available for the two products:

	Plain Fries	Chilli Fries
Sale price per unit	$5	$8
Variable expenses per unit	$3	$6

Total fixed expenses are estimated at $400,000. Two packages of chilli fries are sold for every three packages of plain fries.

Requirements

1. Determine the breakeven sales in units of both products.

2. Compute the target sales in dollars if Super Fries wants to earn $80,000 in operating income.

3. Prove the solution to requirement 2 by calculating net income using the targeted sales.

19-6.   Chancellor Industries incurred the following costs for its potato chip manufacturing business in July 2013:

Direct materials cost per crate	$ 10.00
Direct labor cost per crate	$ 4.00
Variable manufacturing overhead cost per crate	$ 2.25
Total fixed manufacturing overhead costs	$85,000
Total fixed selling and administrative costs	$42,000
Crates of potato chips produced	25,000
Sales price per crate of potato chips	$ 24.50

What is Chancellor's inventoriable product cost per crate under both absorption costing and variable costing?

	Absorption Costing	Variable Costing
Direct materials		
Direct labor		
Variable manufacturing overhead		
Fixed manufacturing overhead		
Total cost per crate		

Do It Yourself! Question 1

Easy Wear T-shirts prints T-shirts for local organizations. The average amount they charge for a printed T-shirt is $10. Easy Wear has calculated the average variable cost of a printed T-shirt to be $6. Its monthly fixed cost is $18,000.

Requirements

[2] Use CVP analysis to compute breakeven points

1. Use the contribution margin approach to calculate how many T-shirts Easy Wear must sell in a month to break even.

[2] Use CVP analysis to compute breakeven points

2. Use the contribution margin ratio approach to determine Easy Wear's breakeven point in sales dollars.

[2] Use CVP analysis to compute breakeven points

3. Use the income statement approach to prove that the solutions to requirements 1 and 2 are correct.

[3] Use CVP analysis for profit planning, and graph the CVP relations

4. The owner of Easy Wear currently works for another T-shirt company and earns $3,200 per month. He does not want to incur the risk of owning his own business unless he believes that he can have profit of at least the amount he currently earns. Determine the number of T-shirts Easy Wear must print in a month to earn profit of $3,200.

Do It Yourself! Question 2

Cool Board sells a snowboard for $240 that it can purchase for $100. It has additional variable costs of $40 and a monthly fixed cost of $22,000.

Requirements

NOTE: Solve each requirement as a separate and independent situation.

2 Use CVP analysis to compute breakeven points

1. Calculate Cool Board's breakeven point in units.

4 Use CVP methods to perform sensitivity analyses

2. Cool Board is considering raising its selling price to $249. Calculate the new breakeven in units.

4 Use CVP methods to perform sensitivity analyses

3. Cool Board has found a new supplier for the snowboards, who will sell the board to Cool for $95. Calculate the new breakeven in units.

5 Calculate the breakeven point for multiple products or services

4. Cool Board has had many requests from customers for bindings to go along with the board. Cool believes that for every three boards it sells, it could sell two bindings. Cool can purchase the bindings for $25 and would incur another $5 in other variable costs for a total variable cost on the bindings of $30. Cool can sell the bindings for $55. Total fixed costs should remain the same at $22,000 per month. Calculate the breakeven point in units for snowboards and bindings.

5 Calculate the breakeven point for multiple products or services

5. Use a contribution margin income statement to prove the breakeven point calculated in requirement 4.

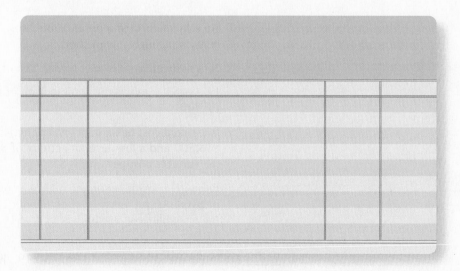

Quick Practice Solutions

True/False

___T___ 1. Total fixed costs don't change as production levels decrease. (p. 926)

___T___ 2. On a CVP graph, the vertical distance between the total expense line and the total sales revenue line equals the operating income or loss. (p. 934)

___T___ 3. Sensitivity analysis is a "what if" technique that asks what a result will be if a predicted amount is not achieved or if an underlying assumption changes. (p. 937)

___F___ 4. The margin of safety is the excess of breakeven sales over expected sales.

  False—The margin of safety is the excess of *actual* sales over *breakeven* sales. (p. 939)

___F___ 5. The contribution margin is the band of volume where total fixed costs remain constant and the variable cost *per unit* remains constant.

  False—The *relevant range* is the band of volume where total fixed costs remain constant and the variable cost per unit remains constant. (p. 929)

___F___ 6. Gray Company sells two products, X and Y. For the coming year, Gray predicts the sale of 5,000 units of X and 10,000 units of Y. The contribution margins of the two products are $2 and $3, respectively. The weighted-average contribution margin would be $2.50.

  False—The weighted-average contribution margin would be $2.67. (p. 931)

> Sales mix: 5,000 units/15,000 units = 1/3;
> 10,000 units/15,000 units = 2/3;
> sales mix = 1:2.
> $(1 \times \$2) = \$2 + (2 \times \$3) = \$8;$
> $(\$2 + \$6)/3 = \$2.67/\text{unit}.$

___T___ 7. An easy method to separate mixed costs into variable and fixed components is the high-low method. (p. 927)

___F___ 8. Sensitivity analysis is the combination of products that make up total sales.

  False—*Sales mix* is the combination of products that make up total sales. (p. 940)

___F___ 9. If a mixed cost has a high level of activity of 1,200 hours and a cost of $16,500 and a low level of activity of 800 hours and a cost of 12,500, the variable cost per unit is $5.

  False—If a mixed cost has a high level of activity of 1,200 hours and a cost of $16,500 and a low level of activity of 800 hours and a cost of 12,500, the variable cost per unit is *$10*. ($16,500 − $12,500)/(1,200 − 800) = $10/hour. (p. 927)

___T___ 10. Using the information in Question 9, the fixed cost would be $4,000. (p. 926)

Multiple Choice

1. A cost whose total amount changes in direct proportion to a change in volume is what type of cost? (p. 925)
   a. Fixed cost
   b. Variable cost
   c. Mixed cost
   d. Irrelevant cost

2. Which of the following is a fixed cost? (p. 926)
   a. Salary of plant manager
   b. Sales commissions
   c. Direct materials
   d. Delivery costs

3. What is the effect on total variable costs of changes in production? (p. 925)
   a. Remain the same as production levels change
   b. Decrease as production increases
   c. Decrease as production decreases
   d. Increase as production decreases

4. What is the effect on fixed costs per unit of changes in production? (p. 926)
   a. Increase as production increases
   b. Decrease as production decreases
   c. Increase as production decreases
   d. Remain the same as production levels change

5. What is contribution margin? (p. 931)
   a. Fixed expenses plus variable expenses
   b. Sales revenues minus variable expenses
   c. Fixed expenses minus variable expenses
   d. Sales revenues minus fixed expenses

6. If the sale price per unit is $75, variable expenses per unit are $40, target operating income is $22,000, and total fixed expenses are $20,000, what is the total number of units that must be sold to reach the target operating income? (p. 933)
   a. 571
   b. 629
   c. 1,050
   d. 1,200

7. Canine Company produces and sells dog treats for discriminating pet owners. The unit selling price is $10, unit variable costs are $7, and total fixed costs are $3,300. How many dog treats must Canine Company sell to break even? (p. 931)
   a. 194
   b. 330
   c. 471
   d. 1,100

8. Fixed Company produces a single product selling for $30 per unit. Variable costs are $12 per unit and total fixed costs are $4,000. What is the contribution margin ratio? (p. 932)

a. 0.40
b. 0.60
c. 1.67
d. 2.50

9. Which of the following will decrease the breakeven point assuming no other changes in the cost-volume-profit relationship? (pp. 932–935)

a. A decrease in the sale price per unit
b. An increase in the sale price per unit
c. An increase in total fixed costs
d. An increase in the variable costs per unit

10. Gould Enterprises sells computer disks for $1.50 per disk. Unit variable expenses total $0.90. The breakeven sales in units are 3,000 and budgeted sales in units are 4,300. What is the margin of safety? (p. 939)

a. $ 780
b. $1,950
c. $2,580
d. $4,500

Quick Exercises

19-1. Place an F in the space provided if the cost is typically a fixed cost, a V if it is a variable cost, or an M if it is a mixed cost. (pp. 925–927)

a.	V	Units-of-production depreciation
b.	F	Property taxes
c.	V	Packing materials
d.	M	Building rent ($2,000 plus 5% of sales revenue per month)
e.	V	Sales commissions
f.	V	Delivery expenses
g.	F	Insurance expense
h.	V	Direct materials
i	M	Photocopying machine rent (X amount per month plus Y amount per copy)
j.	F	Executive salaries

19-2. Calculate the unknowns for the following situations based on the given data. (pp. 930–939)

Actual total sales revenue	$600,000
Total fixed cost	130,000
Unit variable cost	$ 15
Contribution margin ratio	40%

a. Breakeven point in dollars

$130,000 / 0.40 = $325,000

b. Unit selling price

$15 / (100% − 40%) = $25

c. Unit contribution margin

$$\$25 \times 0.40 = \$10 \text{ or } \$25 - \$15 = \$10$$

d. Breakeven point in units

$$\$130,000 / \$10 = 13,000 \text{ units}$$

e. Margin of safety

$$\$600,000 - \$325,000 = \$275,000$$

19-3. Taylor Company produces handheld games and has gathered the following information: (pp. 929–933)

Total fixed costs	$256,000
Unit variable cost	$ 6
Planned sales in units	48,000

Requirement

1. Assuming breakeven sales in units of 30,000, compute:

   a. Sales price per unit

$$\text{Let } X = \text{contribution margin per unit}$$
$$\$256,000 / X = 30,000$$
$$\$256,000 = 30,000X$$
$$X = \$256,000 / 30,000 = \$8.53$$
$$\$8.53 + \$6 = \$14.53$$

   b. Contribution margin ratio

$$\$8.53/\$14.53 = 0.587$$

   c. Breakeven sales in dollars

$$30,000 \times \$14.53 = \$435,900 \text{ or } \$256,000 / 0.587 = \text{approximately } \$435,900, \text{ rounded}$$

19-4. Calculate the unknowns for the following situations based on the data below. All situations are independent of each other. (pp. 929–933)

Total fixed costs	$231,000
Unit sale price	$ 100
Unit variable cost	$ 40

   a. Calculate the breakeven point in units.

$$\$231,000 / (\$100 - \$40) = 3,850$$

b. Calculate the breakeven point in dollar sales.

> 3,850 units × $100 = $385,000 or $231,000 / 0.60 = $385,000

c. Assume the unit sale price increases by 10%. Other data are unchanged. Calculate the breakeven point in units.

> $100 × 1.10 = $110
> $110 − $40 = $70
> $231,000 / $70 = 3,300 units (rounded)

d. Assume the unit variable cost increases by 5%. Other data are unchanged. Calculate the breakeven point in units.

> $40 × 1.05 = $42
> $100 − $42 = $58
> $231,000 / $58 = 3,983 units (rounded)

e. Assume total fixed costs increase by $6,000. Other data are unchanged. Calculate the breakeven point in units.

> ($231,000 + $6,000)/$60 = 3,950 units (rounded)

19-5. **Super Fries Company produces two different types of frozen french fries, one plain and one with chilli. The following information is available for the two products:** (pp. 929–933)

	Plain Fries	Chilli Fries
Sale price per unit	$5	$8
Variable expenses per unit	$3	$6

Total fixed expenses are estimated at $400,000. Two packages of chilli fries are sold for every three packages of plain fries.

Requirements

1. Determine the breakeven sales in units of both products.

> $5 − $3 = $2
> $2 × 2 = $4
> $8 − $6 = $2
> $2 × 3 = $6
> $4 + $6 = $10
> $10 / 5 = $2 weighted-average contribution margin
> $400,000 / $2 = 200,000 sets
> 200,000 × 2 / (2 + 3) = 80,000 packages of chilli fries
> 200,000 × 3 / (2 + 3) = 120,000 packages of plain fries

2. Compute the target sales in dollars if Super Fries wants to earn $80,000 in operating income.

$$\$400,000 + \$80,000 = \$480,000$$
$$\$480,000 \,/\, \$2 = 240,000 \text{ packages}$$
$$\$240,000 \times 2 \,/\, (2 + 3) = 96,000 \text{ units}$$
$$96,000 \times \$5 = \$480,000$$
$$240,000 \times 3 \,/\, (2 + 3) = 144,000$$
$$144,000 \times \$8 = \$1,152,000$$
$$\$480,000 + \$1,152,000 = \$1,632,000$$

3. Prove the solution to requirement 2 by calculating net income using the targeted sales.

$$\text{Revenue} - \text{Variable costs} - \text{Fixed costs} = \text{Net income}$$
$$\$1,632,000 - (96,000 \times \$3) - (144,000 \times \$6) - \$400,000 = \$80,000$$

19-6 Chancellor Industries incurred the following costs for its potato chip manufacturing business in July 2013: (p. 938)

Direct materials cost per crate	$ 10.00
Direct labor cost per crate	$ 4.00
Variable manufacturing overhead cost per crate	$ 2.25
Total fixed manufacturing overhead costs	$85,000
Total fixed selling and administrative costs	$42,000
Crates of potato chips produced	25,000
Sales price per crate of potato chips	$ 24.50

What is Chancellor's inventoriable product cost per crate under both absorption costing and variable costing?

	Absorption Costing	Variable Costing
Direct materials	$10.00	$10.00
Direct labor	$ 4.00	$ 4.00
Variable manufacturing overhead	$ 2.25	$ 2.25
Fixed manufacturing overhead ($85,000/25,000 crates)	$ 3.40	
Total cost per crate	$19.65	$16.25

Do It Yourself! Question 1 Solutions

Requirements

1. Use the contribution margin approach to calculate how many T-shirts Easy Wear must sell in a month to break even.

Contribution margin per unit = Sales price per unit – Variable cost per unit	
Sales price per unit	$10
Variable cost per unit	(6)
Contribution margin per unit	$ 4

Breakeven in units = Fixed cost/Contribution margin per unit

= $18,000/$4

= 4,500 T-shirts

2. Use the contribution margin ratio approach to determine Easy Wear's breakeven point in sales dollars.

Contribution margin ratio = Contribution margin per unit/sales revenue per unit

= $4/$10

= 0.40 (or 40%)

Breakeven in sales dollars = Fixed cost/Contribution margin ratio

= $18,000/0.40

= $45,000

3. Use the income statement approach to prove that the solutions to requirements 1 and 2 are correct.

Sales revenue ($10 × 4,500 units)	$45,000
Less: Variable costs (4,500 × $6)	27,000
Total contribution margin	18,000
Less: Fixed costs	18,000
Operating income	$ 0

4. The owner of Easy Wear currently works for another T-shirt company and earns $3,200 per month. He doesn't want to incur the risk of owning his own business unless he believes that he can have profit of at least the amount he currently earns. Determine the number of T-shirts Easy Wear must print in a month to earn profit of $3,200.

Desired profit sales level in units = (Fixed cost + Desired profit)/Contribution margin
= ($18,000 + $3,200)/($10 − $6)
= $21,200/$4
= 5,300 units

Another way to think of this is to divide your desired profit by your contribution margin and add the difference to your breakeven:

3,200/$4 = 800 units
800 units + 4,500 breakeven = 5,300 units

Do It Yourself! Question 2 Solutions

Requirements

1. Calculate Cool Board's breakeven point in units.

> Breakeven in units = Fixed cost/(Selling price per unit − Variable cost per unit)
>
> = $22,000/($240 − $140)
>
> = **220 boards**

2. Cool Board is considering raising its selling price to $249. Calculate the new breakeven in units.

> Breakeven in units = Fixed cost/(Selling price per unit − Variable cost per unit)
>
> = $22,000/($249 − $140)
>
> = 201.83, **rounded to 202 snowboards**

3. Cool Board has found a new supplier for the snowboards, who will sell the board to Cool for $95. Calculate the new breakeven in units.

> Breakeven in units = Fixed cost/(Selling price per unit − Variable cost per unit)
>
> = $22,000/($240 − $135)
>
> = 209.52, **rounded to 210 snowboards**

4. Cool Board has had many requests from customers for bindings to go along with the board. Cool believes that for every three boards they sell they could sell two bindings. Cool can purchase the bindings for $25 and would incur another $5 in other variable costs for a total variable cost on the bindings of $30. Cool can sell the bindings for $55. Total fixed costs should remain the same at $22,000 per month. Calculate the breakeven point in units for snowboards and bindings.

Step 1: Calculate the weighted-average contribution margin.

	Boards	Bindings	Total
Sales price per unit	$240	$55	
Deduct: Variable cost per unit	(140)	(30)	
Contribution margin per unit	$100	$25	
Sales mix in units	× 3	× 2	5
Contribution margin	$300	$50	$350
Weighted-average contribution margin per unit ($350/5)			$ 70

Step 2: Calculate the breakeven point in units for the total of both products combined.

> Total sales in units = Fixed cost/Weighted-average contribution margin per unit
>
> $\qquad$ = \$22,000/\$70
>
> $\qquad$ = **314.28**, rounded to 315

Step 3: Calculate the breakeven in units for each product line.

> Breakeven sales of boards [315 × (3/5)] = **189 snowboards**
> Breakeven sales of bindings [315 × (2/5)] = **126 bindings**
> $\qquad\qquad\qquad\qquad\qquad\qquad\qquad$ = 315 total units

5. Use a contribution margin income statement to prove the breakeven point calculated in requirement 4.

COOL BOARDS Contribution Margin Income Statement				
		Boards	Bindings	Total
Sales revenue:				
$\quad$ Boards (189 × \$240)		\$45,360		
$\quad$ Bindings (126 × \$55)			\$6,930	\$52,290
Variable costs:				
$\quad$ Boards (189 × \$140)		26,460		
$\quad$ Bindings (126 × \$30)			3,780	\$30,240
Contribution margin		\$18,900	\$3,150	\$22,050
Fixed costs				(22,000)
Operating income				\$ 50

There is a slight \$50 profit at the breakeven level because of rounding to whole units.

The Power of Practice

For more practice using the skills learned in this chapter, visit MyAccountingLab. There you will find algorithmically generated questions that are based on these Demo Docs and your main textbook's Review and Assess Your Progress sections.

Go to MyAccountingLab and follow these steps:

1. Direct your URL to www.myaccountinglab.com.
2. Log in using your name and password.
3. Click the MyAccountingLab link.
4. Click Study Plan in the left navigation bar.
5. From the table of contents, select Chapter 19, Cost-Volume-Profit Analysis.
6. Click a link to work tutorial exercises.

20 Short-Term Business Decisions

What You Probably Already Know

You often make choices between alternatives using both financial and nonfinancial information. Assume you are planning a week-long vacation from Florida to New York. You may consider whether you should fly to New York and rent a car for the week or take the Amtrak auto train from Florida to Virginia and then drive 5 hours in your own car to New York. Some of the nonfinancial considerations might include your enjoyment (or lack thereof) of flying, taking a train trip, driving 5 hours between Virginia and New York and the increased amount of time required for train and car travel. *Relevant costs, expected future data that differs among alternatives,* should also be considered. Some of the relevant costs would include the cost of the plane ticket, train ticket, rental car, and the highway tolls between Virginia and New York. If you need to purchase luggage for your trip, would that cost affect your decision to go by train or plane? No, because that cost does not differ between your two choices, therefore it is *not* relevant. Businesses, like you, only consider relevant costs when making decisions between alternatives.

Learning Objectives/Success Keys

 Describe and identify information relevant to business decisions.

To make business decisions, management compares relevant information between alternative courses of action. Relevant information includes items that will differ between alternatives and be incurred in the future. Relevant information, therefore, affects the decisions that are made. *See Exhibits 20-1 and 20-2 (p. 963).*

 Make special order and pricing decisions.

A special order offer at a reduced sales price should only be considered when there is excess capacity. Consideration should also be given to the impact that accepting the order will have on existing customers, competitors, and future sales. Assuming that excess capacity is available and no adverse future financial effects will be incurred, an analysis should be performed to determine whether accepting the special order results in an increase to net income. When the revenue from the special sale exceeds the expenses related to the special order, net income is produced and the offer should be accepted. *See Exhibits 20-4 through 20-6 (p. 966, 968), Summary Problem 1 (p. 975–976), and Demo Doc 1.*

To determine the appropriate pricing, companies should consider the desired profit, the price customers would be willing to pay, and whether the product permits the company to be a price-taker or price-setter. *See Exhibits 20-7 and 20-8 (pp. 969–970).*

3 **Make dropping a product and product-mix decisions.**

The analysis performed to decide whether to drop a product, department, or division is similar to that of the special order. Consideration should also be given to the impact that dropping this portion of the business may have on other segments. An analysis should be performed to determine whether dropping the segment will result in an increase to net income. When the revenue generated from the segment under consideration is *less* than the *variable and fixed costs that relate only to this segment of the business*, it should be dropped.

In terms of product mix, a **constraint** is something that restricts the production or sale of a product, such as labor hours, machine hours, or available materials. Given sufficient demand, the products that generate the highest contribution margin *per constrained resource* will maximize operating income. *See Exhibits 20-13 through 20-18 (pp. 977–980), and Summary Problem 2 (pp. 989–990).*

4 **Make outsourcing and sell as is or process further decisions.**

Similar to the decision whether to drop a segment, an analysis should be performed to determine whether making or outsourcing the product results in a higher profit. Note that some fixed costs may be avoidable if the product is outsourced. If the decision to outsource includes an opportunity to generate revenue, this *opportunity cost* should be added to the "make option" as another cost in the analysis.

When deciding to sell a product as is or process it further, management should consider the **split-off point**, which is the point at which the product is complete and can be sold or continues to be processed further and then sold after incurring more costs. The analysis compares the revenue from selling the product as it is to the higher revenue, less additional costs, from selling the product after processing further. Whichever option results in a higher net revenue is the more profitable alternative. *See Exhibits 20-21 through 20-24 (pp. 981–986), Summary Problem 2 (pp. 989–990), and Demo Doc 2.*

Demo Doc 1

Special Business Decisions

Learning Objectives 1–4

Part 1

Doctor "C" produces sunglasses. An Australian company has offered to purchase 2,000 pairs of sunglasses at a unit price of $20. Assume selling to the Australian company will not affect regular customers, will not change fixed costs, will not require any additional variable nonmanufacturing expenses, and will use manufacturing capacity that would otherwise be idle.

DOCTOR "C" Income Statement (without considering the special sale)	
Sales revenue (35,000 pairs @ $27 per pair)	$945,000
Less: Manufacturing cost of goods sold	420,000
Gross profit	525,000
Less: Marketing and administrative expenses	370,000
Operating income	$155,000

Requirement 1

Assuming $300,000 of the manufacturing costs is fixed and $180,000 of the marketing and administrative costs is fixed, should Doctor accept the order from the Australian company?

Part 2

Quick Pack has offered to package the glasses for Doctor "C." Currently, Doctor "C" packages the product themselves at the following per-pair cost:

Direct materials	$27,000
Direct labor	43,500
Variable overhead	5,000
Fixed overhead	12,000
Total manufacturing cost	$87,500
Cost per unit ($87,500/35,000)	$2.50

Requirement 2

Quick Pack's price per pair is $2.30. Doctor would avoid all variable costs associated with the packaging and would reduce the fixed cost by $1,000 if Quick Pack packages Doctor's glasses. Should Doctor outsource the packaging work to Quick Pack?

Part 3

Of Doctor's 35,000 unit sales, 3,000 units are for sunglasses with special colored lenses made for one customer. The colored lenses sell for the same price, $27, as all the other glasses, but seem to be more costly to produce. Doctor is considering dropping the colored lenses. An analysis has determined that the variable cost of producing the colored lenses is $19 per unit. If the colored glasses were not produced, fixed costs would not change.

Requirement 3

Should Doctor stop producing the colored lenses?

Part 4

Assume that Doctor "C" is a price-setter and decides to use the cost-plus price approach to pricing. The stockholders expect to see a return of 15% on the company assets of $1,500,000.

Requirement 4

Using the cost-plus price approach, what would the sales price per unit be? (Use the same information in Part 1.)

Demo Doc 1 Solutions

Requirement 1

1 Describe and identify information relevant to business decisions

4 Make outsourcing and sell as is or process further decisions

Assuming $300,000 of the manufacturing costs is fixed and $180,000 of the marketing and administrative costs is fixed, should Doctor accept the order from the Australian company?

Part 1	Part 2	Part 3	Part 4	Demo Doc Complete

The key to this problem is to determine what effect the special sale would have on Doctor's operating income. Fixed costs will not change as a result of the sale; therefore, we will compare only the change in revenue with the change in variable costs as a result of the special sale. The decision to accept a special order will be made if the incremental revenues exceed the incremental expenses for the special order.

The increase in revenue is determined by multiplying the additional pairs sold, 2,000, by the offered selling price per pair of $20. Thus, the increase in revenue will be $40,000.

To determine the variable cost of producing the additional 2,000 units, we must first determine the variable cost per unit. The manufacturing cost of producing 35,000 units was $420,000. Of the $420,000, fixed cost makes up $300,000. Therefore, manufacturing variable cost is $120,000. The variable marketing and administrative cost is determined by subtracting the fixed portion, $180,000, from the total marketing and administrative cost of $370,000, to get variable marketing and administrative cost of $190,000. Thus, the total variable cost of producing the 35,000 units is:

$$\$120,000 + \$190,000 = \$310,000$$

The variable cost per unit is computed by dividing the total variable cost, $310,000, by the 35,000 units, which equals $8.86 per pair.

The increase in variable cost with the special sales order is:

$$2,000 \text{ pairs} \times \text{the variable cost per unit of } \$8.86 = \$17,720$$

Incremental Analysis of Special Sales Order

Increase in revenues:	
Sale of 2,000 pairs @ $20 per pair	$40,000
Increase in variable expenses:	
2,000 pairs × $8.86	17,720
Increase in operating income	$22,280
Profit per pair:	
$22,280/2,000 pairs = $11.14	

Doctor should **accept** the special order because it would increase operating income.

Requirement 2

1 Describe and identify information relevant to business decisions

4 Make outsourcing and sell as is or process further decisions

Quick Pack's price per pair is $2.30. Doctor would avoid all variable costs associated with the packaging and would reduce the fixed cost by $1,000 if Quick Pack packages Doctor's lenses. Should Doctor outsource the packaging work to Quick Pack?

Part 1	**Part 2**	Part 3	Part 4	Demo Doc Complete

Outsourcing decisions consider whether management will make or buy (outsource) their products or services. Incremental analysis can be performed by comparing: (1) the cost to make the product, which includes direct materials, direct labor, and overhead, to (2) the cost to buy, which includes the purchase price plus possibly some portion of the fixed overhead that will continue with outsourcing.

In addition, a relevant opportunity cost may be involved. An **opportunity cost** represents the benefit forgone by not choosing an alternative course of action. If the production process is outsourced and the goods are purchased, opportunities to use the idle resources to generate profits may be available. The opportunity cost reduces the cost of outsourcing.

In this case, the key to this decision is to compare the Doctor's cost savings of not packaging their glasses with the cost charged by Quick Pack. On the surface, it might seem that Quick Pack is making an attractive offer to package the lenses for $0.20 cheaper per pair than Doctor spends to package the glasses themselves.

But an incremental analysis is necessary to consider the overall effects of total costs and savings on the make-or-buy decision.

The following shows the differences in costs between making and outsourcing (buying) the packaging:

Packaging Costs	Make	Buy	Difference
Direct materials	$27,000		$ 27,000
Direct labor	43,500		43,500
Variable factory overhead	5,000		5,000
Avoidable fixed costs	12,000	11,000	1,000
Purchase cost from Quick Pack			
(35,000 units × $2.30 per unit)		80,500	(80,500)
Total cost of labels	$87,500	$91,500	$ (4,000)
Cost per unit (divide by 35,000 pairs)	$ 2.50	$ 2.61*	$ (0.11)

*Rounded

This analysis makes it clear that the fixed costs have an impact on this decision. In this case, Doctor will incur $11,000 in fixed costs whether it outsources the packaging to Quick Pack or packages its own glasses. This factor puts the total cost for the 35,000 pairs at $4,000 higher if Doctor decided to outsource the packaging to Quick Pack.

So it would make sense for Doctor to continue packaging its own product.

Requirement 3

Should Doctor stop producing the colored lenses?

Part 1	Part 2	**Part 3**	Part 4	Demo Doc Complete

Management should consider whether discontinuing a product line, department, or component of the business would increase the operating income. The decision to eliminate a business segment may be made if dropping the segment will result in a decrease in total expenses *greater* than the decrease in revenues.

In this case, fixed costs remain the same whether or not the colored lenses product line is dropped; therefore, fixed costs are not relevant to the decision. Only the revenues and variable expenses are relevant.

Segment margin is calculated as:

Sales	
Less:	Variable costs
=	Contribution margin
Less:	Discretionary fixed costs
=	Segment margin

In the absence of any discretionary fixed costs, contribution margin is the criteria for deciding whether a product or product line should be dropped.

If the colored lenses product line is dropped, revenues will decrease by:

Revenue	$3,000 \times \$27$	= $(81,000)$
Variable costs will decrease as well:		
	$3,000 \times \$19$	= $(57,000)$
Contribution margin will decrease by:		
	$3,000 \times \$18$	= $(24,000)$

The actual revenue generated from having this line is $81,000.

$81,000 is greater than $57,000 (a $24,000 difference); therefore, the company is better off by NOT dropping this product.

A decision rule might be: If the actual revenue of the product *exceeds* the cost savings (in reduced costs, either variable or fixed or both), then the product should *not* be dropped.

Requirement 4

Using the cost-plus price approach, what would the sales price per pair be? (Use the same information in Part 1.)

Part 1	Part 2	Part 3	**Part 4**	Demo Doc Complete

The computation of the cost-plus price approach used by price-setters begins with the **full product cost**. All of the variable and fixed manufacturing, marketing, and administrative costs are included in the full product cost.

The *desired profit* is added to the full cost. The desired profit is the amount expected by the shareholders, a 15% return on assets (net income/total assets). Because total assets are $1,500,000, the desired profit is $225,000 ($1,500,000 × 0.15).

Manufacturing cost of goods sold		$ 420,000
Marketing and administrative costs		370,000
Full product cost		790,000
Desired profit		225,000
Target revenue		1,015,000
Divided by number of units		35,000
Cost-plus price per unit	$	29

Part 1	Part 2	Part 3	Part 4	**Demo Doc Complete**

Demo Doc 2

Capital Investment Decisions

Learning Objectives 3, 4

Pattie's Tea Pots makes two types of teapots. The Deluxe pot requires more machine hours to produce than the Standard one. Due to increased demand for both pots, Pattie is wondering whether she should be producing more of the Deluxe or Standard type.

		Standard	Deluxe
Sales price		$30	$40
Variable expenses		15	24

Each year, 10,000 machine hours are available. The Standard pot takes 5 minutes to produce while the Deluxe pot takes 10 minutes.

Requirements

1. What should Pattie do to maximize her net income assuming sufficient demand to sell either type exclusively?

2. Pattie is purchasing another factory to manufacture teapots. This site will produce teapots that will be hand painted and trimmed in gold. Pattie is considering whether she should produce the basic ceramic pot and sell it to another company to do the hand painting and trim or have her company complete the processing. She plans on producing 36,000 pots this year. She can sell the unfinished pots at $26 per unit (the cost per unit is $17) or she can finish the painting and trim at a cost of $8 per unit and sell them for $45. What should Pattie do?

Demo Doc 2 Solutions

3 Make dropping a product and product-mix decisions

Requirement 1

What should Pattie do to maximize her net income assuming sufficient demand to sell either type exclusively?

Part 1	Part 2	Demo Doc Complete

Even though Pattie has sufficient demand for both the standard and deluxe teapots, the constraint on this company is the 10,000 machine hours available. In the *long run*, the company could expand its facilities, but for now Pattie faces a short-run business decision.

The product that should be produced, given sufficient demand as we have in this case, is the one that generates the *greatest contribution margin per unit of constraint*. This approach will result in the largest net income for the company.

First the calculation of the contribution margin (sales price less variable expenses) must be made.

	Per Unit	
	Standard	Deluxe
Sales price	$30	$40
Less: Variable expenses	15	24
Contribution margin	$15	$16

As shown, the Deluxe pots have a higher contribution margin, $16 per unit. However, we cannot assume that the Deluxe pots should be produced exclusively. The *contribution margin per unit of constraint (machine hours)* must now be calculated.

	Standard	Deluxe
Units that can be produced each machine hour*	12	6
Contribution margin per unit	$ 15	$ 16
Contribution margin per machine hour	$ 180	$ 96
Available capacity (number of machine hours)	10,000	10,000
Total contribution margin at full capacity	$1,800,000	$960,000

*A Standard pot requires 5 minutes to produce. 60 minutes/5 minutes = 12 pots per hour.
*A Deluxe pot requires 10 minutes to produce. 60 minutes/10 minutes = 6 pots per hour.

The Standard pots will generate the most contribution margin. Even though the Deluxe pot has a contribution margin of $16, $1 greater than the Standard pot, twice as many Standard pots can be produced within an hour than the Deluxe. Based on ample customer demand, the increased level of production will result in a much greater contribution margin for Pattie.

Requirement 2

4 Make outsourcing and sell as is or process further decisions

Pattie is purchasing another factory to manufacture teapots. This site will produce teapots that will be hand painted and trimmed in gold. Pattie is considering whether she should produce the basic ceramic pot and sell it to another company to do the hand painting and trim or have her company complete the processing. She plans on producing 36,000 pots this year. She can sell the unfinished pots at $26 per unit (the cost per unit is $17) or she can finish the painting and trim at a cost of $8 per unit and sell them for $45. What should Pattie do?

Part 1	Part 2	Demo Doc Complete

Again, short-run business decisions require that the relevant information and a contribution margin approach be used. The relevant information includes the following:

1. **Sales price for the pot as is, $26**

2. **Future costs of processing, $8**

3. **Sales price of the fully processed pot, $45**

Sell as Is or Process Further Decision	Sell as Is	Process Further	Difference
Expected revenue from selling 36,000 pots as is (36,000 × $26)	$936,000		
Expected revenue from selling 36,000 fully processed pots (36,000 × $45)		$1,620,000	684,000
Additional costs to paint and trim pots (36,000 × $8)		(288,000)	(288,000)
Total net revenue	$936,000	$1,332,000	
Differrence in net revenue			$396,000

The decision rule states that if the extra revenue from processing further exceeds the extra cost of processing, then the decision should be to process further. Pattie should process the teapots further.

Part 1	Part 2	**Demo Doc Complete**

Quick Practice Questions

True/False

_____ 1. Relevant information is future data that differ among alternatives.

_____ 2. If the lost revenue from dropping a product exceeds the cost savings from dropping the product, it should be retained.

_____ 3. A company that has unique and distinctive products and enjoys lesser competition is usually a price-taker.

_____ 4. A sunk cost is a past cost that cannot be changed regardless of which future action is taken.

_____ 5. The absorption costing income statement does not include the fixed portion of cost of goods sold.

_____ 6. To maximize profits, produce the product with the highest contribution margin per unit of the constraint.

_____ 7. If a product line has a negative contribution margin, it should be dropped.

_____ 8. Fixed costs are irrelevant to a special decision when those fixed costs differ between alternatives.

_____ 9. When a company is a price-setter, it emphasizes a target price approach to pricing.

_____ 10. A company considers only the variable costs when using the cost-plus pricing approach.

Multiple Choice Questions

1. **For incremental analysis, which of the following would be irrelevant?**
   a. The cost of an asset that the company is considering replacing
   b. Fixed overhead costs that differ among alternatives
   c. The cost of further processing a product that could be sold as is
   d. The expected increase in sales of one product line as a result of a decision to drop a separate unprofitable product line

2. **Which of the following is an irrelevant cash inflow or outflow?**
   a. Future disposal value of an asset
   b. Future operating cash flows
   c. Current cash outlay to acquire a new asset
   d. Cash outlay to acquire equipment 10 years ago

3. Lowwater Sailmakers manufactures sails for sailboats. The company has the capacity to produce 25,000 sails per year, but is currently producing and selling 20,000 sails per year. The following information relates to current production:

Sale price per unit	$ 150
Variable costs per unit:	
Manufacturing	$ 55
Marketing and administrative	$ 25
Total fixed costs:	
Manufacturing	$640,000
Marketing and administrative	$280,000

If a special sales order is accepted for 5,000 sails at a price of $125 per unit, and fixed costs remain unchanged, what would the effect on operating income be?
a. Decrease by $5,000
b. Increase by $190,000
c. Decrease by $125,000
d. Increase by $225,000

4. Using the data in Question 3, compute the effect on operating income if a special sales order is accepted for 2,500 sails at a price of $70 per unit, when fixed costs increase by $10,000, and variable marketing and administrative costs for the order decrease by $5 per unit?
a. Decrease by $82,500
b. Increase by $10,000
c. Increase by $22,500
d. Decrease by $22,500

5. DC Electronics uses a standard part in the manufacture of several of its radios. The cost of producing 30,000 parts is $90,000, which includes fixed costs of $33,000 and variable costs of $57,000. The company can buy the part from an outside supplier for $2.50 per unit, and avoid 30% of the fixed costs. If DC Electronics makes the part, what is the effect on its operating income?
a. $6,500 greater than if the company bought the part
b. $8,100 greater than if the company bought the part
c. $15,000 less than if the company bought the part
d. $5,100 less than if the company bought the part

6. The following data are available for the Forte, Co.:

	Toaster Ovens	Bread Machines
Sale price	$60	$135
Variable costs	38	62

The company can manufacture five toaster ovens per machine hour and three bread machines per machine hour. The company's production capacity is 1,500 machine hours per month. To maximize profits, what should the company produce?
a. 4,500 bread machines
b. 2,250 toaster ovens and 3,750 bread machines
c. 3,750 toaster ovens and 2,250 bread machines
d. 7,500 toaster ovens

7. Shine Bright Company has three product lines: D, E, and F. The following information is available:

	D	E	F
Sales	$60,000	$38,000	$26,000
Variable costs	36,000	18,000	12,000
Contribution margin	24,000	20,000	14,000
Fixed expenses	12,000	15,000	16,000
Operating income (loss)	$12,000	$ 5,000	$ (2,000)

Shine Bright Company is thinking of dropping product line F because it is reporting an operating loss. Assuming Shine Bright Company drops line F and does not replace it, what is the effect on the operating income?
a. Increase $2,000
b. Increase $14,000
c. Decrease $14,000
d. Increase $16,000

8. Using the data in Question 7, assume that Shine Bright Company drops line F and rents the space formerly used to produce product F for $17,000 per year. What is the effect on the operating income?
a. Decrease $3,000
b. Increase $3,000
c. Decrease $14,000
d. Increase $15,000

9. Mike's Sneaker Shop expects to sell 10,000 sneakers this year at the current market price of $55 a pair. He would like to earn a return of 10% on the $2 million of assets invested in the shop. What is the target full cost?
a. $550,000
b. $200,000
c. $350,000
d. $750,000

10. Florence's Fine Furniture Company is considering selling her wood tables unfinished for $900 apiece. If the decision is made to process them further and complete the finishing required, the table could be sold for $1,200 but the additional cost to process would be $275. What should Florence do?
a. Sell the table unfinished and have $25 more net income per unit.
b. Sell the table finished and have $300 more net income per unit.
c. Sell the table finished and have $25 more net income per unit.
d. It cannot be determined; other factors need to be considered.

Quick Exercises

20-1. Label each of the following items as relevant or irrelevant in making a decision.

_____ a. Accumulated depreciation on old equipment being evaluated for replacement

_____ b. Cost of insurance on a new vehicle

_____ c. Original cost of old equipment that is being evaluated for replacement

_____ d. Cost of previous year's insurance policy on old equipment being evaluated for replacement

_____ e. Cost of new equipment under evaluation to replace used equipment

_____ f. Cost of roof repair made on rental property last year

20-2. Picard Enterprises produces and sells a part used in the production of computing equipment. The unit costs associated with this part are as follows:

Direct materials	$0.25
Direct labor	0.32
Variable manufacturing overhead	0.15
Fixed manufacturing overhead	0.14
Total cost	$0.86

Data Company has approached Picard Enterprises with an offer to purchase 20,000 units of this part at a price of $0.75 per unit. Accepting this special sales order will put idle manufacturing capacity to use and will not affect regular sales. Total fixed costs will not change.

Requirement

1. Determine whether the special order should be accepted. Justify your conclusion.

20-3. Jun Outerwear manufactures coats and jackets. The company's product line income statement follows:

	Total	Coats	Jackets
Sales revenue	$900,000	$580,000	$320,000
Cost of goods sold			
Variable	230,000	116,000	114,000
Fixed	280,000	184,000	96,000
Total cost of goods sold	510,000	300,000	210,000
Gross profit	390,000	280,000	110,000
Marketing and administrative expenses			
Variable	186,000	58,000	128,000
Fixed	135,000	79,000	56,000
Total marketing and administrative expenses	321,000	137,000	184,000
Operating income (loss)	$ 69,000	$143,000	$ (74,000)

Management is considering dropping the jackets product line. Accountants for the company estimate that dropping the jackets line will decrease fixed costs of goods sold by $50,000 and fixed marketing and administrative expenses by $8,000.

Requirement

1. Prepare an analysis supporting your opinion about whether to drop the jackets product line.

	Current—Jackets	If Jackets Dropped

20-4. We Play Company makes a part used in the manufacture of video game systems. Management is considering whether to continue manufacturing the part, or to buy the part from an outside source at a cost of $23 per part. We Play needs 125,000 parts per year. The cost of manufacturing 125,000 parts is computed as follows:

Direct materials	$1,265,000
Direct labor	812,000
Variable manufacturing overhead	510,000
Fixed manufacturing overhead	663,000
Total manufacturing cost	$3,250,000

We Play would pay $0.20 per unit to transport the parts to its manufacturing plant. Purchasing the part from an outside source would enable the company to avoid 30% of fixed manufacturing overhead. We Play's factory space freed up by purchasing the part from an outside supplier could be used to manufacture another product with a contribution margin of $65,000.

Requirement

1. Prepare an analysis to show which alternative makes the best use of We Play factory space, assuming that We Play does the following:

1. Makes the part
2. Buys the part and leaves facilities idle
3. Buys the part and uses facilities to make another product

20-5. Hunter's Hats, Co., had the following financial information for the year ended December 31, 2013.

- Sales of 150,000 hats at $5 per unit
- Variable manufacturing costs of $1.20 per unit
- Fixed manufacturing costs of $105,000
- Variable selling and administrative expenses of $.50 per unit
- Fixed selling and administrative expenses of $80,000

Requirement

1. Prepare an income statement for the company using the absorption costing format and contribution margin format.

Absorption Costing Income Statement

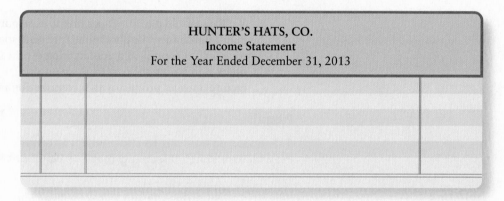

HUNTER'S HATS, CO.
Income Statement
For the Year Ended December 31, 2013

Contribution Margin Income Statement

HUNTER'S HATS, CO.
Income Statement
For the Year Ended December 31, 2013

Do It Yourself! Question 1

Special Business Decisions

Part 1

Easy Access produces keyless entry remotes for automobiles. A Yemen company has offered to purchase 500 cases of keyless entry remotes at a per-unit price of $80. Assume selling to the Yemen company will not affect regular customers, will not change fixed costs, will not require any additional variable nonmanufacturing expenses, and will use manufacturing capacity that would otherwise be idle.

EASY ACCESS Income Statement (without considering the special sale)	
Sales revenue (5,000 cases @ $140 per case)	$700,000
Less: Manufacturing cost of goods sold	400,000
Gross profit	300,000
Less: Marketing and administrative expenses	220,000
Operating income	$ 80,000

Requirement 1

2 Make special order and pricing decisions

Assuming $250,000 of the manufacturing costs is fixed and $100,000 of the marketing and administrative cost is fixed, should Easy Access accept the order from the Yemen company?

Part 2

Great Graphics has offered to print the graphics on the keyless remotes. Currently, Easy Access does the printing themselves at the following per-case costs:

Direct materials	$20,000
Direct labor	40,000
Variable overhead	5,000
Fixed overhead	15,000
Total manufacturing cost	$80,000
Cost per case ($80,000/5,000)	$ 16

Requirement 2

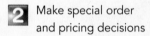
Make special order
and pricing decisions

Great Graphics price per case is $15. Easy Access would avoid all variable costs associated with the printing and would reduce the fixed cost by $3,000 if Great Graphics prints Easy Access's graphics. Should Easy Access outsource the printing work to Great Graphics?

Part 3

Of Easy Access's 5,000 case sales, 200 cases are for a specially shaped keyless remote made for one customer. The special keyless remote sells for the same price, $140, as all the other keyless remotes, but seems to require more expenses. Easy Access is considering dropping the specially shaped keyless remote. An analysis has determined that the variable cost of producing the special keyless remote is $135 per case. If the special keyless remote was not produced, fixed costs would not change.

Requirement 3

Make special order
and pricing decisions

Should Easy Access stop producing the specially shaped keyless remote?

Do It Yourself! Question 2

Special Business Decisions: Dropping a Product and Product Mix Choices

The top managers of Massive, Co., are concerned about their operating losses. They are considering dropping the Free Weights product line and continue selling only Exercise Machines. Company accountants prepared the following analysis to help make this decision:

	Total	Exercise Machines	Free Weights
Sales revenue	$850,000	$630,000	$220,000
Variable expenses	490,000	340,000	150,000
Contribution margin	360,000	290,000	70,000
Fixed expenses:			
Manufacturing	230,000	140,000	90,000
Marketing and administrative	140,000	100,000	40,000
Total fixed expenses	370,000	240,000	130,000
Operating income (loss)	$ (10,000)	$ 50,000	$ (60,000)

Part 1

Requirements

3 Make dropping a product and product-mix decisions

1. Total fixed costs will not change if the company stops selling Free Weights. Prepare an incremental analysis to show whether Massive, Co., should drop the Free Weights product line. Will dropping Free Weights add $60,000 to operating income? Explain.

3 Make dropping a product and product-mix decisions

2. Refer to requirement 1 and assume that Massive, Co., can now avoid $80,000 of fixed expenses by dropping the Free Weights product line (these costs are direct fixed costs of the Free Weights product line). Prepare an incremental analysis to show whether Massive, Co., should stop selling Free Weights.

Part 2

Ignore Part 1. Assume that customer demand is sufficient for as many Exercise Machines and Free Weights as the company can produce. Following are the sales price, variable expense, and allocated fixed expense per unit for Exercise Machines and Free Weights:

	Exercise Machines	Free Weights
Average sale price	$250	$35
Average variable expenses	145	8
Average contribution margin	105	27
Average fixed expenses (allocated)	30	10
Average operating income	$ 75	$17

Requirements

3 Make dropping a product and product-mix decisions

3. The same machines are used to make Exercise Machines as Free Weights. If it takes 120 minutes to produce one Exercise Machine and 30 minutes to produce one Free Weight, compute the sales mix that will maximize operating income. (Assume that the fixed costs are not affected by the sales mix.)

3 Make dropping a product and product-mix decisions

4. Massive, Co., estimates the demand for Exercise Machines is unlimited, but it can only sell 10,000 Free Weights. Assume that the machines can run 12,000 hours this year. How many units of each product should be produced to maximize operating income?

Quick Practice Solutions

True/False

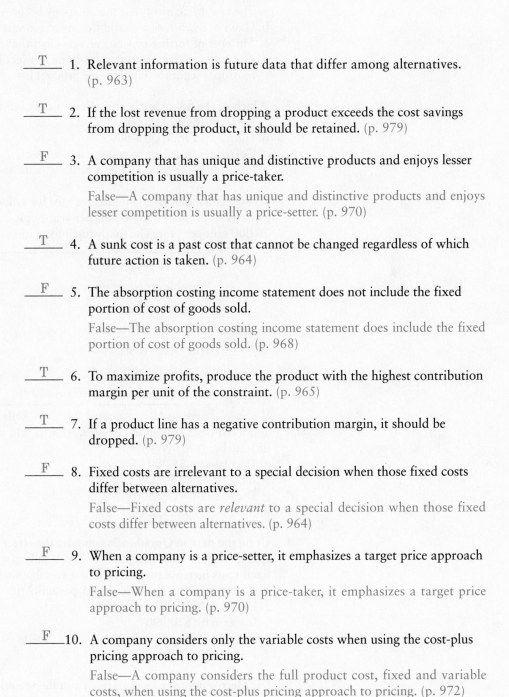

__T__ 1. Relevant information is future data that differ among alternatives. (p. 963)

__T__ 2. If the lost revenue from dropping a product exceeds the cost savings from dropping the product, it should be retained. (p. 979)

__F__ 3. A company that has unique and distinctive products and enjoys lesser competition is usually a price-taker.

   False—A company that has unique and distinctive products and enjoys lesser competition is usually a price-setter. (p. 970)

__T__ 4. A sunk cost is a past cost that cannot be changed regardless of which future action is taken. (p. 964)

__F__ 5. The absorption costing income statement does not include the fixed portion of cost of goods sold.

   False—The absorption costing income statement does include the fixed portion of cost of goods sold. (p. 968)

__T__ 6. To maximize profits, produce the product with the highest contribution margin per unit of the constraint. (p. 965)

__T__ 7. If a product line has a negative contribution margin, it should be dropped. (p. 979)

__F__ 8. Fixed costs are irrelevant to a special decision when those fixed costs differ between alternatives.

   False—Fixed costs are *relevant* to a special decision when those fixed costs differ between alternatives. (p. 964)

__F__ 9. When a company is a price-setter, it emphasizes a target price approach to pricing.

   False—When a company is a price-taker, it emphasizes a target price approach to pricing. (p. 970)

__F__ 10. A company considers only the variable costs when using the cost-plus pricing approach to pricing.

   False—A company considers the full product cost, fixed and variable costs, when using the cost-plus pricing approach to pricing. (p. 972)

Multiple Choice

1. **For incremental analysis, which of the following would be irrelevant?** (p. 965)
   a. The cost of an asset that the company is considering replacing
   b. Fixed overhead costs that differ among alternatives
   c. The cost of further processing a product that could be sold as is
   d. The expected increase in sales of one product line as a result of a decision to drop a separate unprofitable product line

2. **Which of the following is an irrelevant cash inflow or outflow?** (p. 964)
   a. Future disposal value of an asset
   b. Future operating cash flows
   c. Current cash outlay to acquire a new asset
   d. Cash outlay to acquire equipment 10 years ago

3. **Lowwater Sailmakers manufactures sails for sailboats. The company has the capacity to produce 25,000 sails per year but is currently producing and selling 20,000 sails per year. The following information relates to current production:**

Sale price per unit	$ 150
Variable costs per unit:	
Manufacturing	$ 55
Marketing and administrative	$ 25
Total fixed costs:	
Manufacturing	$640,000
Marketing and administrative	$280,000

   If a special sales order is accepted for 5,000 sails at a price of $125 per unit, and fixed costs remain unchanged, what would the effect on operating income be? (pp. 966–969)
   a. Decrease by $5,000
   b. Increase by $190,000
   c. Decrease by $125,000
   d. Increase by $225,000

4. **Using the data in Question 3, compute the effect on operating income if a special sales order is accepted for 2,500 sails at a price of $70 per unit, when fixed costs increase by $10,000, and variable marketing and administrative costs for the order decreases by $5 per unit?** (pp. 966–969)
   a. Decrease by $82,500
   b. Increase by $10,000
   c. Increase by $22,500
   d. Decrease by $22,500

5. **DC Electronics uses a standard part in the manufacture of several of its radios. The cost of producing 30,000 parts is $90,000, which includes fixed costs of $33,000 and variable costs of $57,000. The company can buy the part from an outside supplier for $2.50 per unit, and avoid 30% of the fixed costs. If DC Electronics makes the part, what is the effect on its operating income?** (pp. 982–985)
   a. $6,500 greater than if the company bought the part
   b. $8,100 greater than if the company bought the part
   c. $15,000 less than if the company bought the part
   d. $5,100 less than if the company bought the part

6. The following data are available for the Forte, Co.:

	Toaster Ovens	Bread Machines
Sale price	$60	$135
Variable costs	38	62

The company can manufacture five toaster ovens per machine hour and three bread machines per machine hour. The company's production capacity is 1,500 machine hours per month. To maximize profits, what should the company produce? (pp. 980–982)
a. 4,500 bread machines
b. 2,250 toaster ovens and 3,750 bread machines
c. 3,750 toaster ovens and 2,250 bread machines
d. 7,500 toaster ovens

7. Shine Bright Company has three product lines: D, E, and F. The following information is available:

	D	E	F
Sales	$60,000	$38,000	$26,000
Variable costs	36,000	18,000	12,000
Contribution margin	24,000	20,000	14,000
Fixed expenses	12,000	15,000	16,000
Operating income (loss)	$12,000	$ 5,000	$ (2,000)

Shine Bright Company is thinking of dropping product line F because it is reporting an operating loss. Assuming Shine Bright Company drops line F and does not replace it, what is the effect on the operating income?
(pp. 978–979)
a. Increase $2,000
b. Increase $14,000
c. Decrease $14,000
d. Increase $16,000

8. Using the data in Question 7, assume that Shine Bright Company drops line F and rents the space formerly used to produce product F for $17,000 per year. What is the effect on the operating income? (pp. 978–979)
a. Decrease $3,000
b. Increase $3,000
c. Decrease $14,000
d. Increase $15,000

9. Mike's Sneaker Shop expects to sell 10,000 sneakers this year at the current market price of $55 a pair. He would like to earn a return of 10% on the $2 million of assets invested in the shop. What is the target full cost?
(p. 971)
a. $550,000
b. $200,000
c. $350,000
d. $750,000

10. Florence's Fine Furniture Company is considering selling her wood tables unfinished for $900 apiece. If the decision is made to process them further and complete the finishing required, the table could be sold for $1,200 but the additional cost to process would be $275. What should Florence do? (pp. 986–987)

a. Sell the table unfinished and have $25 more net income per unit.

b. Sell the table finished and have $300 more net income per unit.

c. Sell the table finished and have $25 more net income per unit.

d. It cannot be determined; other factors need to be considered.

Quick Exercises

20-1. Label each of the following items as relevant or irrelevant in making a decision. (pp. 963–965)

<u>irrelevant</u> a. Accumulated depreciation on old equipment being evaluated for replacement

<u>relevant</u> b. Cost of insurance on a new vehicle

<u>irrelevant</u> c. Original cost of old equipment that is being evaluated for replacement

<u>irrelevant</u> d. Cost of previous year's insurance policy on old equipment being evaluated for replacement

<u>relevant</u> e. Cost of new equipment under evaluation to replace used equipment

<u>irrelevant</u> f. Cost of roof repair made on rental property last year

20-2. Picard Enterprises produces and sells a part used in the production of computing equipment. The unit costs associated with this part are as follows:

Direct materials	$0.25
Direct labor	$0.32
Variable manufacturing overhead	$0.15
Fixed manufacturing overhead	$0.14
Total cost	$0.86

Data Company has approached Picard Enterprises with an offer to purchase 20,000 units of this part at a price of $0.75 per unit. Accepting this special sales order will put idle manufacturing capacity to use and will not affect regular sales. Total fixed costs will not change.

Requirement

1. Determine whether the special order should be accepted. Justify your conclusion. (pp. 966–969)

Variable manufacturing expenses per unit:

$0.25 + $0.32 + $0.15 = $0.72
$0.75 − $0.72 = $0.03/unit × 20,000 units = $600 increase in operating income

Picard Enterprises should accept the offer as this would increase operating income by $600.

Points to consider:
Total fixed costs will not change.
Idle capacity exists.
No effect on regular sales.

20-3. Jun Outerwear manufactures coats and jackets. The company's product line income statement follows:

	Total	Coats	Jackets
Sales revenue	$900,000	$580,000	$321,000
Cost of goods sold			
Variable	230,000	116,000	114,000
Fixed	280,000	184,000	96,000
Total cost of goods sold	510,000	300,000	210,000
Gross profit	390,000	280,000	110,000
Marketing and administrative expenses			
Variable	186,000	58,000	128,000
Fixed	135,000	79,000	56,000
Total marketing and administrative expenses	321,000	137,000	184,000
Operating income (loss)	$ 69,000	$143,000	$ (74,000)

Management is considering dropping the jackets product line. Accountants for the company estimate that dropping the jackets line will decrease fixed costs of goods sold by $50,000 and fixed marketing and administrative expenses by $8,000.

Requirement

1. Prepare an analysis supporting your opinion about whether or not the jackets product line should be dropped. (pp. 978–979)

Contribution Margin Income Statement for jackets

	Current—Jackets	If Jackets Dropped
Sales revenue	$321,000	$ 0
Variable expenses:		
Manufacturing	114,000	0
Marketing and administrative	128,000	0
Contribution margin	78,000	0
Fixed expenses:		
Manufacturing	96,000	46,000
Marketing and administrative	56,000	18,000
Operating income (loss)	$ (74,000)	$(94,000)

The company should keep producing and selling jackets because operating income will decrease by $94,000 – $74,000 = $20,000 if the product line is dropped.

20-4. We Play Company makes a part used in the manufacture of video game systems. Management is considering whether to continue manufacturing the part, or to buy the part from an outside source at a cost of $23 per part. We Play needs 125,000 parts per year. The cost of manufacturing 125,000 parts is computed as follows:

Direct materials	$1,265,000
Direct labor	812,000
Variable manufacturing overhead	510,000
Fixed manufacturing overhead	663,000
Total manufacturing cost	$3,250,000

We Play would pay $0.20 per unit to transport the parts to its manufacturing plant. Purchasing the part from an outside source would enable the company to avoid 30% of fixed manufacturing overhead. We Play's factory space freed up by purchasing the part from an outside supplier could be used to manufacture another product with a contribution margin of $65,000.

Requirement

1. Prepare an analysis to show which alternative makes the best use of Sharp Image's factory space, assuming that We Play does the following: (pp. 982–987)

1. Makes the part
2. Buys the part and leaves facilities idle
3. Buys the part and uses facilities to make another product

	Make	Buy Part and Leave Facilities Idle	Buy Part and Use Facilities to Make Another Project
Direct materials	$1,265,000		
Direct labor	812,000		
Variable manufacturing overhead	510,000		
Variable transportation		$ 37,500	$ 37,500
Fixed manufacturiing overhead	663,000	464,100	464,100
Purchase price		2,875,000	2,875,000
Profit contribution from another product			(65,000)
Total cost	$3,250,000	$3,376,600	$3,311,600

We Play should continue to manufacture the part. This alternative results in the lowest cost.

Calculations (for buying parts):

Variable Transportation = 125,000 × $0.20 = $37,500
Fixed Manufacturing Overhead = 663,000 × (1 − 30%) = $464,100
Purchase Price = 125,000 × $23 = $2,875,000

20-5. Hunter's Hats, Co., had the following financial information for the year ended December 31, 2013.

- Sales of 150,000 hats at $5 per unit
- Variable manufacturing costs of $1.20 per unit
- Fixed manufacturing costs of $105,000
- Variable selling and administrative expenses of $.50 per unit
- Fixed selling and administrative expenses of $80,000

Requirement

1. Prepare an income statement for the company using the absorption costing and contribution margin formats. (p. 968)

Absorption Costing Income Statement

<table>
<tr><td colspan="2" align="center">**HUNTER'S HATS, CO.**
Income Statement
For the Year Ended December 31, 2013</td></tr>
<tr><td>Sales revenue</td><td>$ 750,000</td></tr>
<tr><td>Less: Cost of goods sold</td><td>(285,000)</td></tr>
<tr><td>Gross profit</td><td>465,000</td></tr>
<tr><td>Less: Selling and administrative expenses</td><td>(155,000)</td></tr>
<tr><td>Operating income</td><td>$ 310,000</td></tr>
</table>

Calculations:

Sales revenue = 150,000 × $5 = $750,000
Cost of goods sold = (150,000 × $1.20) + $105,000 = $285,000
Selling and administrative expenses = (150,000 × $0.50) + $80,000 = $155,000

Contribution Margin Income Statement

<table>
<tr><td colspan="3" align="center">**HUNTER'S HATS, CO.**
Income Statement
For the Year Ended December 31, 2013</td></tr>
<tr><td>Sales revenue</td><td></td><td>$750,000</td></tr>
<tr><td>Less: Variable expenses</td><td></td><td></td></tr>
<tr><td>Manufacturing</td><td>$(180,000)</td><td></td></tr>
<tr><td>Selling and administrative</td><td>(75,000)</td><td>(255,000)</td></tr>
<tr><td>Contribution margin</td><td></td><td>495,000</td></tr>
<tr><td>Less: Fixed expenses</td><td></td><td></td></tr>
<tr><td>Manufacturing</td><td>(105,000)</td><td></td></tr>
<tr><td>Selling and administrative</td><td>(80,000)</td><td>(185,000)</td></tr>
<tr><td>Operating income</td><td></td><td>$ 310,000</td></tr>
</table>

Calculations:

Sales revenue = 150,000 × $5 = $750,000
Variable manufacturing = 150,000 × $1.20 = $180,000
Variable selling and administrative = 150,000 × $0.50 = $75,000

Do It Yourself! Question 1 Solutions

Part 1

Requirement 1

Assuming $250,000 of the manufacturing costs is fixed and $100,000 of the marketing and administrative cost is fixed, should Easy Access accept the order from the Yemen company?

$$\text{Variable cost per unit} = \frac{(\$400,000 - \$250,000) + (\$220,000 - \$100,00)}{5,000 \text{ cases}}$$

$$\frac{\$150,000 + \$120,000}{5,000 \text{ cases}}$$

$$\frac{\$270,000}{5,000 \text{ cases}}$$

$$= \$54 \text{ per case}$$

Increase in revenues:

Sale of 500 cases @ $80	$40,000

Increase in expenses variable costs:

500 cases @ $54/case	27,000
Increase in operating income	$13,000

Easy Access should accept the special order because an increase in operating income will result.

Part 2

Requirement 2

Great Graphics price per case is $15. Easy Access would avoid all variable costs associated with the printing and would reduce the fixed cost by $3,000 if Great Graphics prints Easy Access's graphics. Should Easy Access outsource the printing work to Great Graphics?

Graphics Costs	Make	Buy	Difference
Direct materials	$20,000		$ 20,000
Direct labor	40,000		40,000
Variable factory overhead	5,000		5,000
Fixed costs	$15,000	$12,000	3,000
Purchase cost from Great Graphics			
(5,000 cases × $15 per case)		75,000	(75,000)
Total cost of graphics	$80,000	$87,000	$ (7,000)
Cost per unit (divide by 5,000 cases)	$ 16.00	$ 17.40	$ (1.40)

Easy Access should not accept the printing offer from Great Graphics. It costs $1.40 less to make than to buy.

Part 3

Requirement 3

Should Easy Access stop producing the specially shaped keyless remote?

Reduction in revenue by dropping special keyless remote:

200 × $140 = **$28,000**

Reduction in expenses by dropping special keyless remote:

200 × $135 = **$27,000**

Decrease in operating income = **$ 1,000**

Because the difference between the absolute value of the loss of revenue less the cost savings from dropping the product is positive, Easy Access should not drop the special keyless remote.

Do It Yourself! Question 2 Solutions

Part 1

Requirements

1. Total fixed costs will not change if the company stops selling Free Weights. Prepare an incremental analysis to show whether Massive, Co., should drop the Free Weights product line. Will dropping Free Weights add $60,000 to operating income? Explain.

Because fixed costs will not change in this case the focus will be on the expected decrease in revenues and the expected decrease in variable expenses. Any *decrease* in operating income means the product should *not* be dropped.

When fixed costs do not change it is always advisable to *not* drop the product line if the contribution margin remains positive.

Expected decrease in revenues:	
Sale of free weights...	$220,000
Expected decrease in expenses:	
Variable expenses	150,000
Expected decrease in operating income	$ 70,000

Dropping Free Weights will result in a decrease in operating income of $70,000. Free Weights should not be dropped.

2. Refer to Requirement 1 and assume that Massive, Co., can now avoid $80,000 of fixed expenses by dropping the Free Weights product line. (These costs are direct fixed costs of the Free Weights product line.) Prepare an incremental analysis to show whether Massive, Co., should stop selling Free Weights.

Relevant costs continue to be the focus, but now the fixed costs are relevant because they are no longer constant.

Expected decrease in revenues:		
Sale of free weights..................................		$220,000
Expected decrease in expenses:		
Variable expenses	150,000	
Fixed expenses..	80,000	
Expected decrease in total expenses............		230,000
Expected increase in operating income		$ 10,000

Massive, Co., should stop selling Free Weights. This decision will result in an increase in operating income of $10,000.

Part 2

Requirements

3. The same machines that are used to make Exercise Machines also make Free Weights. If it takes 120 minutes to produce one Exercise Machine and 30 minutes to produce one Free Weight, compute the sales mix that will maximize operating income. (Assume that the fixed costs are not affected by the sales mix.)

Identify the constraint that restricts producing as many units as Massive, Co., can sell.

Calculate which product(s) generate the highest contribution margin per unit of the constraint.

Because fixed costs are not affected by the sale mix (not unusual for short-range decision making), it is not necessary to consider the impact on fixed costs of selecting one product instead of others in this case.

	Exercise Machines	Free Weights
(1) Units that can be produced each hour	.5	2
(2) Contribution margin per unit	$105.00	$27.00
Contribution margin per hour (1) × (2)	$ 52.50	$54.00

Given sufficient customer demand, it is advisable to produce all Free Weights because its contribution margin per hour is higher than Exercise Machines.

The contribution margin per *unit* is higher for the Exercise Machines than the Free Weights. Since the number of hours the machines can run is limited *and* there is sufficient demand for both products, the product with the higher contribution margin per unit of constraint (hours in this case) is the product that you want to produce.

4. Massive, Co., estimates the demand for Exercise Machines is unlimited, but it can only sell 10,000 Free Weights this year. Assume that the machines can run 12,000 hours annually. How many units of each product should be produced this year to maximize operating income?

The Free Weights have the higher contribution margin per hour. This product will be allocated machine hours first, 10,000 hours, to satisfy customer demand. Exercise Machines will be produced with the excess available machine hours.

Maximum machine hours this year	= 12,000 hours
Free weights: 10,000 units × 1/2 hour =	5,000
Remaining available hours this year	7,000
Exercise machines produced per hour	× 1/2
Total exercise machines produced	3,500

10,000 Free Weights and 3,500 Exercise Machines should be produced this year.

The Power of Practice

For more practice using the skills learned in this chapter, visit MyAccountingLab. There you will find algorithmically generated questions that are based on these Demo Docs and your main textbook's Review and Assess Your Progress sections.

To go to MyAccountingLab, follow these steps:

1. Direct your URL to www.myaccountinglab.com.
2. Log in using your name and password.
3. Click the MyAccountingLab link.
4. Click Study Plan in the left navigation bar.
5. From the table of contents, select Chapter 20, Short-Term Business Decisions.
6. Click a link to work tutorial exercises.

21 Capital Investment Decisions and the Time Value of Money

What You Probably Already Know

People purchase lottery tickets in the hopes of winning the grand jackpot. In March, 2011, seven New York state employees won the Mega Millions grand prize of $319 million. Winners can choose to receive the money in 26 equal payments over the upcoming 25 years or in a lump sum. The seven winners decided to take a lump-sum payment. You probably already know that opting for the lump-sum payment means that something less than $319,000,000 is received because of the time value of money. Receiving a dollar now is worth more than receiving it in a year, 5 years, or 25 years in the future. The winnings are "discounted," reduced to the present value. The seven winners received $202 million. In this chapter, we will study how to calculate the present value of future cash flows and how that information is used to help management make decisions.

Learning Objectives/Success Keys

 Describe the importance of capital investments and the capital budgeting process.

The investment of **capital assets**, long-term assets, is vitally important to a business. New equipment and technologies are necessary to stay competitive. Because resources are limited it is crucial to use a process to make decisions among competing investments; this process is called capital budgeting analysis.

2 Use the payback period and accounting rate of return methods to make capital investment decisions.

The focus of capital budgeting is on the net cash inflows that are projected in the future. One tool that is used to assess capital investments is the payback period. The **payback period** is the amount of time it takes to recover the initial investment. You will calculate the payback period for two different products in Demo Doc 1. *Review Exhibits 21-2 through 21-4 (pp. 1014–1016) for an illustration of the payback period concept.*

You can use the **accounting rate of return** to determine the rate of return from an asset over its useful life. You will calculate the accounting rate of return for two different products in Demo Doc 1. The average annual operating income can be computed as the net cash inflow from the asset less depreciation expense. The average amount invested in the asset is the average of the cost amount and the residual value. *Review the Rate of Return section of the text (pp. 1016–1018) for an accounting rate of return calculation.*

3 Use the time value of money to compute the present and future values of single lump sums and annuities.

The concepts of present and future values are necessary to make long-term business decisions. To properly compute the present or future value of money the following terms should be understood:

- **Annuity** is a stream of equal installments made at equal time intervals.
- **Principal** (*p*) is the amount invested or borrowed.
- **Number of periods** (*n*) is the length of time from the beginning of the investment until termination.
- **Interest rate** (*i*) is the annual interest rate earned on the investment.

Use the preceding information and the appropriate table in the text to compute the following:

- Present Value of $1: The value today of receiving $1 at some specific date in the future
- Present Value of Annuity of $1: The value today of receiving $1 *every period in the future*
- Future Value of $1: The value in the future of $1 invested today
- Future Value of Annuity of $1: The value in the future of $1 invested *every period for a specified number of periods* Review the text section A Review of the Time Value of Money and Exhibits 21-7 and 21-8 (p. 1022).

Use discounted cash flow models to make capital investment decisions.

Discounted cash flow models use the concept of **present value** or the **time value of money**, which simply means that it is more valuable to receive money now than in the future. To make the best capital budgeting decision, the value of future cash flows must be considered in terms of the current or present value. The discounted cash flow models widely used to evaluate potential expenditures are the **net present value** and the **internal rate of return (IRR)**. You will explore these methods in Demo Doc 2. *Review Exhibit 21-11 (p. 1027) for a computation of the net present value method assuming equal net cash inflows, Exhibit 21-12 (p. 1028) assuming unequal net cash inflows, and Exhibit 21-14 (p. 1030) assuming the asset investment has a residual value. Review Exhibits 21-15 and 21-16 (pp. 1032–1033) for examples of the IRR method.*

Demo Doc 1

Capital Budgeting

Learning Objectives 2, 3, 4

Better Body Fitness produces exercise equipment. They are considering producing one of two possible new products: either a new type of rowing machine or an upper torso piece of equipment. They would need to purchase new machinery to manufacture these items. Each machine would require an additional investment of $500,000. The rower machine would have a useful life of seven years and the torso machine would have a useful life of four years. Neither has a residual value. The expected annual net cash inflows are as follows:

| Useful Life | Net Cash Inflows | | | |
| | Rower | | Torso | |
Years	Annual	Accumulated	Annual	Accumulated
1	$120,000	$120,000	$160,000	$160,000
2	120,000	240,000	160,000	320,000
3	120,000	360,000	160,000	480,000
4	120,000	480,000	160,000	640,000
5	120,000	600,000		
6	120,000	720,000		
7	120,000	840,000		

Requirements

1. Determine the payback period for each product. What is the major weakness of payback analysis?

2. Calculate the accounting rate of return. What is the major weakness of the accounting rate of return?

3. If Better Body Fitness requires a 14% return, what is the net present value of each project?

4. Compute the internal rate of return for each project.

Demo Doc 1 Solutions

Requirement 1

2 Use the payback period and accounting rate of return methods to make capital investment decisions

Determine the payback period for each product. What is the major weakness of payback analysis?

Part 1	Part 2	Part 3	Part 4	Demo Doc Complete

Payback period is a simple approach that is used sometimes to screen potential projects. A company would want to recoup the investment amount as quickly as possible, assuming all other factors are constant.

In this case, payback is the length of time it takes Better Body Fitness to recover, in net cash inflows, the $500,000 initial outlay. The rower and torso have equal cash inflows each year, so the payback period is calculated as:

$$\text{Payback period} = \frac{\text{Amount invested}}{\text{Expected annual net cash inflow}}$$

$$\text{Payback period for rower} = \frac{\$500,000}{\$120,000}$$

$$= \textbf{4.17 years}$$

$$\text{Payback period for torso} = \frac{\$500,000}{\$160,000}$$

$$= \textbf{3.13 years}$$

The payback method favors the torso because it recovers the initial investment more quickly. The major weakness of payback analysis is that it only focuses on time, not on profit. Although the torso recovers the initial investment faster, the rower produces $200,000 more in net cash inflows ($840,000 – $640,000). The payback period must be shorter than the useful life to provide any profit.

Requirement 2

2 Use the payback period and accounting rate of return methods to make capital investment decisions

Calculate the accounting rate of return. What is the major weakness of the accounting rate of return?

Part 1	**Part 2**	Part 3	Part 4	Demo Doc Complete

The accounting rate of return calculated is compared to the required return set by management. The company will invest in the asset if the return is more than that required and will not invest if the return is less than the required return. If several alternatives are being considered, the higher the return, the better it is.

The accounting rate of return is determined by dividing the average operating income from the asset by the average amount invested in the asset.

The average amount invested in the asset is calculated as

$$\frac{\text{Asset cost} - \text{Residual value}}{2}$$

Average amount invested in the rower and torso is

$$\frac{\$500,000 - 0}{2} = \$250,000$$

To determine the average operating income, depreciation must first be calculated. The depreciation associated with the rower is

$$\frac{\$500,000}{7\text{-year life}} = \$71,429$$

Depreciation associated with the torso machine is

$$\frac{\$500,000}{4\text{-year life}} = \$125,000$$

The depreciation expense is now subtracted from the expected annual net cash inflows to calculate the average operating income:

$$\text{Rower average operating income} = \$120,000 - \$71,429$$
$$= \$48,571$$

$$\text{Torso average operating income} = \$160,000 - \$125,000$$
$$= \$35,000$$

The accounting rate of return on the rower and torso machines are

$$\text{Rower} = \frac{\$48,571}{\$250,000}$$
$$= 19.428\%$$

$$\text{Torso} = \frac{\$35,000}{\$250,000}$$
$$= 14.00\%$$

The major weakness of the accounting rate of return is that it doesn't consider the timing of the income. The accounting rate of return doesn't consider whether the income is greater early in the life of the asset or near the end of the useful life of the asset. Management would prefer greater income early in the life of the asset so the funds could be used to generate additional income.

3 Use the time value of money to compute the present and future values of single lump sums and annuities

4 Use discounted cash flow models to make capital investment decisions

Requirement 3

If Better Body requires a 14% return, what is the net present value of each project?

Part 1	Part 2	**Part 3**	Part 4	Demo Doc Complete

Net present value brings future cash inflows and future cash outflows to a common time period in order to more easily compare the feasibility of each product.

The net present value (NPV) method compares the present value of the net cash inflows to the initial investment of the capital project. To obtain the present value of the net cash inflows, the minimum desired rate of return is used to find the appropriate discounting factor in the present value tables. If cash flows are equal each year, it is considered to be an annuity and Table B-2 in Appendix B (p. B-2) is used; if the cash flows are unequal, Table B-1 (p. B-1) is used for each year's present value calculation. *If the present value of the inflows to be received is equal or greater to that invested, the project is considered to be desirable.*

Consider the following:

> Net present value = Present value of ALL of the cash flows IN (PVCFI)
> Less: Present value of ALL of the cash flows OUT (PVCFO)

Both of these projects expect a stream of equal periodic cash flows, which is called an annuity. The present value of an annuity is the periodic cash flow multiplied by the present value of an annuity of $1. Table B-2 (reproduced here) shows the present value of annuity factors for various interest rates and numbers of periods:

	Present Value of Annuity of $1						
Period	4%	6%	8%	10%	12%	14%	16%
1	0.962	0.943	0.926	0.909	0.893	0.877	0.862
2	1.886	1.833	1.783	1.736	1.690	1.647	1.605
3	2.775	2.673	2.577	2.487	2.402	2.322	2.246
4	3.630	3.465	3.312	3.170	3.037	2.914	2.798
5	4.452	4.212	3.993	3.791	3.605	3.433	3.274
6	5.242	4.917	4.623	4.355	4.111	3.889	3.685
7	6.002	5.582	5.206	4.868	4.564	4.288	4.039
8	6.733	6.210	5.747	5.335	4.968	4.639	4.344
9	7.435	6.802	6.247	5.759	5.328	4.946	4.607
10	8.111	7.360	6.710	6.145	5.650	5.216	4.833

Appendix C-2 provides a more comprehensive table for the present value of an annuity of $1.

As shown in Table B-2, the present value factor for the rower investment, 14% and 7 periods, is 4.288, and the present value factor for the torso investment, 14% and 4 periods, is 2.914.

The present value of a project is equal to the present value factor multiplied by one period's cash flow.

The net present value is the present value less the cost of the investment, where the investment is made at time zero, or today at an interest factor of 1.0000, for a "present value" approach.

To calculate net present value for each product:

Rower:

PVCFI	$120,000 × 4.288 =	$ 514,560
PVCFO	$500,000 × 1.000 =	(500,000)
Net present value		= $ 14,560)

Torso Machine:

PVCFI	$160,000 × 2.914 =	$ 466,240
PVCFO	$500,000 × 1.000 =	(500,000)
Net present value	=	$ (33,760)

The torso machine has a negative net present value and that should not be accepted. The rower has a positive net present value of $14,560. Because the net present value is positive the investment must be earning *more than* a 14% return.

If the net present value of a project is *zero*, the investment is earning exactly the amount desired, 14% in this case.

Requirement 4

3 Use the time value of money to compute the present and future values of single lump sums and annuities

4 Use discounted cash flow models to make capital investment decisions

Compute the internal rate of return for each project.

Part 1	Part 2	Part 3	**Part 4**	Demo Doc Complete

The internal rate of return (IRR) method calculates the estimated rate of return Better Body can expect to earn by investing in the project. The IRR uses the same concepts as the net present value. The net present value uses management's minimum desired rate of return to determine whether the present value of the future net cash inflows equals or exceeds the cost of the initial investment. If they are equal, it means that the project is earning exactly the minimum desired rate of return. If the amount is positive, the project is earning a rate of return in excess of the minimum, but it is unknown. The IRR method *calculates* the projected rate of return in the following way:

a. Identify the projected future cash flows (as is done with the net present value method).

b. Estimate the present value of an annuity factor as

$$\text{Annuity PV factor} = \frac{\text{Investment}}{\text{Expected annual net cash flow}}$$

c. Refer to the present value of an annuity table in Appendix B, Table B-2. Find the number of cash flow periods in the left column and follow that row to the right until you locate the factor that is closest to the present value of an annuity factor computed in part b. Follow that number up to the interest rate at the top of the column to determine the rate of return. *If the rate of return calculated is equal to or higher than management's minimum desired rate of return, the project is acceptable.*

To determine the internal rate of return, we must find the discount rate that makes the total present value of the cash inflows equal to the present value of the cash outflows. Work backward to find the discount rate that makes the present value of the annuity of cash inflows equal to the amount of the investment by solving the following equation for the annuity present value factor (which is, in reality, the figure obtained when calculating the payback period, as we did in requirement 1):

$$\text{Annuity PV factor for Rower} = \frac{\$500,000}{\$120,000}$$
$$= 4.17$$

$$\text{Annuity PV factor for Torso} = \frac{\$500,000}{\$160,000}$$
$$= 3.13$$

Look at Table B-2 and scan the row corresponding to the project's expected life— period 7 for the rower, period 4 for the torso machine. Choose the column with the number closest to the annuity PV factor previously calculated. The 4.17 annuity factor for the rower is closest to 4.288, the 14% column and the 3.13 annuity factor for the torso machine is closest to 3.17, the 10% column. Therefore, the internal rate of return for the rower is approximately 14% and the internal rate of return for the torso machine is approximately 10%.

Part 1	Part 2	Part 3	Part 4	**Demo Doc Complete**

Quick Practice Questions

True/False

_____ 1. Capital budgeting focuses on accrual accounting.

_____ 2. After investing in an asset, the company compares the actual net cash inflows generated from the investment to the projection in a process called a post-audit.

_____ 3. Investments with longer payback periods are more desirable, all else being equal.

_____ 4. The internal rate of return (IRR) is the interest rate that makes the NPV of the investment equal to zero.

_____ 5. The payback method can only be used when net cash inflows are the same for each period.

_____ 6. If the net present value of several potential investments is positive and only one may be chosen, it is suggested that the profitability index be computed and the largest selected for investment.

_____ 7. The accounting rate of return is a measure of profitability computed by dividing the average annual cash flows from an asset by the average amount invested in the asset.

_____ 8. The accounting rate of return is sometimes used as a preliminary screen for potential desirable investments.

_____ 9. Net present value and the payback period are examples of discounted cash flow models used in capital budgeting decisions.

_____ 10. In calculating the net present value of an investment in equipment, the required investment and its terminal residual value should be subtracted from the present value of all future cash inflows.

Multiple Choice

1. What is the profitability index of a project that requires an investment of $360,000 and present value of net cash inflows of 403,000? What is the profitability index?
   a. 89%
   b. 112%
   c. 11%
   d. 12%

2. Which of the following is an irrelevant cash inflow or outflow?
   a. Future disposal value of an asset
   b. Future operating cash flows
   c. Current cash outlay to acquire a new asset
   d. Cash outlay to acquire equipment 10 years ago

3. If you won the lottery and would be receiving $100,000 each year for the next 25, which table would you use to compute the value of your winnings in today's dollars?
   a. Present Value of $1
   b. Future Value of $1
   c. Present Value of Annuity of $1
   d. Future Value of Annuity of $1

4. If you started saving $4,000 each year and want to know how much money you will have accumulated at the end of 25 years, which table would you use?
   a. Present Value of $1
   b. Future Value of $1
   c. Present Value of Annuity of $1
   d. Future Value of Annuity of $1

5. Which of the following methods ignores the time value of money?
   a. Accounting rate of return
   b. Net present value
   c. Internal rate of return
   d. None of these ignores the time value of money

6. Lerer, Inc., is considering investing $450,000 in a new piece of machinery. The net cash inflows are $120,000 the first 2 years and $80,000 for the following 4 years. What is the payback period?
   a. 4 years
   b. 5.4 years
   c. 5 years
   d. 4.6 years

Information for Questions 7–10:

Logan, Inc., is evaluating two possible investments in depreciable plant assets. The company uses the straight-line method of depreciation. The following information is available:

	Investment A	Investment B
Initial capital investment	$60,000	$90,000
Estimated useful life	3 years	3 years
Estimated residual value	- 0 -	- 0 -
Estimated annual net cash inflow	$25,000	$40,000
Required rate of return	10%	12%

The present value of $1 due 3 years from now:

8%	0.7938
10%	0.7513
12%	0.7118
14%	0.6750
16%	0.6407

The present value of $1 per year due at the end of each of 3 years:

8%	2.5771
10%	2.4869
12%	2.4018
14%	2.3216
16%	2.2459

7. What is the internal rate of return for Investment A?
   a. 8%
   b. 10%
   c. 12%
   d. 14%

8. What is the internal rate of return for Investment B?
   a. 10%
   b. 12%
   c. 14%
   d. 16%

9. Using the preceding information, what is the net present value of Investment A?
   a. $ 2,173
   b. $ 6,080
   c. $12,825
   d. $60,000

10. Using the preceding information, what is the net present value of Investment B?
    a. $ (164)
    b. $ 6,072
    c. $40,000
    d. $61,528

Quick Exercises

21-1. Your Uncle Buck would like to help you out with your college expenses. He offers to give you $65,000 your first year of school or $20,000 each of the four years. Assuming that the market rate of interest is 8%, which should you choose?

21-2. Tom Jones plans on saving and investing equal amounts of money each year over the next 40 years. His goal is to accumulate $2 million dollars. Tom thinks that he will earn 6% to 8% on her investment over the years. Calculate the minimum and maximum amounts that Tom needs to save each year to reach his goal, assuming that his return may be as low as 6% or as high as 8%.

21-3. Barry, Co., is considering investing $864,000 in a piece of equipment that has a 10-year life and no residual value. The annual net cash inflows from this investment are $98,000 for each of the ten years. Calculate the payback value and the accounting rate of return.

21-4. Barry, Co., (see Exercise 21-3) assumes that the discount rate is 6%.

   a. Calculate the net present value.

   b. Calculate the IRR assuming the same cost of $864,000 and life of 10 years but with net operating inflows of $128,000.

Do It Yourself! Question 1

Capital Budgeting

Home Joy produces various household goods. They want to produce one of two possible new products: either ceramic photo frames or ceramic water fountains. Each product would require a machinery investment of $320,000. Useful life for the frames machinery would be seven years, while the useful life for the fountains machinery would be four years. The expected annual net cash inflows are as follows:

Useful Life Years	Annual	Frames Accumulated	Annual	Fountains Accumulated
1	$60,000	$ 60,000	$90,000	$ 90,000
2	60,000	120,000	90,000	180,000
3	60,000	180,000	90,000	270,000
4	60,000	240,000	90,000	360,000
5	60,000	300,000		
6	60,000	360,000		
7	60,000	420,000		

Requirements

Use the payback period and accounting rate of return methods to make capital investment decisions

1. **Determine the payback period for each product.**

Use the payback period and accounting rate of return methods to make capital investment decisions

2. **Calculate the accounting rate of return.**

3 Use the time value of money to compute the present and future values of single lump sums and annuities

4 Use discounted cash flow models to make capital investment decisions

3 Use the time value of money to compute the present and future values of single lump sums and annuities

4 Use discounted cash flow models to make capital investment decisions

3. Assuming that Home Joy requires a 12% return on each possible new product, what is the net present value of each project?

4. Compute the internal rate of return for each project.

Quick Practice Solutions

True/False Question Solutions

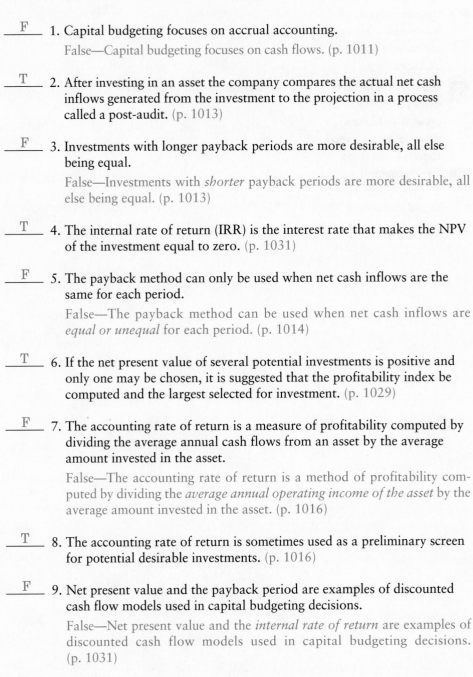

_____ F _____ 1. Capital budgeting focuses on accrual accounting.

   False—Capital budgeting focuses on cash flows. (p. 1011)

_____ T _____ 2. After investing in an asset the company compares the actual net cash inflows generated from the investment to the projection in a process called a post-audit. (p. 1013)

_____ F _____ 3. Investments with longer payback periods are more desirable, all else being equal.

   False—Investments with _shorter_ payback periods are more desirable, all else being equal. (p. 1013)

_____ T _____ 4. The internal rate of return (IRR) is the interest rate that makes the NPV of the investment equal to zero. (p. 1031)

_____ F _____ 5. The payback method can only be used when net cash inflows are the same for each period.

   False—The payback method can be used when net cash inflows are _equal or unequal_ for each period. (p. 1014)

_____ T _____ 6. If the net present value of several potential investments is positive and only one may be chosen, it is suggested that the profitability index be computed and the largest selected for investment. (p. 1029)

_____ F _____ 7. The accounting rate of return is a measure of profitability computed by dividing the average annual cash flows from an asset by the average amount invested in the asset.

   False—The accounting rate of return is a method of profitability computed by dividing the _average annual operating income of the asset_ by the average amount invested in the asset. (p. 1016)

_____ T _____ 8. The accounting rate of return is sometimes used as a preliminary screen for potential desirable investments. (p. 1016)

_____ F _____ 9. Net present value and the payback period are examples of discounted cash flow models used in capital budgeting decisions.

   False—Net present value and the _internal rate of return_ are examples of discounted cash flow models used in capital budgeting decisions. (p. 1031)

_____ F _____10. In calculating the net present value of an investment in equipment, the required investment and its terminal residual value should be subtracted from the present value of all future cash inflows.

   False—In calculating the net present value of an investment in equipment, _only_ the required investment should be subtracted from the present value of all future cash inflows. (p. 1029)

Multiple Choice

1. What is the profitability index of a project that requires an investment of $360,000 and present value of net cash inflows of $403,000. What is the profitability index? (p. 1029)
   a. 89%
   b. 112%
   c. 11%
   d. 12%

2. Which of the following is an irrelevant cash inflow or outflow? (p. 1026)
   a. Future disposal value of an asset
   b. Future operating cash flows
   c. Current cash outlay to acquire a new asset
   d. Cash outlay to acquire equipment 10 years ago

3. If you won the lottery and would be receiving $100,000 each year for the next 25, which table would you use to compute the value of your winnings in today's dollars? (p. 1025)
   a. Present Value of $1
   b. Future Value of $1
   c. Present Value of Annuity of $1
   d. Future Value of Annuity of $1

4. If you started saving $4,000 each year and want to know how much money you will have accumulated at the end of 25 years, which table would you use? (p. 1023)
   a. Present Value of $1
   b. Future Value of $1
   c. Present Value of Annuity of $1
   d. Future Value of Annuity of $1

5. Which of the following methods ignores the time value of money? (p. 1016)
   a. Accounting rate of return
   b. Net present value
   c. Internal rate of return
   d. None of these ignores the time value of money

6. Lerer, Inc., is considering investing $450,000 in a new piece of machinery. The net cash inflows are $120,000 the first 2 years and $80,000 for the following 4 years. What is the payback period? (p. 1013)
   a. 4 years
   b. 5.4 years
   c. 5 years
   d. 4.6 years

Information for Questions 7–10:

Logan, Inc., is evaluating two possible investments in depreciable plant assets. The company uses the straight-line method of depreciation. The following information is available:

	Investment A	Investment B
Initial capital investment	$60,000	$90,000
Estimated useful life	3 years	3 years
Estimated residual value	- 0 -	- 0 -
Estimated annual net cash inflow	$25,000	$40,000
Required rate of return	10%	12%

The present value of $1 due 3 years from now:

8%	0.7938
10%	0.7513
12%	0.7118
14%	0.6750
16%	0.6407

The present value of $1 per year due at the end of each of 3 years:

8%	2.5771
10%	2.4869
12%	2.4018
14%	2.3216
16%	2.2459

7. What is the internal rate of return for Investment A? (p. 1031)
   a. 8%
   b. 10%
   c. 12%
   d. 4%

8. What is the internal rate of return for Investment B? (p. 1031)
   a. 10%
   b. 12%
   c. 14%
   d. 16%

9. Using the preceding information, what is the net present value of Investment A? (p. 1027)
   a. $2,173
   b. $6,080
   c. $12,825
   d. $60,000

10. Using the preceding information, what is the net present value of Investment B? (p. 1027)
    a. $(164)
    b. $6,072
    c. $40,000
    d. $61,528

Quick Exercises

21-1. Your Uncle Buck would like to help you out with your college expenses. He offers to give you $65,000 your first year of school or $20,000 each of the four years. Assuming that the market rate of interest is 8%, which should you choose? (p. 1025)

The two cash flow options must both be stated in terms of the present value to make a good decision.

Obviously, the present value of receiving $65,000 today is $65,000. Receiving $20,000 each year is an annuity. To calculate the present value of the annuity, refer to Appendix B, Table B (p. B3). Follow the "periods" column down to 4 (for 4 years) and go across to the 8% column. The discount factor is 3.312. The present value of receiving $20,000 annually is: $20,000 × 3.312 = $66,240. You should choose to take the $20,000 per year because it has a greater present value.

21-2. Tom Jones plans on saving and investing equal amounts of money each year over the next 40 years. His goal is to accumulate $2 million dollars. Tom thinks that he will earn 6% to 8% on his investment over the years. Calculate the minimum and maximum amounts that Tom needs to save each year to reach his goal, assuming that his return may be as low as 6% or as high as 8%. (pp. 1023–1024)

Tom's goal is to accumulate a future value of $2 million by investing equal amounts of money over a period of 40 years. Depending upon the rate of return, the amount required to be invested will vary. To determine the minimum and maximum amounts to be invested, the Future Value of an Annuity of $1, Appendix B, Table B-4 (p. B-4), must be used.

> Future dollars = Factor in Table B-4 × Annuity amount

To calculate the amount necessary to be invested at 6% to generate $2 million, follow the "Periods" column down to 40 and across to the 6% column to find a factor of 154.8. The preceding equation can be used now to solve for the annual amount of cash necessary to invest at a 6% return.

> Future dollars = 154.8 × Annuity amount
> $2,000,000 = 154.8 × Annuity amount
> $2,000,000/154.8 = Annuity amount
> Annuity amount = $12,920

To calculate the amount necessary to be invested at 8% to generate $2 million, follow the "Periods" column down to 40 and across to the 8% column to find a factor of 259.1. The equation can be used now to solve for the annual amount of cash necessary to invest at an 8% return.

> Future dollars = 259.1 × Annuity amount
> $1,000,000 = 259.1 × Annuity amount
> $1,000,000/259.1 = Annuity amount
> Annuity amount = $7,719

The minimum amount to be invested each year is $7,719; assuming an 8% rate of return the future value will be $2 million in 40 years. The maximum amount to be invested each year is $12,920; assuming a 6% rate of return the future value will be $2 million in 40 years.

21-3. **Barry, Co., is considering investing $864,000 in a piece of equipment that has a 10-year life and no residual value. The annual net cash inflows from this investment are $98,000 for each of the ten years. Calculate the payback value and the accounting rate of return.** (pp. 1013, 1027)

Payback value is.calculated as the cost of the investment divided by the annual net cash inflows.

$$\text{Payback value} = \frac{\$864,000}{\$98,000}$$
$$= 8.82 \text{ years}$$

$$\text{Accounting rate of return} = \frac{\text{Average annual operating income from asset}}{\text{Average amount invested in asset}}$$

The average annual operating income is calculated as

Total net cash inflows during life of the asset ($98,000 × 10 years)	$ 980,000
Less: Total depreciation over the life of the asset............................	(864,000)
Total operating income during operating life	116,000
Divide by asset's operating life..	10
Average annual operating income from asset	$ 11,600

$$\text{Average amount invested in asset} = \frac{\$864,000}{2}$$
$$= \$432,000$$

$$\text{Accounting rate of return} = \frac{\$11,600}{\$432,000}$$
$$= 2.69\%$$

21-4. **Barry, Co., (see Exercise 21-3) assumes that the discount rate is 6%.**

a. Calculate the net present value. (p. 1025)

	Annuity PV Factor ($i = 6\%$, $n = 10$)	Net Cash Inflow	Present Value
Present value of annuity of equal annual net cash inflows for 10 years at 6% ($88,000 × 7.360)			$ 721,280
Investment			(864,000)
Net present value			$(142,720)

b. Calculate the IRR assuming the same cost of $864,000 and life of 10 years but with net operating inflows of $128,000. (p. 1063)

Estimate the present value of an annuity factor as

$$\text{Annuity PV factor} = \frac{\text{Investment}}{\text{Expected annual net cash flow}}$$

$$\text{Annuity PV factor} = \frac{\$864,000}{\$128,000}$$

$$\text{Annuity PV factor} = 6.750$$

Go to Appendix B, Table B-2 (p. B-2), and follow the "periods" column down to 10, the life of the asset. Following the number 10 across to the right, stop at 6.710, the closest number in that row to 6.750. The interest rate that corresponds with that column is 8%. The IRR is approximately 8%.

Do It Yourself! Question 1 Solutions

Requirements

1. Determine the payback period for each product.

$$\text{Frame payback} = \frac{\$320,000}{\$60,000}$$
$$= 5.33 \text{ years}$$

$$\text{Fountains payback} = \frac{\$320,000}{\$90,000}$$
$$= 3.56 \text{ years}$$

2. Calculate the accounting rate of return.

$$\text{Average amount invested} = \frac{\$320,000}{2}$$
$$= \$160,000$$

$$\text{Depreciation per year, frames} = \frac{\$320,000}{7}$$
$$= \$45,714$$

$$\text{Depreciation per year, fountains} = \frac{\$320,000}{4}$$
$$= \$80,000$$

$$\text{Average annual operating income from frames} = \$60,000 - \$45,714$$
$$= \$14,286$$

$$\text{Average annual operating income from fountains} = \$90,000 - \$80,000$$
$$= \$10,000$$

$$\text{Accounting rate of return (frames)} = \frac{\$14,286}{\$160,000}$$
$$= 8.929\%$$

$$\text{Accounting rate of return (fountains)} = \frac{\$10,000}{\$160,000}$$
$$= 6.25\%$$

3. **Assuming that Home Joy requires a 12% return on each possible new product, what is the net present value of each project?**

Frames

PVCFI	$ 60,000 × 4.564 = $(273,840
PVCFO	$320,000 × 1.000 = $(320,000)
	Net present value = $ (46,160)

Fountains

$$
\begin{array}{llr}
\text{PVCFI} & \$\ 90{,}000 \times 3.037 = & \$(273{,}330 \\
\text{PVCFO} & \$320{,}000 \times 1.000 = & \$\underline{(320{,}000)} \\
& \text{Net present value} = & \$\ \underline{\underline{(46{,}670)}}
\end{array}
$$

Both projects' net present values are negative, therefore neither project should be accepted.

4. Compute the internal rate of return for each project.

$$
\text{Annuity PV factor} = \frac{\text{Investment}}{\text{Expected annual net cash flow}}
$$

$$
\text{Annuity PV factor for frames} = \frac{\$320{,}000}{\$60{,}000}
$$

$$
= 5.333
$$

Frame internal rate of return = 8% (5.206 is the closest number on period 7 row.)

$$
\text{Annuity PV factor for fountains} = \frac{\$320{,}000}{\$90{,}000}
$$

$$
= 3.56
$$

Fountain internal rate of return = 5% (3.546 is the closest number on period 4 row.)

The Power of Practice

For more practice using the skills learned in this chapter, visit MyAccountingLab. There you will find algorithmically generated questions that are based on these Demo Docs and your main textbook's Review and Assess Your Progress sections.

To go to MyAccountingLab, follow these steps:

1. Direct your URL to www.myaccountinglab.com.
2. Log in using your name and password.
3. Click the My Accounting Lab link.
4. Click Study Plan in the left navigation bar.
5. From the table of contents, select Chapter 21, Capital Investment Decisions and the Time Value of Money.
6. Click a link to work tutorial exercises.

22 The Master Budget and Responsibility Accounting

WHAT YOU PROBABLY ALREADY KNOW

You may have wanted to purchase something you have had to save for over a period of time. To project how you would accomplish your goal, you might have made a plan. You would consider the amount of money available at the beginning of your plan plus the forecasted cash receipts less cash disbursements over the period to reach your goal. You probably already know that by addressing your financial goal and creating a cash budget, you are able to plan for the future and make decisions to facilitate achieving your goal. If the period of time is sufficiently long, you can compare your actual to your budgeted cash flows during interim periods and make changes as warranted. Some of these changes may include the following:

- Initiate steps to increase cash inflows, perhaps work more hours
- Initiate steps to decrease cash outflows, cut back on lesser-important spending
- Initiate steps to finance the shortfall, pursue borrowing opportunities
- Postpone or abandon the purchase plan

In this chapter, we will study the various budgets that companies create and appreciate the usefulness of the budgeting process for all financial entities.

Learning Objectives/Success Keys

 Learn why managers use budgets.

Budgeting helps managers plan and control their actions. Management creates organizational goals. Action steps are planned to achieve those goals. The budget is the anticipated financial results of taking those action steps. The actual results can be compared to the budget and corrective action taken where necessary. *Review Exhibits 22-2 and 22-3 (p. 1052–1053) for the usefulness and benefits of budgets.*

2   Understanding the components of the master budget.

The master budget includes the operating budget, the capital expenditures budget, and the financial budget. The operating budget plans sales, and is the cornerstone of the other budgets. The capital expenditures budget presents the company's plan for purchasing capital assets. The financial budget focuses on the cash budget and projected cash inflows and outflows for the corporation.

3   Prepare an operating budget.

The sales budget is the first part of the operating budget that must be prepared. Expected sales units and future sales prices are used in the budget. This budget will drive the remainder of the operating budget, such as the cost of goods sold, inventory, purchase, and operating expense budgets. *Review Exhibits 22-7 through 22-9 (pp. 1058–1060) for examples of operating budgets.*

4   Prepare a financial budget.

The **financial budget** includes the cash and balance sheet budgets. The **cash budget** contains the beginning cash balance, projected cash collections, cash payments, financing required, and the ending cash balance. The period in which items such as sales and purchases on account result in cash flows must be projected and integrated into the cash budget. After completing all of the operating and cash budgets, a projection of the balance sheet account balances can be determined. This information is used to prepare the balance sheet budget. *Review Exhibits 22-11 through 22-13 (pp. 1063–1065) for components of a cash budget. Review Exhibit 22-14 (p. 1066) for the cash budgets and Exhibit 22-15 (p. 1067) for a budgeted balance sheet.*

5   Use sensitivity analysis in budgeting.

Technology has significantly reduced the amount of manual calculations that were required in budgeting. It is particularly helpful in determining "what if" scenarios. What if sales are greater or less than budgeted? What if the cost of goods sold is greater or less than budgeted? One variable in the budget process can be changed and the entire budgeted results can be recalculated in a moment. Sensitivity analysis provides the various results when an event or circumstance assumed in the budget process changes.

6 Prepare performance reports for responsibility centers and account for traceable and common shared fixed costs.

A **responsibility center** is a part or subunit of an organization whose manager is accountable for specific activities. Performance reports compare the budget to the actual results for each responsibility center. The performance of the managers of each center can then be evaluated. There are four responsibility centers:

- **Cost center**—Only costs or expenses are incurred. The human resources, accounting, and information technology departments are examples of cost centers. The goal of the manager is to minimize costs.

- **Revenue center**—Primarily revenues are incurred although some related expenses may be associated with the revenue center. A sales department would be a revenue center. Managers are assessed based upon the revenues generated. The goal of the manager is to maximize revenues.

- **Profit center**—Responsibility in this center is for revenues and expenses, and ultimately profits or net income. The goal of the manager is to exceed the profit projection. The sales and costs related to the Lipton Cup-a-Soup product line would be an example of a product center.

- **Investment center**—The results of the investment as well as the profits of the entity are evaluated here. Managers are responsible for making sales, maintaining expenses, and managing the investment required to generate profits.

Review Exhibit 22-18 (p. 1075) for examples of responsibility centers and responsibility accounting performance reports in Exhibit 22-20 (p. 1078).

A **common shared fixed cost** is a cost such as payroll or legal, which is shared among many products or divisions. A **traceable fixed cost** is one that would disappear if the company discontinued making the product or operating the division with which it is associated.

Demo Doc 1

Master Budget

Learning Objectives 2, 3

Manuel Mova started a company, Mova Company, that sells computer mice. Actual sales for the month ended September 30 were $30,000. Manuel expects sales to increase 7% in October and increase another 4% over October sales in November. Cash sales are expected to be 60% of total sales and credit sales about 40% of sales. Cost of goods sold should be 60% of total sales. Manuel does not want inventory to fall below $4,000 plus 10% of cost of goods sold for the next month. Sales of $35,000 are expected for December. Inventory on September 30 is $6,000.

Operating expenses include sales commission, 10% of sales; rent expense of $1,000; depreciation expense of $1,200; utility expense of $800; and insurance expense of $400.

Round all figures to the nearest dollar.

Requirement

1. Prepare the following budgets for October and November:

   a. Sales budget

   b. Inventory, purchases, and cost of goods sold budget

   c. Operating expense budget

   d. Budgeted income statement

Demo Doc 1 Solution

Requirement 1

Prepare the following budgets for October and November:

2 Understand the components of the master budget

3 Prepare an operating budget

a. Sales budget

Part 1	Part 2	Part 3	Part 4	Demo Doc Complete

We prepare the sales budget first because sales affect most elements of the other budgets we will be preparing for this period.

In order to complete the sales budget, we start by calculating the total sales for each month. We will then compute the split between cash sales and credit sales for each month based on the company's estimation that cash sales will be 60% of the total sales for each month and credit sales will be 40% of total sales for each month.

Let's begin by calculating the total sales for October and November. The question tells us that actual sales for the month ended September 30 were $30,000, and that sales are expected to increase by 7% over that in October and another 4% over October's sales in November:

$$\text{October total sales} = \text{September sales} \times 107\%$$

$$\begin{aligned} \text{October total sales} &= \$30,000 \times 107\% \\ &= \$32,100 \end{aligned}$$

$$\text{November total sales} = \text{October sales} \times 104\%$$

$$\begin{aligned} \text{November total sales} &= \$32,100 \times 104\% \\ &= \$33,384 \end{aligned}$$

So we begin to build our sales budget with these data:

MOVA COMPANY
Sales Budget
Two Months Ended November 30

	October	November	Total
Cash sales, 60%			
Credit sales, 40%			
Total sales	$32,100	$33,384	

Now we work backwards to calculate the split between cash and credit sales for each month. In this case, cash sales are 60% of total sales and credit sales are 40% of total sales for the current months:

$$
\begin{aligned}
\text{Cash sales} &= \text{Total sales} \times 60\% \\
\text{October cash sales} &= \$32,100 \times 60\% \\
&= \$19,260 \\
\text{November cash sales} &= \$33,384 \times 60\% \\
&= \$20,030.40 \text{ (rounded to \$20,030)} \\
\\
\text{Credit sales} &= \text{Total sales} \times 40\% \\
\text{October credit sales} &= \$32,100 \times 40\% \\
&= \$12,840 \\
\text{November credit sales} &= \$33,384 \times 40\% \\
&= \$13,353.60 \text{ (rounded to \$13,354)}
\end{aligned}
$$

Following is the completed sales budget:

MOVA COMPANY
Sales Budget
Two Months Ended November 30

	October	November	Total
Cash sales, 60%	$19,260	$20,030	$39,290
Credit sales, 40%	12,840	13,354	26,194
Total sales	$32,100	$33,384	$65,484

The calculations give us a total sales budget for October and November of $65,484, with 60% of that ($39,290) from cash and 40% ($26,194) from credit.

Because the sales budget calculates values that you will use when preparing other budgets, it is always a good idea to check your work. These calculations can be performed in a number of ways. Here is one alternative:

$$
\begin{aligned}
\text{October total sales} &= \text{Previous month's sales} \times 107\% \\
&= \$30,000 \times 107\% \\
&= \$32,100
\end{aligned}
$$

$$
\begin{aligned}
\text{October cash sales} &= \text{October expected sales} \times 60\% \\
&= \$32,100 \times 60\% \\
&= \$19,260
\end{aligned}
$$

$$
\begin{aligned}
\text{October credit sales} &= \text{October expected sales} \times 40\% \\
&= \$32,100 \times 40\% \\
&= \$12,840
\end{aligned}
$$

$$
\begin{aligned}
\text{November total sales} &= \text{Previous month's sales} \times 104\% \\
&= \$32,100 \times 104\% \\
&= \$33,384
\end{aligned}
$$

$$
\begin{aligned}
\text{November cash sales} &= \text{November expected sales} \times 60\% \\
&= \$33,384 \times 60\% \\
&= \$20,030
\end{aligned}
$$

$$
\begin{aligned}
\text{November credit sales} &= \text{November expected sales} \times 40\% \\
&= \$33,384 \times 40\% \\
&= \$13,354
\end{aligned}
$$

2 Understand the components of the master budget

3 Prepare an operating budget

b. Inventory, purchases, and cost of goods sold budget

Part 1	**Part 2**	Part 3	Part 4	Demo Doc Complete

The inventory, purchases, and cost of goods sold budget statement takes the following format:

Cost of goods sold
+ Desired ending inventory
= Total inventory required
– Beginning inventory
= Purchases

So we first calculate the cost of goods sold. We know from the question that cost of goods sold is expected to be 60% of total sales for the period. From the sales budget, we know that total sales for October are expected to be $32,100, and total sales for November are expected to be $33,384. So we can calculate cost of goods sold as follows:

Cost of goods sold = 60% of budgeted sales from the sales budget
October = $32,100 × 60%
= $19,260
November = $33,384 × 60%
= $20,030

So here is our budget so far:

MOVA COMPANY
Inventory, Purchases, and Cost of Goods Sold Budget
Two Months Ended November 30

	October	November
Cost of goods sold	$19,260	$20,030
+ Desired ending inventory		
= Total inventory required		
– Beginning inventory		
= Purchases		

Next, we need to add the desired ending inventory for each month. The question states that the company does not want inventory to fall below $4,000 plus 10% of cost of goods sold for the next month. In order to calculate the desired ending inventory for November, we need to know the cost of goods sold for December. The question tells us that December's sales are expected to be $35,000. Returning to our calculation for cost of goods sold:

Cost of goods sold = 60% of budgeted sales from the sales budget
December = $35,000 × 60%
= $21,000

Desired ending inventory is now calculated as follows:

Desired ending inventory = [$4,000 + (10% of cost of goods sold for the next month)]
October = $4,000 + (10% × 20,030)
= $6,003
November = $4,000 + (10% × 21,000)
= $6,100

We can now calculate the total ending inventory required:

MOVA COMPANY
Inventory, Purchases, and Cost of Goods Sold Budget
Two Months Ended November 30

	October	November
Cost of goods sold	$19,260	$20,030
+ Desired ending inventory	6,003	6,100
= Total inventory required	$25,263	$26,130
– Beginning inventory		
= Purchases		

Beginning inventory is equal to the previous month's desired ending inventory. We are told in the question that the inventory on September 30 is $6,000, so this amount becomes October's beginning inventory. Once we determine beginning inventory, we subtract it from the total inventory required to determine total purchases for the period:

MOVA COMPANY
Inventory, Purchases, and Cost of Goods Sold Budget
Two Months Ended November 30

	October	November
Cost of goods sold	$19,260	$20,030
+ Desired ending inventory	6,003	6,100
= Total inventory required	$25,263	$26,130
– Beginning inventory	6,000	6,003
= Purchases	$19,263	$20,127

c. Operating expense budget

2 Understand the components of the master budget

3 Prepare an operating budget

Part 1	Part 2	**Part 3**	Part 4	Demo Doc Complete

With the exception of the sales commission, which we know from the question to be 10% of sales, all expenses remain constant between October and November, as follows:

MOVA COMPANY Operating Expense Budget Two Months Ended November 30			
	October	November	Total
Variable operating expenses:			
Sales commission, 10% of sales			
Total variable operating expenses			
Fixed operating expenses			
Rent expense (fixed amount)	$1,000	$1,000	$2,000
Insurance expense (fixed amount)	400	400	800
Depreciation expense (fixed amount)	1,200	1,200	2,400
Utility expense (fixed amount)	800	800	1,600
Total fixed operating expenses	$3,400	$3,400	$6,800
Total operating expenses			

The only calculation to perform here is sales commission. We can compute sales commissions for October and November using the respective sales computations ($32,100 and $33,384) from the sales budget:

$$\text{Sales commission} = \text{Expected sales} \times 10\%$$
$$\text{October sales commission} = \$32,100 \times 10\%$$
$$= \$3,210$$

$$\text{November sales commision} = \$33,384 \times 10\%$$
$$= \$3,338.40 \text{ (rounded to } \$3,338)$$

Here is our completed operating expense budget for October and November:

MOVA COMPANY Operating Expense Budget Two Months Ended November 30			
	October	November	Total
Variable operating expenses:			
Sales commission, 10% of sales	$3,210	$3,338	$ 6,548
Total variable operating expenses	$3,210	$3,338	$ 6,548
Fixed operating expenses			
Rent expense (fixed amount)	$1,000	$1,000	$ 2,000
Insurance expense (fixed amount)	400	400	800
Depreciation expense (fixed amount)	1,200	1,200	2,400
Utility expense (fixed amount)	800	800	1,600
Total fixed operating expenses	$3,400	$3,400	$ 6,800
Total operating expenses	$6,610	$6,738	$13,348

2 Understand the components of the master budget

3 Prepare an operating budget

d. Budgeted income statement

Part 1	Part 2	Part 3	**Part 4**	Demo Doc Complete

The results of the budgets you have created so far are carried over into the fourth element: the budgeted income statement.

Sales revenue is traced from the sales budget in part **a**.

Cost of goods sold is traced from the inventory, purchases, and cost of goods sold budget in part **b**.

We compute gross profit by subtracting the cost of goods sold from sales revenue:

MOVA COMPANY
Budgeted Income Statement
Two Months Ended November 30

	October	November	Total
Sales revenue	$32,100	$33,384	$65,484
Cost of goods sold	19,260	20,030	39,290
Gross profit	12,840	13,354	26,194
Operating expenses			
Net income			

Operating expenses are traced from the operating expenses budget from part **c**.

We compute net income (loss) by subtracting operating expenses from gross profit. Our completed budgeted income statement looks this way:

MOVA COMPANY
Budgeted Income Statement
Two Months Ended November 30

	October	November	Total
Sales revenue	$32,100	$33,384	$65,484
Cost of goods sold	19,260	20,030	39,290
Gross profit	12,840	13,354	26,194
Variable operating expenses:			
Salary and commissions	$ 3,210	$ 3,338	$ 6,548
Total variable operating expenses	$ 3,210	$ 3,338	$ 6,548
Contribution margin	$ 9,630	$10,016	$19,646
Fixed operating expenses:			
Rent expense	$ 1,000	$ 1,000	$ 2,000
Depreciation expense	1,200	1,200	2,400
Insurance expense	400	400	800
Utility expense	800	800	1,600
Total fixed operating expenses	$ 3,400	$ 3,400	$ 6,800
Net income	$ 6,230	$ 6,616	$12,846

For the period, our totals are as follows:

MOVA COMPANY
Budgeted Income Statement
Two Months Ending November 30

Sales revenue			$65,484
Cost of goods sold			39,290
Gross profit			26,194
Variable operating expenses:			
Salary and commissions		$6,548	
Total variable operating expenses			$ 6,548
Contribution margin			$19,646
Fixed operating expenses:			
Rent expense		$2,000	
Depreciation expense		2,400	
Insurance expense		800	
Utility expense		1,600	
Total fixed operating expenses			$ 6,800
Operating income			12,846

Part 1	Part 2	Part 3	Part 4	**Demo Doc Complete**

Demo Doc 2

Financial Budget

Learning Objectives 2, 4

Manuel Mova Company prepared its sales budget; inventory, purchases, and cost of goods sold budget; operating expense budget; and budgeted income statement. Manuel would like to prepare the cash budget for the months of October and November.

Actual sales for the month ended September 30 were $30,000. Actual sales for the month ended August 31 were $26,000. Manuel believes that sales will increase 7% in October and increase another 4% over October sales in November. Cash sales are expected to be 60% of sales and credit sales about 40% of sales.

Cost of goods sold is expected to be 60% of total sales. Manuel does not want inventory to fall below $4,000 plus 10% of cost of goods sold for the next month. Sales of $25,000 are expected for December. Manuel purchased $11,000 of inventory during September and ended the month with $6,000 in ending inventory.

Operating expenses include sales commission, 10% of sales; rent expense of $1,000; depreciation expense of $1,200; utility expense of $800; and insurance expense of $400.

The September 30 cash balance was $4,000.

Of the credit sales, Manuel expects to collect 70% in the month following the sale and the remaining 30% in the next month. Purchases made by Mova Company are paid for in the month after the purchase. Sales commissions are paid 50% in the month incurred and 50% in the next month. Rent, utility, and insurance are paid in the month incurred.

Requirement

1. For the months of October and November, prepare the following:

    a. Budgeted cash collections from customers

    b. Budgeted cash payments for purchases

    c. Budgeted cash payments for operating expenses

    d. Cash budget

Demo Doc 2 Solution

Requirement 1

For the months of October and November, prepare the following:

a. Budgeted cash collections from customers

Part 1	Part 2	Part 3	Part 4	Demo Doc Complete

Armed with the budget data we calculated in Demo Doc 1 of this chapter, we can begin to prepare the cash budget. We start with the budgeted cash collections from customers, which we will use in part **d** of this demo doc to calculate total cash available for the period.

We computed the cash sales for October and November on the sales budget as $19,260 and $20,030, respectively. To these figures we will add any credit collections that Manuel makes in this period.

Manuel expects to collect on credit sales at a rate of 70% in the month following the sale and 30% in the next month. In October, Manuel expects to collect 70% of any credit sales made in September and 30% of credit sales made in August. Likewise, in November, Manuel will collect 70% of October's credit sales and 30% of September's credit sales.

Before we can calculate how much in credit sales Manuel will collect in October and November, we need to see the sales budget data for August and September because collections are being made from those two months. We know from the question that total August sales were $26,000 and total September sales were $30,000. We also know that Manuel expects 40% of total sales each month to be credit sales. So if we were to figure Manuel's sales budget data for August and September, credit sales would look this way:

$$\text{August credit sales} = \text{August total sales} \times 40\%$$
$$= \$26,000 \times 40\%$$
$$= \$10,400$$

$$\text{September credit sales} = \text{September total sales} \times 40\%$$
$$= \$30,000 \times 40\%$$
$$= \$12,000$$

Given these data, Manuel's sales budget for the period August–November would appear this way (although note that the only data you are interested in at this point are the highlighted data):

MOVA COMPANY
Sales Budget
The Four Months Ending November 30

	August	September	October	November
Cash sales, 60%	$15,600	$18,000	$19,260	$20,030
Credit sales, 40%	10,400	12,000	12,840	13,354
Total sales	$26,000	$30,000	$32,100	$33,384

Remember that credit sales for October and November came from the sales budget in Demo Doc 1.

So for October, Manuel expects to collect 30% of credit sales made in August and 70% of credit sales made in September:

> October collections from August credit sales = $10,400 × 30%
> = $3,120
>
> October collections from September credit sales = $12,000 × 70%
> = $8,400

For November, Manuel expects to collect 30% of credit sales made in September and 70% of credit sales made in October:

> November collections from September credit sales = $12,000 × 30%
> = $3,600
>
> November collections from October credit sales = $12,840 × 70%
> = $8,988

Cash sales on the statement come directly from the sales budget and result in the following completed budget:

MOVA COMPANY
Budgeted Cash Collections from Customers
The Two Months Ending November 30

	October	November	Total
Cash sales	$19,260	$20,030	$39,290
Collections of previous month's credit sales	8,400	8,988	17,388
Collections of 2nd previous month's credit sales	3,120	3,600	6,720
Total collections	$30,780	$32,618	$63,398

Shown another way:

			October	November	Total
Month of Sale:					
August	$26,000				
Cash	60%				
Credit	40%	(26,000 × 40% × 30%)	$ 3,120		$ 3,120
September	$30,000				
Cash					
Credit		(30,000 × 40% × 70%)	8,400		8,400
		(30,000 × 40% × 30%)		3,600	3,600
October	$32,100				
Cash		(60% × 32,100)	19,260		19,260
Credit		(32,100 × 40% × 70%)		8,988	8,988
November	$33,384				
Cash		(60% × 33,384)		20,030	20,030
Credit					
Totals			$30,780	$32,618	$63,398

b. Budgeted cash payments for purchases

Part 1	**Part 2**	Part 3	Part 4	Demo Doc Complete

Purchases made by Manuel are paid in the month following the purchase. So in October, Mova paid for the purchases made in September and in November, Manuel paid for the purchases made in October.

The question states that Manuel purchased $11,000 of inventory in September (which he will pay for in October). We know from the inventory, purchases, and cost of goods sold budget that we prepared in Demo Doc 1 (part **b**) of this chapter that Manuel's purchases in October were $19,263 (which he will pay for in November):

MOVA COMPANY
Budgeted Cash Payments for Purchases
For the Two Months Ended November 30

	October	November	Total
Purchases paid from previous month	$11,000	$19,263	$30,263
Total cash payments for purchases	$11,000	$19,263	$30,263

c. Budgeted cash payments for operating expenses

| Part 1 | Part 2 | **Part 3** | Part 4 | Demo Doc Complete |

Following is Manuel's operating expense budget, which we prepared in Demo Doc 1, part c:

MOVA COMPANY
Operating Expense Budget

	October	November	Total
Variable operating expenses:			
Sales commission, 10% of sales	$3,210	$3,338	$ 6,548
Total variable operating expenses	$3,210	$3,338	$ 6,548
Fixed operating expenses			
Rent expense (fixed amount)	$1,000	$1,000	$ 2,000
Insurance expense (fixed amount)	400	400	800
Depreciation expense (fixed amount)	1,200	1,200	2,400
Utility expense (fixed amount)	800	800	1,600
Total fixed operating expenses	$3,400	$3,400	$ 6,800
Total operating expenses	$6,610	$6,738	$13,348

The question tells us that sales commissions are paid 50% in the month incurred and 50% in the next month. Other expenses are paid in the month incurred. So we must calculate the sales commission payments for the current month and for the previous month each for October and November.

We can calculate commissions from the current month for October and November as:

$$\text{October} = \$3,210 \times 50\% = \$1,605$$

$$\text{November} = \$3,338 \times 50\% = \$1,669$$

So far, we have sales commissions from the current month and all other operating expenses, as follows:

MOVA COMPANY
Budgeted Cash Payments for Operating Expenses

	October	November	Total
Variable operating expenses:			
Sales commissions from current month	$1,605	$1,669	$3,274
Sales commission, from previous month		1,605	1,605
Total variable operating expenses	$3,210	$3,338	$4,879
Fixed operating expenses			
Rent expense (fixed amount)	$1,000	$1,000	$2,000
Insurance expense (fixed amount)	400	400	800
Depreciation expense (fixed amount)	1,200	1,200	2,400
Utility expense (fixed amount)	800	800	1,600
Total fixed operating expenses	$3,400	$3,400	$6,800
Total operating expenses	$6,610	$6,738	$13,348

The question tells us that actual sales for the month ending September 30 were $30,000 and that sales commissions amount to 10% of actual sales. So total sales commissions for September are $30,000 × 10% = $3,000.

Knowing this amount, we can compute the sales commission payments from the previous month for October as:

$$\text{October} = \$3,000 \times 50\%$$
$$= \$1,500$$

Our final statement would appear as follows:

MOVA COMPANY
Budgeted Cash Payments for Operating Expenses

	October	November	Total
Variable operating expenses:			
Sales commissions from current month	$1,605	$1,669	$3,274
Sales commission, 10% of sales		$1,605	$1,605
Total variable operating expenses	$3,210	$3,338	$4,879
Fixed operating expenses			
Rent expense (fixed amount)	$1,000	$1,000	$2,000
Insurance expense (fixed amount)	400	400	800
Depreciation expense (fixed amount)	1,200	1,200	2,400
Utility expense (fixed amount)	800	800	1,600
Total fixed operating expenses	$3,400	$3,400	$6,800
Total operating expenses	$6,610	$6,738	$13,348

Shown another way, we can also compute sales commission payments from the current and previous months using each month's actual sales:

Sales commission from current month =
    Current month sales × 10% sales commission × 50% payment this month
        October = $32,100 × 10% × 50%
            = $1,605
       November = $33,384 × 10% × 50%
            = $1,669
Sales commmission from previous month =
    Previous month sales × 10% sales commission × 50% payment this month
        October = $30,000 × 10% × 50%
            = $1,500
       November = $32,100 × 10% × 50%
            = $1,605

Rent, utilities, and insurance expense are fixed amounts from the operating expense budget.

Remember that depreciation expense is a noncash expense and therefore is not included in the cash budget.

d. Cash budget

Part 1	Part 2	Part 3	**Part 4**	Demo Doc Complete

2 Understand the components of the master budget

4 Prepare a financial budget

To prepare the cash budget, you start with the beginning cash balance and add the budgeted cash collections that you computed in part **a** of this demo doc. Cash payments for purchases and operating expenses are then subtracted to achieve the ending cash balance.

Beginning cash balance is from the ending cash balance of the previous month. September's ending balance as given in the question becomes October's beginning cash balance ($4,000).

Cash collections are from budgeted cash collections from customers. Adding the beginning cash balance to the collections gives you the available cash for the month:

MOVA COMPANY
Cash Budget

	October	November
Beginning cash balance	$ 4,000	
Cash collections	$30,780	$32,618
Cash available	34,780	
Cash payments		
Purchases of inventory		
Operating expenses		
Total cash payments		
Ending cash balance		

Cash payments for purchases of inventory are from the budgeted cash payments for purchases. Cash payments for operating expenses are from the budgeted cash payments from operating budget, giving us the total cash payments:

MOVA COMPANY
Cash Budget

	October	November
Beginning cash balance	$ 4,000	
Cash collections	30,780	32,618
Cash available	34,780	
Cash payments		
Purchases of inventory	11,000	20,003
Operating expenses	5,305	5,474
Total cash payments	16,305	25,477

Ending cash balance is equal to cash available less total cash payments. October's ending cash balance then becomes November's beginning cash balance, and the calculations continue in this manner until the budget is complete:

MOVA COMPANY
Cash Budget

	October	November
Beginning cash balance	$ 4,000	$18,475
Cash collections	30,780	32,618
Cash available	34,780	51,093
Cash payments		
Purchases of inventory	11,000	20,003
Operating expenses	5,305	5,474
Total cash payments	16,305	25,477
Ending cash balance	$18,475	$25,616

Part 1	Part 2	Part 3	Part 4	**Demo Doc Complete**

Quick Practice Questions

True/False

_____ 1. Many companies budget their cash flows monthly, weekly, or even on a daily basis.

_____ 2. The first budget that is prepared is the sales budget.

_____ 3. A company's plan for purchases of property, plant, equipment, and other long-term assets is part of the financial budget.

_____ 4. The cash budget is a projection of the cash inflows and cash outflows for a future period.

_____ 5. The cash budget is prepared before the budgeted balance sheet is prepared.

_____ 6. Sensitivity analysis is a what-if technique that asks what a result will be if a predicted amount is not achieved or if an underlying assumption changes.

_____ 7. Responsibility accounting is a system for evaluating the performance of each responsibility center and its manager.

_____ 8. The master budget is the set of budgeted financial statements and supporting schedules for one division of an organization.

_____ 9. Most companies consider company divisions as cost centers.

_____ 10. The research and development department would be considered a profit center.

Multiple Choice Questions

1. **Which of the following statements regarding the budgeting process is (are) true?**
   a. Managers prepare short-term and long-term budgets.
   b. The budget should be approved by the company's external auditors.
   c. The budget should be designed by top management and communicated to lower-level personnel.
   d. All the above statements are true regarding the budgeting process.

2. **Which of the following budgets is an operating budget?**
   a. Capital expenditures budget
   b. Budgeted balance sheet
   c. Budgeted income statement
   d. Cash budget

3. Which of the following alternatives reflects the proper order of preparing components of the master budget?

   1. Financial budget
   2. Operating budget
   3. Capital expenditures budget

   a. 2, 3, 1
   b. 1, 3, 2
   c. 1, 2, 3
   d. 3, 1, 2

4. Desired ending inventory is 80% of beginning inventory. If cost of goods sold is $300,000, purchases will always have what relationship with cost of goods sold?
   a. Be more than cost of goods sold
   b. Be 80% of cost of goods sold
   c. Equal cost of goods sold
   d. Be less than cost of goods sold

5. During April, Cherry Company had actual sales of $180,000 compared to budgeted sales of $195,000. Actual cost of goods sold was $135,000, compared to a budget of $136,500. Monthly operating expenses, budgeted at $28,000, totaled $25,000. Interest revenue of $2,500 was earned during April but had not been included in the budget. What is the net income variance on the performance report for April?
   a. $(8,000)
   b. $(13,000)
   c. $8,000
   d. $13,000

6. Heath Company has beginning inventory of 21,000 units and expected sales of 48,000 units. If the desired ending inventory is 15,500 units, how many units should be purchased?
   a. 27,000
   b. 42,500
   c. 45,000
   d. 53,500

7. York Enterprises recorded sales of $160,000 during March. Management expects sales to increase 5% in April, 3% in May, and 5% in June. Cost of goods sold is expected to be 70% of sales. What is the budgeted gross profit for June?
   a. $ 54,508
   b. $112,000
   c. $127,184
   d. $181,692

8. Which of the following is an example of a financial budget?
   a. Sales budget
   b. Budgeted balance sheet
   c. Budgeted income statement
   d. Operating expense budget

9. Jay Corporation desires a December 31 ending inventory of 1,500 units. Budgeted sales for December are 2,300 units. The November 30 inventory was 850 units. What are budgeted purchases?
a. 2,350
b. 2,950
c. 3,150
d. 3,800

10. Bolin's, an elite clothier, expects its November sales to be 30% higher than its October sales of $200,000. Purchases were $100,000 in October and are expected to be $150,000 in November. All sales are on credit and are collected as follows: 30% in the month of the sale and 70% in the following month. Purchases are paid 25% in the month of purchase and 75% in the following month. The beginning cash balance on November 1 is $9,000. What is the ending cash balance on November 30?
a. $ 87,000
b. $114,500
c. $140,000
d. $149,000

Quick Exercises

22-1. Solve for the following independent situations:

a. An appliance store has budgeted cost of goods sold for February of $30,200 for its microwave ovens. Management also wants to have $18,000 of microwave ovens in inventory at the end of the month to prepare for the next month. Beginning inventory in February was $16,000. What dollar amount of microwave ovens should be purchased to meet these objectives?

b. An electronics product retailer store budgeted May purchases of high definition televisions at $84,000. The store had televisions costing $13,000 on hand at the beginning of May, and to cover part of anticipated June sales, it expects to have $48,000 of televisions on hand at the end of May. What was the budgeted cost of goods sold for May?

22-2. Rawlins Company prepared the following forecasts of monthly sales:

	September	October	November	December
Sales (in units)	4,500	5,200	4,700	2,800

Rawlins decided that the number of units in its inventory at the end of each month should equal 60% of next month's sales. The budgeted cost per unit is $25.

a. How many units should be in September's beginning inventory?

b. What amount should be budgeted for the cost of merchandise purchases in September?

c. How many units should be purchased in September and October?

22-3. The sales budget of Cider Company for the second quarter of 2013 is as follows:

	April	May	June
Sales	$91,000	$76,000	$108,000

Sales are 35% cash, 65% credit.

April purchases were $61,000 and May purchases were $58,000.

Collections on credit sales are as follows:

50% in the month of sale
30% in the month following sale
15% in the second month following sale
 5% uncollectible

Payments for inventory are 70% in the month following purchase and 30% two months following purchase.

a. Compute the cash collections for June.

b. Compute the cash disbursements for purchases during June.

22-4. Shanti Inc. gathered the following information as of August 31, 2013:

August 31 inventory balance	$22,100
August payments for inventory	16,300
August payments of accounts payable and accrued liabilities	18,800
August 31 accounts payable balance	10,400
July 31 equipment balance	74,500
July 31 accumulated depreciation–equipment balance	40,900
Cash purchase of equipment in August	4,700
August operating expenses, excluding depreciation (75% paid in August, 25% accrued on August 31)	8,200
August depreciation expense	1,600
July 31 stockholders' equity	88,580
July 31 cash balance	54,040
August budgeted sales	50,300
August cash receipts from sales on account	24,110

Cost of goods sold is 80% of sales.

August 31 accounts receivable balance is 30% of August sales.

Prepare the budgeted balance sheet on August 31, 2013.

22-5. **Answer the following completely.**

a. Define the term *budget.* _____

_____

_____

b. Identify four benefits of budgeting. _____

_____

_____

c. Should employees participate in the budgeting process or should management prepare the budgets alone? Explain. _____

_____

_____

Do It Yourself! Question 1

Suzie's Stencils sells a variety of stencils for multiple purposes. Actual sales for the month ended June 30 was $90,000. Suzie believes that sales will increase 2% in July and an additional 3% in August. Cash sales are expected to be 10% of sales and credit sales are 90% of sales.

Cost of goods sold is expected to be 75% of total sales. Suzie does not want inventory to fall below $10,000 plus 5% of cost of goods sold for the next month. Sales of $95,000 are expected for September. Inventory on June 30 is $13,000.

Operating expenses include sales commission, 5% of sales; rent expense of $6,000; depreciation expense of $4,000; utility expense of $1,500; and insurance expense of $1,400.

Round all figures to the nearest dollar.

Requirement 1

Prepare the following budgets for July and August:

2 Understand the components of the master budget

3 Prepare an operating budget

a. Sales budget

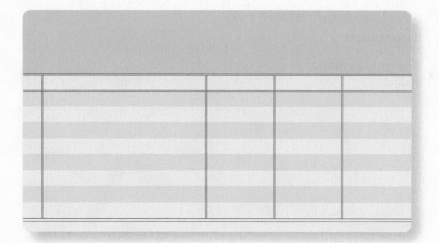

2 Understand the components of the master budget

3 Prepare an operating budget

b. Inventory, purchases, and cost of goods budget

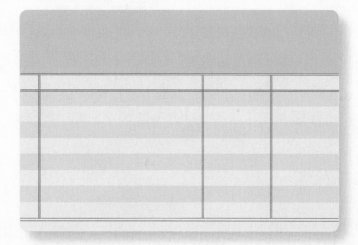

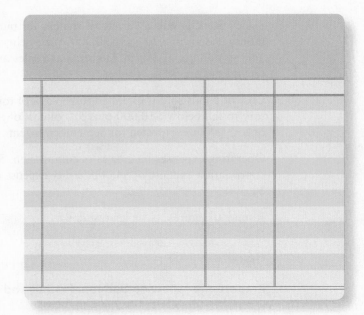

2 Understand the components of the master budget

3 Prepare an operating budget

c. Operating expense budget

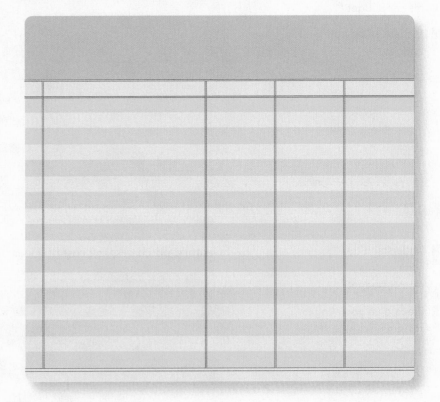

2 Understand the components of the master budget

3 Prepare an operating budget

d. Budgeted income statement

Do It Yourself! Question 2

Suzie's Stencils prepared its sales budget; inventory, purchases, and cost of goods budget; operating expense budget; and budgeted income statement for July and August. Suzie would now like to prepare the cash budget for the months of July and August.

Actual sales for the month ended June 30 were $90,000. Actual sales for the month ended May 30 were $75,000. Suzie believes that sales will increase 2% in July and increase another 3% over July sales in August. Cash sales are expected to be 10% of sales and credit sales are 90% of sales.

Cost of goods sold is expected to be 75% of total sales. Suzie doesn't want inventory to fall below $12,000 plus 5% of cost of goods sold for the next month. Sales of $85,000 are expected for September. Suzie purchased $56,000 of inventory during June and ended the month with $13,000 in ending inventory.

Operating expenses include sales commission, 5% of sales: rent expense of $6,000; depreciation expense of $4,000; utility expense of $1,500; and insurance expense of $1,400.

The June 30 cash balance is $14,000.

Of the credit sales, Suzie expects to collect 20% in the month of the sale, 50% in the month following the sale and the remaining 30% in the next month. Purchases are paid for in the month after the purchase. Sales commissions are paid 50% in the month incurred and 50% in the next month. Rent, utility and insurance are paid in the month incurred.

Requirement 1

For the months of July and August, prepare the following:

2 Understand the components of the master budget

4 Prepare a financial budget

a. Budgeted cash collections from customers

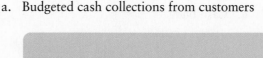

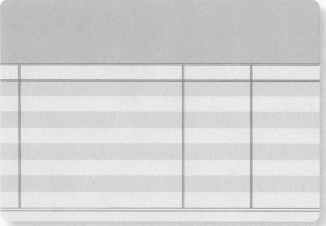

2 Understand the
components of the
master budget

4 Prepare a financial
budget

b. Budgeted cash payments for purchases

2 Understand the
components of the
master budget

4 Prepare a financial
budget

c. Budgeted cash payments for operating expenses

2 Understand the
components of the
master budget

4 Prepare a financial
budget

d. Cash budget

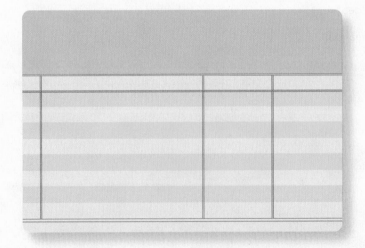

Quick Practice Solutions

True/False

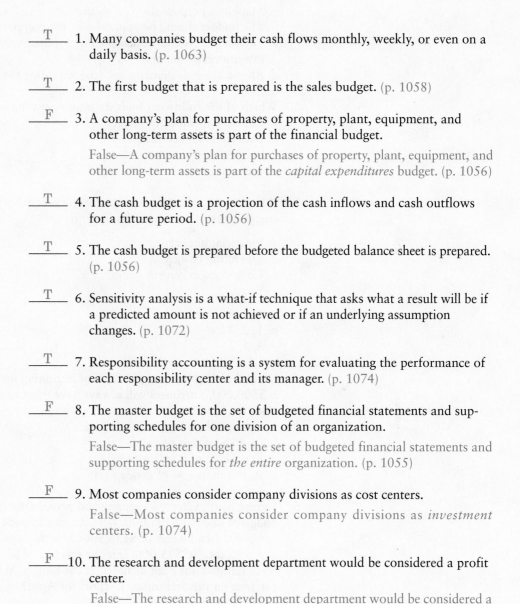

_____T_____ 1. Many companies budget their cash flows monthly, weekly, or even on a daily basis. (p. 1063)

_____T_____ 2. The first budget that is prepared is the sales budget. (p. 1058)

_____F_____ 3. A company's plan for purchases of property, plant, equipment, and other long-term assets is part of the financial budget.

False—A company's plan for purchases of property, plant, equipment, and other long-term assets is part of the _capital expenditures_ budget. (p. 1056)

_____T_____ 4. The cash budget is a projection of the cash inflows and cash outflows for a future period. (p. 1056)

_____T_____ 5. The cash budget is prepared before the budgeted balance sheet is prepared. (p. 1056)

_____T_____ 6. Sensitivity analysis is a what-if technique that asks what a result will be if a predicted amount is not achieved or if an underlying assumption changes. (p. 1072)

_____T_____ 7. Responsibility accounting is a system for evaluating the performance of each responsibility center and its manager. (p. 1074)

_____F_____ 8. The master budget is the set of budgeted financial statements and supporting schedules for one division of an organization.

False—The master budget is the set of budgeted financial statements and supporting schedules for _the entire_ organization. (p. 1055)

_____F_____ 9. Most companies consider company divisions as cost centers.

False—Most companies consider company divisions as _investment_ centers. (p. 1074)

_____F_____ 10. The research and development department would be considered a profit center.

False—The research and development department would be considered a _cost_ center because the managers only control costs. (p. 1075)

Multiple Choice

1. Which of the following statements regarding the budgeting process is (are) true? (p. 1052)
   a. Managers prepare short-term and long-term budgets.
   b. The budget should be approved by the company's external auditors.
   c. The budget should be designed by top management and communicated to lower-level personnel.
   d. All the above statements are true regarding the budgeting process.

2. Which of the following budgets is an operating budget? (p. 1060)
   a. Capital expenditures budget
   b. Budgeted balance sheet
   c. Budgeted income statement
   d. Cash budget

3. Which of the following alternatives reflects the proper order of preparing components of the master budget? (p. 1058)

   1. Financial budget
   2. Operating budget
   3. Capital expenditures budget

   a. 2, 3, 1
   b. 1, 3, 2
   c. 1, 2, 3
   d. 3, 1, 2

4. Desired ending inventory is 80% of beginning inventory. If cost of goods sold is $300,000, purchases will always have what relationship with cost of goods sold? (p. 1059)
   a. Be more than cost of goods sold
   b. Be 80% of cost of goods sold
   c. Equal cost of goods sold
   d. Be less than cost of goods sold

5. During April, Cherry Company had actual sales of $180,000 compared to budgeted sales of $195,000. Actual cost of goods sold was $135,000, compared to a budget of $136,500. Monthly operating expenses, budgeted at $28,000, totaled $25,000. Interest revenue of $2,500 was earned during April but had not been included in the budget. What is the net income variance on the performance report for April? (p. 1064)
   a. $(8,000)
   b. $(13,000)
   c. $8,000
   d. $13,000

6. Heath Company has beginning inventory of 21,000 units and expected sales of 48,000 units. If the desired ending inventory is 15,500 units, how many units should be purchased? (p. 1059)
   a. 27,000
   b. 42,500
   c. 45,000
   d. 53,500

7. York Enterprises recorded sales of $160,000 during March. Management expects sales to increase 5% in April, 3% in May, and 5% in June. Cost of goods sold is expected to be 70% of sales. What is the budgeted gross profit for June? (p. 1060)
   a. $54,508
   b. $112,000
   c. $127,184
   d. $181,692

8. Which of the following is an example of a financial budget? (p. 1056)
   a. Sales budget
   b. Budgeted balance sheet
   c. Budgeted income statement
   d. Operating expense budget

9. Jay Corporation desires a December 31 ending inventory of 1,500 units. Budgeted sales for December are 2,300 units. The November 30 inventory was 850 units. What are budgeted purchases? (p. 1059)
   a. 2,350
   b. 2,950
   c. 3,150
   d. 3,800

10. Bolin's, an elite clothier, expects its November sales to be 30% higher than its October sales of $200,000. Purchases were $100,000 in October and are expected to be $150,000 in November. All sales are on credit and are collected as follows: 30% in the month of the sale and 70% in the following month. Purchases are paid 25% in the month of purchase and 75% in the following month. The beginning cash balance on November 1 is $9,000. What is the ending cash balance on November 30? (p. 1066)
    a. $ 87,000
    b. $114,500
    c. $140,000
    d. $149,000

Quick Exercises

22-1. Solve for the following independent situations: (p. 1059)

a. An appliance store has budgeted cost of goods sold for February of $30,200 for its microwave ovens. Management also wants to have $18,000 of microwave ovens in inventory at the end of the month to prepare for the next month. Beginning inventory in February was $16,000. What dollar amount of microwave ovens should be purchased to meet the above objectives?

$$\text{Let } x = \text{Purchases}$$
$$\$16,000 + x - \$30,200 = \$18,000$$
$$x - \$14,200 = \$18,000$$
$$x = \$32,200$$

b. An electronic products retailer store budgeted May purchases of high definition televisions at $84,000. The store had televisions costing $13,000 on hand at the beginning of May, and to cover part of anticipated June sales they expect to have $48,000 of televisions on hand at the end of May. What was the budgeted cost of goods sold for May?

$$\text{Let } x = \text{Cost of goods sold}$$
$$\$13,000 + \$84,000 - x = \$48,000$$
$$\$97,000 - x = \$48,000$$
$$x = \$46,000$$

22-2. Rawlins Company prepared the following forecasts of monthly sales:

	September	October	November	December
Sales (in units)	4,500	5,200	4,700	2,800

Rawlins decided that the number of units in its inventory at the end of each month should equal 60% of next month's sales. The budgeted cost per unit is $25. (p. 1059)

a. How many units should be in September's beginning inventory?

$$60\% \times 4,500 \text{ units} = 2,700 \text{ units}$$

b. What amount should be budgeted for the cost of merchandise purchases in September?

$$5,025 \text{ units} \times \$25 = \$25,625$$

c. How many units should be purchased in September and October?

	September	October
Next month's budgeted sales (units)	5,200	4,700
Ratio of inventory to future sales	× 60%	× 60%
Desired ending inventory	3,120	2,820
Budgeted sales for the month (units)	4,500	5,200
Required units of available merchandise	7,620	8,020
Deduct beginning inventory	3,375	3,900
Number of units to be purchased	4,245	4,120

22-3. The sales budget of Cider Company for the second quarter of 2013 is as follows:

	April	May	June
Sales	$91,000	$76,000	$108,000
Purchases	61,000	58,800	65,000

Sales are 35% cash, 65% credit.

April purchases were $61,000 and May purchases were $58,000.

Collections on credit sales are as follows:

50% in the month of sale
30% in the month following sale
15% in the second month following sale
 5% uncollectible

Payments for inventory are 70% in the month following purchase and 30% two months following purchase.

a. Compute the cash collections for June. (p. 1063)

April credit sales	= $ 8,874 ($91,000 × 0.65 × 0.15)
May credit sales	= 14,820 ($76,000 × 0.65 × 0.30)
June cash sales	= 37,800 ($108,000 × 0.35)
June credit sales	= 35,100 ($108,000 × 0.65 × 0.50)
June cash collections = $96,594	

b. Compute the cash disbursements for purchases during June. (p. 1064)

April purchases ($61,000 × 0.30)	$18,300
May purchases ($58,000 × 0.70)	40,600
June cash disbursements for purchases = $58,900	

22-4. Shanti Inc. gathered the following information as of August 31, 2013:

August 31 inventory balance	$22,100
August payments for inventory	16,300
August payments of accounts payable and accrued liabilities	18,800
August 31 accounts payable balance	10,400
July 31 equipment balance	74,500
July 31 accumulated depreciation–equipment balance	40,900
Cash purchase of equipment in August	4,700
August operating expenses, excluding depreciation (75% paid in August, 25% accrued on August 31)	8,200
August depreciation expense	1,600
July 31 stockholders' equity	88,580
July 31 cash balance	54,040
August budgeted sales	50,300
August cash receipts from sales on account	24,110

Cost of goods sold is 80% of sales.

August 31 Accounts receivable balance is 30% of August sales.

Prepare the budgeted balance sheet on August 31, 2013. (p. 1067)

SHANTI INC. Budgeted Balance Sheet August 31, 2013		
Assets		
Current assets:		
Cash	$32,200*	
Accounts receivable ($34,300 × 0.30)	10,290	
Inventory	22,100	
Total current assets		64,590
Plant assets:		
Equipment	79,200**	
Less: accumulated depreciation	(42,500)**	36,700
Total assets		$101,290
Liabilities		
Current liabilities:		
Accounts payable	$10,400	
Accrued liabilities ($8,200 × 0.25)	2,050	
Total current liabilities		$ 12,450
Stockholders' equity		88,840***
Total liabilities and stockholders' equity		$101,290

*[$54,040 − $16,300 − $18,800 − $4,700 − (0.75 × $8,200) + $24,110] = $32,200
**74,500 + 4,700 = 79,200; 40,900 + 1,600 = 42,500
***Net income for August = $50,300 − (0.80 × $50,300) − $8,200 − $1,600 = $260
    $88,580 + $260 = $88,840

22-5. **Answer the following completely.** (pp. 1051–1053)

   a. Define the term *budget*.

      A budget is a quantitative expression of a plan of action that helps managers coordinate and implement the plan.

   b. Identify four benefits of budgeting.

      The four benefits of budgeting include:

      1. Budgeting compels planning. Budgeting helps managers set realistic goals by requiring them to plan specific actions to meet their goals. Budgeting also helps managers prepare for a range of conditions and plan for contingencies.

      2. Budgeting promotes coordination and communication. The master budget coordinates the activities of the organization. It forces managers to consider relationships among operations across the entire value chain.

      3. Budgeting aids performance evaluation. To evaluate a department or activity, its actual results may be compared either to its budget or its past performance. In general, the budget is a better benchmark because it considers current changes stemming from past conditions.

      4. Budgeting can affect behavior and motivate employees. The budgeting process prompts managers to look further into the future than they would look otherwise. This process helps them to foresee and avoid problems.

   c. Should employees participate in the budgeting process or should management prepare the budgets alone? Explain.

      Employees should participate in the budgeting process so that they can bear ownership of the plan. If employees are excluded from this process and unrealistic goals are set, employee morale can be deflated, especially if the employees' performance is judged against these unfair standards. If employees help to create the budget, it can be a motivating factor to achieve the desired outcome.

Do It Yourself! Question 1 Solutions

Requirement 1

Prepare the following budgets for July and August:

a. Sales budget

SUZIE'S STENCILS Sales Budget For the Two Months Ending August 31			
	July	August	Total
Cash sales, 10%	$ 9,180	$ 9,455	$ 18,635
Credit sales, 90%	82,620	85,099	167,719
Total	$91,800	$94,554	$186,354

b. Inventory, purchases, and cost of goods sold budget

SUZIE'S STENCILS Inventory, Purchases, and Cost of Goods Sold Budget For the Two Months Ending August 31		
	July	August
Cost of goods sold	$68,850	$70,916
+ Desired ending inventory	13,546	13,563
= Total inventory required	82,396	84,479
− Beginning inventory	13,000	13,546
= Purchases	$69,396	$70,933

c. Operating expense budget

SUZIE'S STENCILS Operating Expense Budget For the Two Months Ending August 31			
	July	August	Total
Variable operating expenses:			
Sales commission	$ 4,590	$ 4,728	$ 9,318
Total variable operating expenses	$ 4,590	$ 4,728	$ 9,318
Fixed operating expenses			
Rent expense (amount)	$ 6,000	$ 6,000	$12,000
Depreciation expense (amount)	4,000	4,000	8,000
Utility expense (amount)	1,500	1,500	3,000
Insurance expense (amount)	1,400	1,400	2,800
Total fixed operating expenses	$12,900	$12,900	$25,800
Total operating expenses	$17,490	$17,628	$35,118

d. Budgeted income statement

SUZIE'S STENCILS
Budgeted Income Statement
For the Two Months Ending August 31

	July	August	Total
Sales revenue	$91,800	$94,554	$186,354
Cost of goods sold	68,850	70,916	139,766
Gross profit	22,950	23,638	46,588
Variable operating expenses:			
Sales commission	$ 4,590	$ 4,728	$ 9,318
Total variable operating expenses	$ 4,590	$ 4,728	$ 9,318
Contribution margin	$18,360	$18,910	$37,270
Fixed operating expenses:			
Rent expense (fixed amount)	$ 6,000	$ 6,000	$12,000
Depreciation expense	4,000	4,000	8,000
Utility expense	1,500	1,500	3,000
Insurance expense	1,400	1,400	2,800
Total fixed operating expenses	$ 3,400	$ 3,400	$25,800
Operating income	$ 5,460	$ 6,010	$ 11,470

Do It Yourself! Question 2 Solutions

Requirement 1

For the months of July and August, prepare the following:

a. Budgeted cash collections from customers

SUZIE'S STENCILS
Budgeted Cash Collections from Customers
For the Two Months Ending August 31

	July	August
Cash sales	$ 9,180	$ 9,455
Collections from current month credit sales	16,524	17,020
Collections from previous month credit sales	40,500	41,310
Collections from 2nd previous month credit sales	20,250	24,300
Total collections	$86,454	$92,085

b. Budgeted cash payments for purchases

SUZIE'S STENCILS
Budgeted Cash Payments for Purchases
For the Two Months Ending August 31

	July	August	Total
Payment of last month's purchases	$56,000	$69,396	$125,396

c. Budgeted cash payments for operating expenses

SUZIE'S STENCILS
Budgeted Cash Payments for Operating Expenses

	July	August	Total
Variable operating expenses:			
Sales commission from this month	$ 2,295	$ 2,364	$ 4,659
Sales commission from last month	$ 2,250	$ 2,285	$ 4,535
Total variable operating expenses	$ 4,545	$ 4,649	$ 9,194
Fixed operating expenses			
Rent expense (fixed amount)	$ 6,000	$ 6,000	$12,000
Utility expense (fixed amount)	1,500	1,500	3,000
Insurance expense (fixed amount)	1,400	1,400	2,800
Total fixed operating expenses	$ 8,900	$ 8,900	$17,800
Total operating expenses	$13,445	$13,559	$27,004

d. Cash budget

SUZIE'S STENCILS
Cash Budget

	July	August
Beginning cash balance	$ 14,000	$ 31,009
Cash collections	86,454	92,085
Cash available	100,454	123,094
Cash payments		
Purchase of inventory	56,000	69,396
Operating expenses	13,445	13,559
Total cash payments	69,445	82,955
Ending cash balance	$ 31,009	$ 41,139

The Power of Practice

For more practice using the skills learned in this chapter, visit MyAccountingLab. There you will find algorithmically generated questions that are based on these demo docs and your main textbook's Review and Assess Your Progress sections.

To go to MyAccountingLab, follow these steps:

1. Direct your URL to www.myaccountinglab.com.
2. Log in using your name and password.
3. Click the MyAccountingLab link.
4. Click Study Plan in the left navigation bar.
5. From the table of contents, select Chapter 22, The Master Budget and Responsibility Accounting.
6. Click a link to work tutorial exercises.

23 Flexible Budgets and Standard Costs

WHAT YOU PROBABLY ALREADY KNOW

You should already be familiar with various budgets including cash budgets. Assume you had budgeted $500 as your monthly automobile expenditures and found that you actually spent $545. At first glance, it appears that there is an unfavorable difference. The budget of $500 was created assuming that your travel would be 1,000 miles and your costs consist of auto insurance of $100, gasoline $225 (1,000 miles / 20 miles per gallon × $4.50 per gallon), and $175 repayment of the car loan. If you find that you used the car 1,200 miles this month, you probably already know that you should not be held to the original, static budget. The budget should be "flexible" to allow for differences in the level of activity that impacts costs. The flexible budget for 1,200 miles should be $545 [($100 + $175) + 1,200 miles / 20 miles per gallon × $4.50 per gallon]. When the actual results are compared to the flexible budget, it appears that there is no variance. In this chapter, we will study the creation and evaluation of flexible budgets.

Learning Objectives/Success Keys

1 Prepare a flexible budget for the income statement.

Flexible budgets are budgets that summarize cost and revenue information for several different volume levels within a relevant range. To prepare a flexible budget, the variable cost per unit and total fixed costs must be determined. You will prepare a flexible budget in Demo Doc 1. *Review the flexible budget in Exhibit 23-2 (p. 1107).*

2 Prepare an income statement performance report.

The income statement performance report shows the difference between the actual results and expected results. The difference between the actual results at actual volume and the budgeted results at expected sales volume is the static budget variance. A component of the variance may be due to the actual sales volume differing from the budgeted sales volume; this is called the **sales volume variance**. The other component of the variance may be due to the actual amounts at actual volume differing from the budgeted amounts at actual volume; this is called the **flexible budget variance**. The **static budget variance** is the total of the sales volume variance and the flexible budget variance. *Review Exhibit 23-3 (p. 1108) for an illustration of the relationship between the static budget variance, the flexible budget variance, and the sales volume variance. Review the income statement performance report in Exhibit 23-4 (p. 1109).*

3 Identify the benefits of standard costs and learn how to set standards.

Many companies use standard costing because it helps them better plan and control levels of performance and provide a goal for employees to work toward. In addition, record-keeping costs are reduced because it's easier to value all inventory at standard and it provides cost information that helps to determine the sales prices. *See Exhibit 23-5 (p. 1113) for standard setting issues relating to standard costing.*

4 Compute standard cost variances for direct materials and direct labor.

The actual production costs are compared to the standard costs periodically. There may be a variance due to the price or the quantity used. A **price variance** measures the difference between the actual price and the standard price multiplied by the actual quantity.

A quantity or efficiency variance measures how well the business uses its materials or human resources. The quantity variance measures the difference in the actual and standard quantities multiplied by the standard price per unit. *Review Exhibit 23-6 (p. 1116) for an illustration of the relationship between the variances and Exhibit 23-7 (p. 1116) for a computation of price and quantity variances.*

5 Analyze manufacturing overhead in a standard cost system.

The total manufacturing overhead variance is the difference between the actual overhead incurred and the standard overhead. The standard overhead amount is the product of the standard overhead rate and the standard allocation base at the actual volume. Recall that the standard overhead rate is computed before the period begins as

$$\text{Standard overhead rate} = \frac{\text{Expected manufacturing overhead costs}}{\text{Expected quantity of allocation base}}$$

The total overhead variance can be separated between the overhead flexible budget variance and the production volume variance. The **overhead flexible budget variance** shows how well management has controlled overhead costs. It is computed in exactly the same way as the flexible budget variances for direct materials and direct labor. The overhead flexible budget variance can be measured as the difference between the actual overhead cost and the flexible budget overhead for the actual number of outputs. The production volume variance arises when actual production differs from expected production. It is the difference between the flexible budget for the actual outputs and the standard overhead allocated to actual production. *Review Exhibit 23-8 (p. 1118) to see the total overhead, overhead flexible budget, and production volume variances and the surrounding text for the calculations of the standard prices.*

6 Record transactions at standard cost and prepare a standard cost income statement.

The standard cost system requires that the cost of inventory be recorded at the standard amount. This procedure permits variances to be recorded as soon as possible. If the variance is unfavorable, actual costs exceed the standard costs. The unfavorable variance is recorded as a debit to the Variance account and is treated as an expense on the income statement. If the variance is favorable, actual costs are less than the standard costs. The favorable variance is recorded as a credit to the Variance account and is treated as a contra-expense on the income statement. The recorded variances are shown on the standard cost income statement as an adjustment to the cost of goods sold. *Review the "Standard Cost Accounting System section in the main text for sample journal entries and Exhibit 22-13 (p. 1127) for the flow of costs in a standard costing system. Review Exhibit 23-14 (p. 1128) for a sample standard cost income statement.*

Demo Doc 1

Flexible Budgets and Income Statement Performance Report _____

Learning Objectives 1, 2

Management at Virus Detection Sensors predicted 2013 sales of 5,400 sensors at a price of $1,000 per sensor. Actual sales for the year were 5,200 sensors at $1,050 per sensor. Following is a breakdown of their costs for 2013:

Units Sold	Budgeted 5,400	Actual 52,00
Variable costs	$ 620	$ 630
Fixed costs	$2,100,000	$2,050,000

Requirements

1. Why would Virus Detection prepare a flexible budget? Using Virus Detection's estimated budget values for costs and sales price, develop flexible budgets for 5,200; 5,400; 5,600; and 6,000 sensors. Would Virus Detection Sensors' managers use this flexible budget for planning or controlling? What specific insights can Virus Detection Sensors' managers gain from this flexible budget?

2. Using the format shown in Exhibit 23-4 (p. 1109) of the textbook, prepare Virus Detection's income statement performance report for 2013.

3. What was the effect on Virus Detection's operating income of selling 200 units less than the static budget level of sales?

Demo Doc 1 Solutions

Requirement 1

1 Prepare a flexible budget for the income statement

Why would Virus Detection prepare a flexible budget? Using their estimated budget values for costs and sales price, develop flexible budgets for 5,200; 5,400; 5,600; and 6,000 sensors. Would Virus Detection Sensors' managers use this flexible budget for planning or controlling? What specific insights can Virus Detection Sensors' managers gain from this flexible budget?

Part 1	Part 2	Part 3	Demo Doc Complete

It is difficult for management to analyze results when the actual volume differs from the static budget. Therefore, companies will produce flexible budgets, which are budgets that summarize cost and revenue information for several different volume levels within a relevant range. Virus Detection would prepare a flexible budget if they weren't sure about their projected sales volume of 5,400 sensors. Virus Detection's flexible budget would show how its revenues and expenses should vary at different volume levels.

Depending upon the volume within the relevant range, a budget can be determined for each amount of activity using the following formula:

Flexible budget total cost = (Number of output units × Variable cost per output unit) + Total fixed cost

For Virus Detection Sensors, the following would be its flexible budget for 5,200; 5,400; 5,600; and 6,000 sensors:

VIRUS DETECTION SENSORS
Flexible Budget
Year Ended December 31, 2013

	Flexible Budget per Output Unit	Output Units (sensors)			
		5,200	5,400	5,600	6,000
Sales revenue	$1,000	$5,200,000	$5,400,000	$5,600,000	$6,000,000
Variable expenses	620	3,224,000	3,348,000	3,472,000	3,720,000
Fixed expenses		2,100,000	2,100,000	2,100,000	2,100,000
Total expenses		5,324,000	5,448,000	5,572,000	5,820,000
Operating income (loss)		$ (124,000)	$ (48,000)	$ 28,000	$ 180,000

Notice how the total fixed expenses stay constant at $2,100,000 across all four scenarios, yet revenue and variable expenses change. Remember that variable expenses are constant *per unit*—they are called variable because total variable costs change with level of activity.

As you can see, with an output of 5,200 units, Virus Detection would generate 5,200 × $1,000 per unit = $5,200,000 in sales revenue. Meanwhile, its expenses would be 5,200 × $620 = $3,224,000 variable expenses, plus $2,100,000 fixed expenses = $5,324,000 in total expenses.

So with an output of 5,200 units, Virus Detection would incur a loss of $5,200,000 − $5,324,000 = $124,000.

Because the output levels in the flexible budget are estimated levels of sales, these flexible budgets are being developed *before* the period to help managers *plan*. In this case, the budgets indicate that there is a danger of Virus Detection Sensors operating at a loss for 2013 at sales levels below 5,600 units. Managers should devote considerable effort to ensure that Virus Detection Sensors sells more than 5,600 sensors, or find ways to either decrease the expenses associated with manufacturing each sensor or increase the sales price per unit.

Requirement 2

2 Prepare an income statement performance report

Using the format shown in Exhibit 23-4 (p. 1108) of the textbook, prepare Virus Detection's income statement performance report for 2013.

Part 1	**Part 2**	Part 3	Demo Doc Complete

Columns 1 and 5 of the income statement performance report represent Virus Detection's actual 2013 results and its expected (budgeted) results, respectively. These figures come directly from the comparison of actual results with a static budget statement for 5,400 units.

Actual results at actual prices are what actually happened. This column (1) represents Virus Detection's true income statement for 2013. This is calculated by multiplying actual quantity by actual price.

Static budget (column 5) represents Virus Detection's original budget with budgeted volume and costs. This budget uses output of 5,400 sensors, when in reality Virus Detection only had a volume of 5,200 sensors in 2013.

We can begin to build our performance report using the actual results and the static budget.

	1	2	3	4	5
VIRUS DETECTION SENSORS **Income Statement Performance Report** Year Ended December 31, 2013					
	Actual Results at Actual Prices	Flexible Budget Variance	Flexible Budget for Actual Number of Output Units	Sales Volume Variance	Static (Master) Budget
Output Units	5,200				5,400
Sales revenue	$5,460,000				$5,400,000
Variable costs	3,276,000				3,348,000
Fixed costs	2,050,000				2,100,000
Total costs	5,326,000				5,448,000
Operating income (loss)	$ 134,000				$ (48,000)

The next column that we can complete is the flexible budget for actual number of output units (column 3), which represents budgeted amounts based on what Virus Detection actually sold (the other two *variance* columns depend on the values calculated in this column). So for this column, we forget about the number of units that Virus Detection *expected* to sell in 2013, but we instead calculate what its operating income *would have been* had it sold the 5,200 sensors using its actual budget figures for revenues and expenses. This gives management the basis with which to compare the flexible budget variance with the sales volume variance.

Remember that a flexible budget based upon actual outputs provides the greatest ability to evaluate and control because you are comparing what you expected it to be against what it actually is.

From the question, we know that Virus Detection had budgeted to sell each sensor at $1,000. Regardless of how many sensors it *expected* to sell, if it had priced the 5,200 sensors it *did* sell at its original estimate of $1,000 per sensor, Virus Detection's sales revenue *would have been* 5,200 × $1,000 = **$5,200,000**. This is called the flexible budget for sales revenue based on actual units produced.

Virus Detection had budgeted its variable costs at $620 per sensor. If its budgeted variable costs had stayed at $620, then its **flexible budget for variable costs** would be 5,200 sensors × $620 = **$3,224,000**.

Similarly, had Virus Detection's budgeted fixed costs remained at $2,100,000, then its **flexible budget for total costs** would be $3,224,000 variable costs + $2,100,000 fixed costs = $5,324,000.

Given this data, then, Virus Detection's flexible budgeted operating income would be calculated as

$5,200,000 sales revenue − $5,324,000 total costs = $(124,000) operating loss

VIRUS DETECTION SENSORS
Income Statement Performance Report
Year Ended December 31, 2013

	1 Actual Results at Actual Prices	2 Flexible Budget Variance	3 Flexible Budget for Actual Number of Output Units	4 Sales Volume Variance	5 Static (Master) Budget
Output Units	5,200		5,200		5,400
Sales revenue	$5,460,000		$5,200,000		$5,400,000
Variable costs	3,276,000		3,224,000		3,348,000
Fixed costs	2,050,000		2,100,000		2,100,000
Total costs	5,326,000		5,324,000		5,448,000
Operating income (loss)	$ 134,000		$ (124,000)		$ (48,000)

So, how do we use this data? We use it to complete the two variance columns of the income statement performance report. The differences between columns 1 and 3 are presented in column 2, which shows us the flexible budget variance.

Flexible budget variance is the difference between the actual results (at actual prices) and the flexible budget (for actual number of output units). This variance represents more or less revenue earned than expected, and more or less expenses incurred than expected, for the actual level of output. For sales revenue, the variance is favorable if the actual is greater than the flexible budget. In this case, actual sales revenue of $5,460,000 exceeds the flexible budget of $5,200,000 by $260,000, so this is a favorable outcome.

For costs, the variance is unfavorable if the actual is greater than the flexible budget. In this case, actual total costs of $5,326,000 exceed the flexible budget of $5,324,000 by $2,000, which is unfavorable. However, total operating income demonstrates a favorable result of $258,000.

VIRUS DETECTION SENSORS
Income Statement Performance Report
Year Ended December 31, 2013

	1 Actual Results at Actual Prices	2 Flexible Budget Variance	3 Flexible Budget for Actual Number of Output Units	4 Sales Volume Variance	5 Static (Master) Budget
Output Units	5,200	0	5,200		5,400
Sales revenue	$5,460,000	$260,000 F	$5,200,000		$5,400,000
Variable costs	3,276,000	52,000 U	3,224,000		3,348,000
Fixed costs	2,050,000	50,000 F	2,100,000		2,100,000
Total costs	5,326,000	2,000 U	5,324,000		5,448,000
Operating income (loss)	$ 134,000	$258,000 F	$ (124,000)		$ (48,000)

So what does this mean? The flexible budget variance of $260,000 for sales revenue indicates that Virus Detection actually received $260,000 more for the 5,200 sensors than they would have had they sold the 5,200 units at their budgeted sales price of $1,000. On average, they received $50 more per sensor than they thought they would. At the same time, they spent $52,000 more in variable costs than they expected to, and while fixed costs were trimmed by $50,000, they still spent $2,000 more than they budgeted for on total costs. Even though the overall results are favorable, management will still want to know why costs exceeded expectations.

The last column to compute is the sales volume variance column (4). The differences between columns 3 and 5 are presented in column 4.

Sales volume variance is the difference between flexible budget (for actual number of output units) and the static budget. The only reason for this variance is because the number of units actually sold differs from the static budget, but knowing whether these variances are favorable or unfavorable gives managers insight into how sales and marketing are performing in relation to the overall report.

For sales revenue, this variance is favorable if the flexible budget is greater than the static budget. That is not the case with Virus Detection, however. The flexible budget sales revenue of $5,200,000 is lower than the budgeted sales of $5,400,000. This is because the sales force sold fewer units than expected.

For costs, this variance is favorable if the flexible budget is less than the static budget. In this case, the results are favorable, with the flexible budget showing $5,324,000 in total costs and the static budget showing $5,448,000, for a favorable variance of $124,000 in total costs. However, this variance results from the fact that the sales force sold fewer units than expected. In actuality, variable costs *increased* by $10 per unit over what Virus Detection had budgeted. This is favorable only because Virus Detection budgeted costs for more units than it actually made.

	VIRUS DETECTION SENSORS Income Statement Performance Report Year Ended December 31, 2013				
	1 Actual Results at Actual Prices	2 Flexible Budget Variance	3 Flexible Budget for Actual Number of Output Units	4 Sales Volume Variance	5 Static (Master) Budget
Output Units	5,200	0	5,200	200U	5,400
Sales revenue	$5,460,000	$260,000 F	$5,200,000	$200,000 U	$5,400,000
Variable costs	3,276,000	52,000 U	3,224,000	124,000 F	3,348,000
Fixed costs	2,050,000	50,000 F	2,100,000	0	2,100,000
Total costs	5,326,000	2,000 U	5,324,000	124,000 F	5,448,000
Operating income (loss)	$ 134,000	$258,000 F	$ (124,000)	$ 76,000 U	$ (48,000)

Requirement 3

2 Prepare an income statement performance report

What was the effect on Virus Detection's operating income of selling 200 units less than the static budget level of sales?

Part 1	Part 2	**Part 3**	Demo Doc Complete

Virus Detection's sales volume variance is $200,000 unfavorable. So, Virus selling 200 units less than budgeted reduced their sales volume by $200,000. Virus was able to more than overcome this reduction in sales volume by selling at a higher price than anticipated, as indicated by the favorable flexible budget sales revenue variance of $260,000 favorable. Had Virus Detection sold what it had budgeted for, it would have incurred a loss of $48,000. But, by increasing the sales price and reducing the fixed expense costs, even selling 200 fewer units, Virus incurred an operating income of $134,000 instead of incurring the loss.

Part 1	Part 2	Part 3	**Demo Doc Complete**

Demo Doc 2

Standard Costs

Learning Objectives 3–6

Bumpy Road Maps manufactures road maps. Bumpy uses a standard cost system to control manufacturing costs.

The following standard unit cost information is based on the static budget volume of 120,000 road maps per month:

Direct materials (40 sq. yards @ $0.015 per sq. yard)		$0.60
Direct labor (0.10 hours @ $12.00 per hour)		1.20
Manufacturing overhead:		
Variable (0.10 hours @ $3.00 per hour)	0.30	
Fixed (0.10 hours @ $8.00 per hour)	0.80	1.10
Total cost per map		$2.90

In this example, total budgeted fixed manufacturing overhead = $0.80 × 120,000 road maps = $96,000.

Actual cost and production volume information is as follows:

- Actual production was 118,000 maps.
- Actual direct materials usage was 41 square yards per map, at an actual cost of $0.016 per square yard.
- Actual direct labor usage was 11,600 hours at $12.10 per hour, a total cost of $140,360.
- Total actual overhead was $126,000.

Requirements

1. Bumpy has developed their standards. What are the five benefits of standard costing?

2. Compute the price and efficiency variances for direct materials and direct labor. Are these variances favorable or unfavorable? Why?

3. Journalize the usage of direct materials, including the related variance.

4. For manufacturing overhead, compute the total variance, the flexible variance, and the production volume variance. Are these variances favorable or unfavorable? Why?

Demo Doc 2 Solutions

Requirement 1

3 Identify the benefits of standard costs and learn how to set standards

Bumpy has developed their standards. What are the five benefits of standard costing?

| Part 1 | Part 2 | Part 3 | Part 4 | Part 5 | Part 6 | Part 7 | Demo Doc Complete |

A **standard cost** is a budget for a single unit. A standard is developed for the quantity and price of direct materials, direct labor, and manufacturing overhead.

Material price standards consider the cost of purchases plus freight in and receiving costs less discounts. Direct labor cost standards include the labor rates, payroll taxes, and fringe benefits. Overhead cost standards are developed by dividing estimated variable and fixed overhead costs by an appropriate allocation base. The quantity standards are usually developed using the input from knowledgeable employees taking into account an expected amount of spoilage, waste, and downtime.

Standards help managers in five areas:

1. Plan by providing unit amounts for budgeting

2. Control by setting target levels of performance

3. Motivate employees by serving as performance benchmarks

4. Set sales prices of products or services by providing unit costs

5. Simplify record keeping and reduce clerical costs

Requirement 2

4 Compute standard cost variances for direct materials and direct labor

Compute the price and efficiency variances for direct materials and direct labor. Are these variances favorable or unfavorable? Why?

| Part 1 | **Part 2** | Part 3 | Part 4 | Part 5 | Part 6 | Part 7 | Demo Doc Complete |

Direct Materials Price Variance

The actual quantity of direct materials used was the total number of maps produced (118,000) multiplied by the amount of direct materials used per map. Actual direct materials usage was 41 square yards per map, for an actual quantity of 4,838,000 square yards of materials.

To compute the variance, multiply the difference between the actual and standard costs per unit by the actual quantity. Bumpy estimated a cost of $0.015 per square yard, but the actual cost was $0.016 per square yard, for a difference of $0.001, which multiplied by 4,838,000 yields a variance of $4,838:

Direct materials price variance = (Actual price − Standard price) × Actual quantity of **material** for maps produced

= ($0.016 − $0.015) × (41 sq. yards usage per unit × 118,000 units)

= $0.001 × 4,838,000

= $4,828 U

This variance is unfavorable because the actual price is greater than the standard price.

Direct Materials Quantity Variance

This variance measures whether the quantity of materials actually used to produce the *actual* number of output units is within the *standard* allowed for that number of outputs. This is calculated by multiplying the difference between quantities of material (actual vs. standard) by the *standard* price per unit of material.

We know from computing the direct materials price variance that the actual quantity of direct materials used was 41 square yards per map × 118,000 maps = 4,838,000 square yards. From this, we subtract the standard quantity (40 square yards per map × 118,000 maps = 4,720,000 square yards) for a difference of 118,000 square yards.

We then multiply that difference in quantity by the standard price per unit. Remember, efficiency variance is measured against the standard (flexible budget, not actual costs), for a total variance of 118,000 × $0.015 = $1,770:

Direct materials quantity variance = (Actual quantity – Standard quantity) × Standard price

$$= [(41 \times 118{,}000) - (40 \times 118{,}000)] \times \$0.015$$
$$= (4{,}838{,}000 - 4{,}720{,}000) \times \$0.015$$
$$= 118{,}000 \times \$0.015$$
$$= \$1{,}770 \text{ U}$$

This variance is unfavorable because the actual material used per map, 41 square yards, was greater than the standard per map, 40 square yards.

Part 1	Part 2	**Part 3**	Part 4	Part 5	Part 6	Part 7	Demo Doc Complete

Direct Labor Rate Variance

This variance measures the difference between the actual price per unit (in this case, rate per hour for labor) and the standard price per unit, multiplied by the actual quantity of input (that is, hours worked).

In this case, Bumpy estimated a rate of $12.00 per hour for labor, and actual costs were $12.10, so the difference is $0.10 per hour, which multiplied by the actual hours of 11,600 yields a variance of $1,160:

Direct labor rate variance = (Actual rate – Standard rate) × Actual hours

$$= (\$12.10 - \$12.00) \times 11{,}600$$
$$= \$0.10 \times 11{,}600$$
$$= \$1{,}160 \text{ U}$$

This variance is unfavorable because the actual hourly rate for labor, $12.10, was greater than the standard rate for labor, $12.00.

Direct Labor Efficiency Variance

This variance measures the difference between the actual quantity of input (in this case, the number of hours Bumpy actually purchased) and the standard quantity of input, multiplied by the standard price per input unit (hourly cost of the labor).

In this case, we know that the actual number of hours purchased was 11,600. To compute standard hours, multiply the standard rate per map, 0.10, by the actual number of maps produced, 118,000 = 11,800. So the difference between actual and standard hours is 200, multiplied by the standard price per hour of $12.00 = $2,400:

$$
\begin{aligned}
\text{Direct labor efficiency variance} &= (\text{Actual hours} - \text{Standard hours}) \times \text{Standard price} \\
&= [11,600 - (0.10 \times 118,000)] \times \$12.00 \\
&= (11,600 - 11,800) \times \$12.00 \\
&= -200 \times \$12.00 \\
&= \$2,400 \text{ F}
\end{aligned}
$$

This variance is favorable because the number of actual hours used was less than standard hours.

Requirement 3

6 Record transactions at standard cost and prepare a standard cost income statement

Journalize the usage of direct materials, including the related variance.

Part 1	Part 2	Part 3	**Part 4**	Part 5	Part 6	Part 7	Demo Doc Complete

Usage of Direct Materials

Bumpy debits (increases) Work in Process Inventory for the standard price multiplied by the standard quantity of direct materials that should have been used for the actual output of 118,000 maps. This maintains inventory at standard cost. Materials Inventory is credited (decreased) for the actual quantity of materials put into production multiplied by the standard price:

Work in process inventory (118,000 × 40 × $0.015)		70,800	
???		1,770	
Materials inventory (118,000 × 41 × $0.015)			72,570

So where does the rest of the debit side of this entry come from?

We learned in requirement 2 that because Bumpy used more materials than the standard, its direct materials quantity variance was $1,770 unfavorable. This unfavorable variance increases the cost of production. Unfavorable variances will always be debited (increased).

Work in process inventory (118,000 × 40 × $0.015)		70,800	
Direct materials quantity variance (118,000 × $0.015)		1,770	
Materials inventory (118,000 × 41 × $0.015)			72,570

Requirement 4

Analyze manufacturing overhead in a standard cost system

For manufacturing overhead, compute the total variance, the flexible variance, and the production volume variance. Are these variances favorable or unfavorable? Why?

Part 1	Part 2	Part 3	Part 4	**Part 5**	Part 6	Part 7	Demo Doc Complete

Total Overhead Variance

Total overhead variance is the difference between actual overhead cost and standard overhead allocated to production.

The standard overhead allocated to production is the standard cost of the overhead per map times the number of maps actually produced. We know from the question that the standard overhead cost per map is $0.30 (variable cost) + $0.80 (fixed cost) = $1.10. So the standard overhead allocated to production = 118,000 × $1.10 = $129,800. Actual overhead cost as given in the question is $126,000, the difference being $3,800:

Total overhead variance = Actual overhead cost − Standard overhead allocated to production

= $126,000 − (118,000 × $1.10)

= $126,000 − $129,800

= $3,800 F

The variance is favorable because the actual overhead is less than the standard overhead. Overapplied overhead is favorable because enough cost was put into production.

Part 1	Part 2	Part 3	Part 4	Part 5	**Part 6**	Part 7	Demo Doc Complete

Overhead Flexible Budget Variance

The flexible budget variance is equal to the difference between the actual overhead cost and the flexible budget overhead for the actual number of maps produced.

To compute the flexible budget overhead variance, the fixed portion of the overhead must be separated from the variable part. The variable part of the overhead is flexible, therefore the variable cost of overhead per map ($0.30) is multiplied by the actual number of maps produced (118,000); the variable part of overhead is thus $35,400.

The fixed portion of the overhead is not flexible within the relevant range, so to compute the full fixed part of the overhead, the fixed cost of overhead per map ($0.80) must be multiplied by the static expected budget output of 120,000 maps. The fixed part of overhead is thus $96,000, the same as the original budgeted amount. Total flexible budget overhead is $35,400 + $96,000 = $131,400.

We know that the actual overhead cost was $126,000, the difference between actual and flexible thus being $5,400:

Overhead flexible budget variance = Actual overhead cost − Flexible budget overhead for the actual number of outputs

$$= \$126,000 - [(118,000 \times \$0.30) + (120,000 \times \$0.80)]$$
$$= \$126,000 - (\$35,400 + \$96,000)$$
$$= \$126,000 - \$131,400$$
$$= \$5,400 \text{ F}$$

The flexible budget variance is favorable because the actual overhead cost is less than the flexible budget.

Part 1	Part 2	Part 3	Part 4	Part 5	Part 6	**Part 7**	Demo Doc Complete

Production Volume Variance

The production volume variance arises when actual production differs from expected production. It is calculated as the difference between the flexible budget overhead for the actual number of outputs and the standard overhead allocated to actual production.

Standard overhead allocated to actual production is calculated by multiplying the number of maps actually produced, 118,000, by the standard overhead per unit, $1.10, which equals $129,800.

We know from calculating the overhead flexible budet variance that the flexible budget overhead for the

$$\text{Actual number of outputs} = [(118,000 \times \$0.30) + (120,000 \times \$0.80)]$$
$$= \$35,400 + \$96,000$$
$$= \$131,400$$

So the difference is calculated as $131,400 − $129,800 = $1,600:

Production volume variance = Flexible budget overhead for the actual number of outputs − Standard overhead allocated to actual production

$$= \$131,400 - (\$1.10 \times 118,000)$$
$$= \$131,400 - \$129,800$$
$$= \$1,600 \text{ U}$$

This variance accounts for Bumpy producing fewer maps, 118,000, than expected output, 120,000. Bumpy didn't use their production capacity as efficiently as possible. Whenever a business produces less than expected, the production volume variance will be unfavorable.

Part 1	Part 2	Part 3	Part 4	Part 5	Part 6	Part 7	**Demo Doc Complete**

Quick Practice Questions

True/False

_____ 1. Total variable costs change as production volume changes in a flexible budget.

_____ 2. At the end of the period, all variance accounts are closed to zero out their balances.

_____ 3. The sales volume variance arises because the number of units actually sold differs from the number of units expected to be sold according to the master budget.

_____ 4. A price variance is the difference between the actual unit price of an input and the standard unit price of the input, multiplied by the standard input quantity.

_____ 5. If the standard quantity allowed is less than the actual quantity used, the efficiency variance is favorable.

_____ 6. An efficiency variance is the difference between the actual quantity of input and the standard quantity of input, multiplied by the actual unit price of input.

_____ 7. Manufacturing overhead allocated to production equals the standard predetermined manufacturing overhead rate times the actual quantity of allocation base allowed for the standard number of outputs.

_____ 8. The overhead flexible budget variance is the difference between the actual overhead cost and the flexible budget overhead for budgeted production.

_____ 9. The production volume variance is favorable whenever actual output is less than expected output.

_____10. In standard costing, the journal entry to record the direct labor costs incurred includes a debit to Manufacturing wages for the actual hours worked at the standard price for direct labor.

Multiple Choice

1. **Which of the following is true for a static budget?**
   a. Adjusted for changes in the level of activity
   b. Prepared for only one level of activity
   c. A budget that stays the same from one period to the next
   d. Also known as a fixed budget

2. Sweet Baby Diaper Company sells disposable diapers for $0.20 each. Variable costs are $0.05 per diaper while fixed costs are $75,000 per month for volumes up to 850,000 diapers and $112,500 for volumes above 850,000 diapers. What is the monthly operating income for 800,000 diapers and 900,000 diapers of volume?
   a. $22,500 and $7,500, respectively
   b. $60,000 and $45,000, respectively
   c. $45,000 and $22,500, respectively
   d. $7,500 and $60,000, respectively

3. A graph of a flexible budget formula reflects fixed costs of $30,000 and total costs of $90,000 at a volume of 6,000 units. Assuming the relevant range is 1,000 to 12,000 units, what is the total cost of 10,000 units on the graph?
   a. $100,000
   b. $130,000
   c. $160,000
   d. $180,000

4. The sales volume variance is the difference between which amounts?
   a. Number of units actually sold and number of units expected to be sold according to the static budget
   b. Amounts in the flexible budget and the static budget
   c. Actual results and amounts in the flexible budget
   d. Actual sales volume and normal sales volume

5. The flexible budget variance is the difference between which amounts?
   a. Actual results and amounts in the static budget
   b. Amounts in the flexible budget and the actual results
   c. Amounts in the flexible budget and the static budget
   d. The budgeted amounts for each level of activity in the flexible budget

6. What does a flexible budget help to measure?
   a. The efficiency of operations at the actual activity levels
   b. The amount by which standard and expected prices differ
   c. Both a and b
   d. None of the above

7. Global Engineering's actual operating income for the current year is $50,000. The flexible budget operating income for actual volume achieved is $40,000, while the static budget operating income is $53,000. What is the sales volume variance for operating income?
   a. $10,000U
   b. $10,000F
   c. $13,000U
   d. $13,000F

8. Tiger's Golf Center reported actual operating income for the current year of $60,000. The flexible budget operating income for actual volume achieved is $55,000, while the static budget operating income is $58,000. What is the flexible budget variance for operating income?
   a. $2,000F
   b. $3,000U
   c. $5,000F
   d. $5,000U

9. What does a favorable direct materials efficiency variance indicate?
    a. Actual cost of direct materials was less than the standard cost of direct materials.
    b. Actual quantity of direct materials used was less than the standard quantity for actual output.
    c. Standard quantity of direct materials for actual output was less than the actual quantity of direct materials used.
    d. Actual quantity of direct materials used was greater than the standard quantity for budgeted output.

10. Western Outfitters Mountain Sports projected 2013 sales of 75,000 units at a unit sale price of $12.00. Actual 2013 sales were 72,000 units at $14.00 per unit. Actual variable costs, budgeted at $4.00 per unit, totaled $4.75 per unit. Budgeted fixed costs totaled $375,000, while actual fixed costs amounted to $400,000. What is the flexible budget variance for variable expenses?
    a. $12,000F
    b. $25,000F
    c. $54,000U
    d. $54,000F

Quick Exercises

23-1. Super Phone Manufacturing projected 2013 sales of 10,000 units at $15 per unit. Actual sales for the year were 12,000 units at $14 per unit. Actual variable expenses, budgeted at $6 per unit, amounted to $5 per unit. Actual fixed expenses, budgeted at $60,000, totaled $65,000.

Requirement

Prepare Super Phone's income statement performance report for 2013, including both flexible budget variances and sales volume variances.

SUPER PHONE MANUFACTURING Income Statement Performance Report Year Ended December 31, 2013					
	1 Actual Results at Actual Prices	2 Flexible Budget Variance	3 Flexible Budget for Actual Number of Output Units	4 Sales Volume Variance	5 Static (Master) Budget
Output Units					
Sales revenue					
Variable costs					
Fixed costs					
Total costs					
Operating income					

23-2. Sadie Company established a master budget volume of 20,000 units for February. Actual overhead costs incurred amounted to $18,000. Actual production for the month was 21,000 units. The standard variable overhead rate was $0.50 per direct labor hour. The standard fixed overhead rate was $0.25 per direct labor hour. One direct labor hour is the standard quantity per finished unit.

Requirements

1. Compute the total manufacturing overhead cost variance.

2. Compute the overhead flexible budget variance.

3. Compute the production volume variance.

23-3. Fantastic Tools Company recognizes variances from standards at the earliest opportunity, and the quantity of direct materials purchased is equal to the quantity used. The following information is available for the most recent month:

	Direct Materials	Direct Labor
Standard quantity/unit	6.00 lbs.	2.5 hrs.
Standard price/lb. or hr.	$8.10/lb.	$8.00/hr.
Actual quantity/unit	6.25 lbs.	2.8 hrs.
Actual price/lb. or hr.	$8.00/lb.	$7.50/hr.
Price variance	$625 F	$400 F
Efficiency variance	$2,025 U	$2,400 U
Static budget volume	900 units	
Actual volume	1,000 units	
Actual overhead	$11,000.00	
Standard variable overhead	$5/unit	
Standard fixed overhead	$5,400	
Overhead flexible budget variance	$900 U	
Production volume variance	$700 F	

Requirements

1. Journalize the purchase and usage of direct materials including the related variances.

Date	Accounts	Debit	Credit

Date	Accounts	Debit	Credit

2. Journalize the direct labor costs incurred and the application of direct labor, including the related variances.

Date	Accounts	Debit	Credit

Date	Accounts	Debit	Credit

3. Journalize the application of overhead costs including the recognition of the overhead variances.

Date	Accounts	Debit	Credit

Date	Accounts	Debit	Credit

23-4. Ringo Industries has the following information regarding direct materials:

Actual pounds purchased and used	58,000
Standard quantity	4 pounds per finished good
Actual production	15,000 finished goods
Direct materials efficiency variance	$10,500 F
Direct materials price variance	$29,000 U

Requirement

Compute Ringo's standard price per pound and actual price per pound.

23-5. Workshop, Inc., sells board games for $15, resulting in a contribution margin of $9 per game. Fixed costs are budgeted at $212,000 per quarter for volumes up to 30,000 games and $242,000 for volumes exceeding 30,000 games.

Requirement

Prepare the flexible budget for the next quarter for volume levels of 25,000; 30,000; and 40,000 games.

WORKSHOP, INC.
Flexible Budget
Year Ended December 31, 2013

	Flexible Budget per Output Unit	Output Units (games)		
		25,000	30,000	40,000
Sales revenue				
Variable expenses				
Fixed expenses				
Total expenses				
Operating income (loss)				

Do It Yourself! Question 1

Flexible Budgets and Income Statement Performance Report

Management at Fluffy Foam Beds predicted 2013 sales of 32,000 beds at a price of $180 per bed. Actual sales for the year were 34,200 beds at $185 per bed. Following is a breakdown of Fluffy's costs for 2013:

Units Sold	Budgeted 32,000	Actual 34,200
Variable costs	$ 70	$ 75
Fixed costs	$3,000,000	$3,100,000

Requirements

① Prepare a flexible budget for the income statement

1. Using Fluffy's estimated budget values for costs and sales price, develop flexible budgets for 32,000; 34,000; and 36,000 beds.

FLUFFY FOAM BEDS
Flexible Budget
Year Ended December 31, 2013

	Flexible Budget per Output Unit	Output Units (beds)		
		32,000	34,000	36,000
Sales revenue				
Variable expenses				
Fixed expenses				
Total expenses				
Operating income (loss)				

2 Prepare an income statement performance report

2. Prepare Fluffy's income statement performance report for 2013.

	1 Actual Results at Actual Prices	2 Flexible Budget Variance	3 Flexible Budget for Actual Number of Output Units	4 Sales Volume Variance	5 Static (Master) Budget
Output Units					
Sales revenue					
Variable costs					
Fixed costs					
Total costs					
Operating income					

FLUFFY FOAM BEDS
Income Statement Performance Report
Year Ended December 31, 2013

Do It Yourself! Question 2

Standard Costs

Circle CD manufactures CD cases. Circle uses a standard cost system to control manufacturing costs.

The following standard unit cost information is based on the static budget volume of 80,000 CD cases per month:

Direct materials (100 sq. ft. @ $0.25 sq. ft.)		$25.00
Direct labor (0.50 hours @ $18.00 per hour)		9.00
Manufacturing overhead:		
Variable (1 hour @ $2.00 per hour)	2.00	
Fixed (2 hours @ $5.00 per hour)	10.00	12.00
Total cost per CD case		$46.00

In this example, total budgeted fixed manufacturing overhead = $10 3 80,000 CD cases = $800,000.

Actual cost and production volume information follows:
- Actual production was 88,000 cases.
- Actual direct materials usage was 102 square feet per case, at an actual cost of $0.24 per square foot.
- Actual direct labor usage of 42,000 hours at $18.15, total cost of $762,300.
- Total actual overhead was $980,000.

Requirements

4 Compute standard cost variances for direct materials and direct labor

1. Compute the price and efficiency variances for direct materials and direct labor.

Direct Materials Price Variance

Direct Materials Efficiency Variance

Direct Labor Rate Variance

Direct Labor Efficiency Variance

5 Analyze manufacturing overhead in a standard cost system

2. For manufacturing overhead, compute the total variance, the flexible variance, and the production volume variance.

Total Overhead Variance

Overhead Flexible Budget Variance

Production Volume Variance

Quick Practice Solutions

True/False

<u>T</u> 1. Total variable costs change as production volume changes in a flexible budget. (p. 1109)

<u>T</u> 2. At the end of the period, all variance accounts are closed to zero out their balances. (p. 1127)

<u>T</u> 3. The sales volume variance arises because the number of units actually sold differs from the number of units expected to be sold according to the master budget. (p. 1108)

<u>F</u> 4. A price variance is the difference between the actual unit price of an input and the standard unit price of the input, multiplied by the standard input quantity.

False—A price variance is the difference between the actual unit price of an input and the standard unit price of the input, multiplied by the actual input quantity. (p. 1116)

<u>F</u> 5. If the standard quantity allowed is less than the actual quantity used, the efficiency variance is favorable.

False—If the standard quantity allowed is less than the actual quantity used, the efficiency variance is unfavorable. (p. 1116)

<u>F</u> 6. An efficiency variance is the difference between the actual quantity of input and the standard quantity of input, multiplied by the actual unit price of input.

False—An efficiency variance is the difference between the actual quantity of input and the standard quantity of input, multiplied by the standard unit price of input. (p. 1116)

<u>F</u> 7. Manufacturing overhead allocated to production equals the standard predetermined manufacturing overhead rate times the actual quantity of allocation base allowed for the standard number of outputs.

False—Manufacturing overhead allocated to production equals the standard predetermined manufacturing overhead rate times the standard quantity of allocation base allowed for the actual number of outputs. (p. 1121)

<u>F</u> 8. The overhead flexible budget variance is the difference between the actual overhead cost and the flexible budget overhead for budgeted production.

False—The overhead flexible budget variance is the difference between the actual overhead cost and the flexible budget overhead for the actual number of outputs. (p. 1116)

<u>F</u> 9. The production volume variance is favorable whenever actual output is less than expected output.

False—The production volume variance is unfavorable whenever actual output is less than expected output. (p. 1124)

__T__10. In standard costing, the journal entry to record the direct labor costs incurred includes a debit to Manufacturing wages for the actual hours worked at the standard price for direct labor. (p. 1126)

Multiple Choice

1. Which of the following is true for a static budget? (p. 1106)
   a. Adjusted for changes in the level of activity
   b. Prepared for only one level of activity
   c. A budget that stays the same from one period to the next
   d. Also known as a fixed budget

2. Sweet Baby Diaper Company sells disposable diapers for $0.20 each. Variable costs are $0.05 per diaper while fixed costs are $75,000 per month for volumes up to 850,000 diapers and $112,500 for volumes above 850,000 diapers. What is the monthly operating income for 800,000 diapers and 900,000 diapers of volume? (p. 1109)
   a. $22,500 and $7,500, respectively
   b. $60,000 and $45,000, respectively
   c. $45,000 and $22,500, respectively
   d. $7,500 and $60,000, respectively

3. A graph of a flexible budget formula reflects fixed costs of $30,000 and total costs of $90,000 at a volume of 6,000 units. Assuming the relevant range is 1,000 to 12,000 units, what is the total cost of 10,000 units on the graph? (p. 1116)
   a. $100,000
   b. $130,000
   c. $160,000
   d. $180,000

4. The sales volume variance is the difference between which amounts? (p. 1108)
   a. Number of units actually sold and number of units expected to be sold according to the static budget
   b. Amounts in the flexible budget and the static budget
   c. Actual results and amounts in the flexible budget
   d. Actual sales volume and normal sales volume

5. The flexible budget variance is the difference between which amounts? (p. 1108)
   a. Actual results and amounts in the static budget
   b. Amounts in the flexible budget and the actual results
   c. Amounts in the flexible budget and the static budget
   d. The budgeted amounts for each level of activity in the flexible budget

6. What does a flexible budget help to measure? (p. 1107)
   a. The efficiency of operations at the actual activity levels
   b. The amount by which standard and expected prices differ
   c. Both a and b
   d. None of the above

7. Global Engineering's actual operating income for the current year is $50,000. The flexible budget operating income for actual volume achieved is $40,000 while the static budget operating income is $53,000. What is the sales volume variance for operating income? (p. 1108)
   a. $10,000U
   b. $10,000F
   c. $13,000U
   d. $13,000F

8. Tiger's Golf Center reported actual operating income for the current year of $60,000. The flexible budget operating income for actual volume achieved is $55,000 while the static budget operating income is $58,000. What is the flexible budget variance for operating income? (p. 1108)
   a. $2,000F
   b. $3,000U
   c. $5,000F
   d. $5,000U

9. What does a favorable direct materials efficiency variance indicate? (p. 1119)
   a. Actual cost of direct materials was less than the standard cost of direct materials.
   b. Actual quantity of direct materials used was less than the standard quantity for actual output.
   c. Standard quantity of direct materials for actual output was less than the actual quantity of direct materials used.
   d. Actual quantity of direct materials used was greater than the standard quantity for budgeted output.

10. Western Outfitters Mountain Sports projected 2013 sales of 75,000 units at a unit sale price of $12.00. Actual 2013 sales were 72,000 units at $14.00 per unit. Actual variable costs, budgeted at $4.00 per unit, totaled $4.75 per unit. Budgeted fixed costs totaled $375,000 while actual fixed costs amounted to $400,000. What is the flexible budget variance for variable expenses? (p. 1108)
    a. $12,000F
    b. $25,000F
    c. $54,000U
    d. $54,000F

Quick Exercises

23-1. Super Phone Manufacturing projected 2013 sales of 10,000 units at $15 per unit. Actual sales for the year were 12,000 units at $14 per unit. Actual variable expenses, budgeted at $6 per unit, amounted to $5 per unit. Actual fixed expenses, budgeted at $60,000, totaled $65,000.
(pp. 1108–1109)

Requirement

Prepare Super Phone's income statement performance report for 2013, including both flexible budget variances and sales volume variances.

	1 Actual Results at Actual Prices	2 Flexible Budget Variance	3 Flexible Budget for Actual Number of Output Units	4 Sales Volume Variance	5 Static (Master) Budget
	SUPER PHONE MANUFACTURING Income Statement Performance Report Year Ended December 31, 2013				
Output Units	12,000	0	12,000	2,000 F	10,000
Sales revenue	$168,000	$12,000 U	$180,000	$30,000 F	$150,000
Variable costs	72,000	12,000 U	60,000		60,000
Fixed costs	65,000	5,000 U	60,000	0	60,000
Total costs	137,000	2,000 F	120,000		120,000
Operating income	$ 31,000	$29,000 U	$ 60,000	$30,000 F	$ 30,000

23-2.   Sadie Company established a master budget volume of 20,000 units for February. Actual overhead costs incurred amounted to $18,000. Actual production for the month was 21,000 units. The standard variable overhead rate was $0.50 per direct labor hour. The standard fixed overhead rate was $0.25 per direct labor hour. One direct labor hour is the standard quantity per finished unit. (pp. 1121–1125)

Requirements

$$\text{Actual overhead} = \$18,000$$

$$\text{Flexible budget overhead for actual production} = (\$0.50 \times 21,000) + (\$0.25 \times 20,000)$$
$$= \$15,500$$

$$\text{Standard overhead allocated to production} = (\$0.50 \times 21,000) + (\$0.25 \times 21,000)$$
$$= \$15,750$$

1. Compute the total manufacturing overhead cost variance.

$$\text{Total manufacturing overhead cost variance} = \$18,000 - \$15,750$$
$$= \$2,250 \text{ U}$$

2. Compute the overhead flexible budget variance.

$$\text{Overhead flexible budget variance} = \$18,000 - \$15,500$$
$$= \$2,500 \text{ U}$$

3. Compute the production volume variance.

$$\text{Production volume variance} = \$15,500 - \$15,750$$
$$= \$250 \text{ F}$$

23-3. Fantastic Tools Company recognizes variances from standards at the earliest opportunity, and the quantity of direct materials purchased is equal to the quantity used. The following information is available for the most recent month: (pp. 1125–1127)

	Direct Materials	Direct Labor
Standard quantity/unit	6.00 lbs.	2.5 hrs.
Standard price/lb. or hr.	$8.10/lb.	$8.00/hr.
Actual quantity/unit	6.25 lbs.	2.8 hrs.
Actual price/lb. or hr.	$8.00/lb.	$7.50/hr.
Price variance	$625 F	$1,400 F
Efficiency variance	$2,025 U	$2,400 U
Static budget volume	900 units	
Actual volume	1,000 units	
Actual overhead	$11,000.00	
Standard variable overhead	$5/unit	
Standard fixed overhead	$5,400	
Overhead flexible budget variance	$900 U	
Production volume variance	$700 F	

Requirements

1. Journalize the purchase and usage of direct materials including the related variances.

		General Journal		
Date	Accounts		Debit	Credit
	Materials inventory (6.25 × $8.10 × 1,000)		50,625	
	Accounts payable (6.25 × $8.00 × 1,000)			50,000
	Direct material price variance			625

		General Journal		
Date	Accounts		Debit	Credit
	Work in process inventory (6.00 × $8.10 × 1,000)		48,600	
	Direct materials efficiency variance		2,025	
	Materials inventory			50,625

2. Journalize the direct labor costs incurred and the application of direct labor, including the related variances.

	Date	Accounts		Debit	Credit
		General Journal			
		Manufacturing wages (2.8 × $8.00 × 1,000)		22,400	
		Wages payable (2.8 × $7.50 × 1,000)			21,000
		Direct labor price variance			1,400

	Date	Accounts		Debit	Credit
		General Journal			
		Work in process inventory (2.5 × $8.00 × 1,000)		20,000	
		Direct labor efficiency variance		2,400	
		Manufacturing wages			22,400.00

3. Journalize the application of overhead costs including the recognition of the overhead variances.

	Date	Accounts		Debit	Credit
		General Journal			
		Work in process inventory		11,000	
		Manufacturing overhead ([$5,400/900 + $5.00] × 1,000)			11,000

	Date	Accounts		Debit	Credit
		General Journal			
		Overhead flexible budget variance		900.00	
		Production volume variance			700.00
		Manufacturing overhead			200.00

23-4. **Ringo Industries has the following information regarding direct materials:** (pp. 1113–1117)

Actual pounds purchased and used	58,000
Standard quantity	4 pounds per finished good
Actual production	15,000 finished goods
Direct materials efficiency variance	$10,500 F
Direct materials price variance	$29,000 U

Requirement

Compute Ringo's standard price per pound and actual price per pound.

Let Y = standard price per pound
Direct materials efficiency variance = $[(4 \times 15,000) - 58,000]Y = \$10,500$
$$2,000Y = \$10,500$$
$$Y = \$5.25$$

Let Y = actual price per pound
Direct materials price variance = $(Y - \$5.25) \times 58,000 = \$29,000$
$$Y - \$5.25 = \$29,000/58,000$$
$$Y - \$5.25 = \$0.50$$
$$Y = \$5.75$$

23-5.   Workshop, Inc., sells board games for $15, resulting in a contribution
        margin of $9 per game. Fixed costs are budgeted at $212,000 per quarter
        for volumes up to 30,000 games and $242,000 for volumes exceeding
        30,000 games. (pp. 1117–1125)

Requirement

Prepare the flexible budget for the next quarter for volume levels of
25,000; 30,000; and 40,000 games.

WORKSHOP, INC. Flexible Budget Year Ended December 31, 2013				
	Flexible Budget per Output Unit	**Output Units (games)**		
		25,000	**30,000**	**40,000**
Sales revenue	$15	$375,000	$450,000	$600,000
Variable expenses	6	150,000	180,000	240,000
Fixed expenses		212,000	212,000	242,000
Total expenses		362,000	392,000	482,000
Operating income (loss)		$ 13,000	$ 58,000	$120,000

Do It Yourself! Question 1 Solutions

1. Using Fluffy's estimated budget values for costs and sales price, develop flexible budgets for 32,000; 34,000; and 36,000 beds.

FLUFFY FOAM BEDS
Flexible Budget
Year Ended December 31, 2013

	Flexible Budget per Output Unit	Output Units (beds)		
		32,000	34,000	36,000
Sales revenue	$180	$5,760,000	$6,120,000	$6,480,000
Variable expenses	70	2,240,000	2,380,000	2,520,000
Fixed expenses		3,000,000	3,000,000	3,000,000
Total expenses		5,240,000	5,380,000	5,520,000
Operating income (loss)		$ 520,000	$ 740,000	$ 960,000

2. Prepare Fluffy's income statement performance report for 2013.

FLUFFY FOAM BEDS
Income Statement Performance Report
Year Ended December 31, 2013

	1 Actual Results at Actual Prices	2 Flexible Budget Variance	3 Flexible Budget for Actual Number of Output Units	4 Sales Volume Variance	5 Static (Master) Budget
Output Units	34,200	0	34,200	2,200 F	32,000
Sales revenue	$6,327,000	$171,000 F	$6,156,000	$396,000 F	$5,760,000
Variable costs	2,565,000	171,000 U	2,394,000	154,000 U	2,240,000
Fixed costs	3,100,000	100,000 U	3,000,000	0	3,000,000
Total costs	5,665,000	271,000 U	5,394,000	154,000 U	5,240,000
Operating income	$ 662,000	$100,000 U	$ 762,000	242,000 U	520,000

Do It Yourself! Question 2 Solutions

Requirements

1. Compute the price and efficiency variances for direct materials and direct labor.

Direct Materials Price Variance

$$\begin{aligned} \text{Direct materials price variance} &= (\text{Actual price} - \text{Standard price}) \times \text{Actual quantity} \\ &= (\$0.24 - \$0.25) \times (102 \times 88{,}000 \text{ units}) \\ &= \$89{,}760 \text{ F} \end{aligned}$$

Direct Materials Efficiency Variance

$$\begin{aligned} \text{Direct materials quantity variance} &= (\text{Actual quantity} - \text{Standard quantity}) \times \text{Standard price} \\ &= [(102 \times 118{,}000) - (100 \times 88{,}000)] \times \$0.25 \\ &= \$44{,}000 \text{ U} \end{aligned}$$

Direct Labor Rate Variance

$$\begin{aligned} \text{Direct labor rate variance} &= (\text{Actual rate} - \text{Standard rate}) \times \text{Actual hours} \\ &= (\$18.15 - \$18.00) \times 42{,}000 \\ &= \$6{,}300 \text{ U} \end{aligned}$$

Direct Labor Efficiency Variance

$$\begin{aligned} \text{Direct labor efficiency variance} &= (\text{Actual hours} - \text{Standard hours}) \times \text{Standard price} \\ &= [42{,}000 - (0.50 \times 88{,}000)] \times \$18.00 \\ &= \$36{,}000 \text{ F} \end{aligned}$$

2. For manufacturing overhead, compute the total variance, the flexible variance, and the production volume variance.

Total Overhead Variance

Total overhead variance = Actual overhead cost − Standard overhead allocated to production
= $980,000 − (88,000 × $12)
= $76,000 F

Overhead Flexible Budget Variance

Overhead flexible budget variance = Actual overhead cost − Flexible budget overhead for the actual number of outputs
= $980,000 − [(88,000 × $2.00) + (80,000 × $10.00)]
= $4,000 U

Production Volume Variance

Production volume variance = $\dfrac{\text{Flexible budget output for}}{\text{the actual number of outputs}}$ − $\dfrac{\text{Standard overhead allocated}}{\text{to actual production}}$
= $976,000 − ($12 × 88,000)
= $80,000 F

The Power of Practice

For more practice using the skills learned in this chapter, visit MyAccountingLab. There you will find algorithmically generated questions that are based on these Demo Docs and your main textbook's Review and Assess Your Progress sections.

Go to MyAccountingLab and follow these steps:

1. Direct your URL to www.myaccountinglab.com.
2. Log in using your name and password.
3. Click the MyAccountingLab link.
4. Click Study Plan in the left navigation bar.
5. From the table of contents, select Chapter 23, Flexible Budgets and Standard Costs.
6. Click a link to work tutorial exercises.

24 Performance Evaluation and the Balanced Scorecard

What You Probably Already Know

You may have some extra money in the future that you would like to invest. If you decide to invest in a bank certificate of deposit you would want to place your money in the bank that provides the largest return. If Bank A offers an interest return of $55 on a $1,000 one year investment and Bank B offers a return of $60 for the same $1,000 investment, the choice would be to invest in Bank B. The return on your $1,000 cash asset invested would be $60/$1,000 = 6%. The return on your $1,000 investment at Bank A would have been only $55/$1,000 = 5.5%. This computation of your return on investment (ROI) that you may have already used in your personal life is a performance tool that you will study in this chapter. It can assist you in making informed financial decisions both in your personal and professional life.

Learning Objectives/Success Keys

 Explain why and how companies decentralize.

Decentralization is often necessary as companies grow. Decentralization allows upper management to focus on broad goals and others to focus on their areas of expertise in managing the company increasing motivation and retention. However, decentralization can also create duplicate costs and permit management to deviate from top management's goals.

 Explain why companies use performance evaluation systems.

The goals of performance evaluation systems include:

- Encourage adherence to company goals
- Communicate expectations
- Motivate individual managers
- Provide feedback to top management
- Benchmark, comparing results of the company to others in the industry

Describe the balanced scorecard and identify key performance indicators for each perspective.

The balanced scorecard is a system of measuring financial and operating performance. In addition to evaluating financial results, assessing operational qualities in accordance with the company's goals and strategic plans are also necessary. For example, an airline would want to assess its on-time flights and percentage of lost baggage. This type of feedback could help the company evaluate its long-term performance. *Review Exhibit 24-2 (p. 1156) for the links between goals and key performance indicators and Exhibit 24-3 (p. 1157) for the four perspectives of a balanced scorecard.*

4 Use performance reports to evaluate cost, revenue, and profit centers.

- **Cost center**—The performance report of a cost center identifies the difference between the actual and the budgeted costs. This is a flexible budget approach.

- **Revenue center**—The performance report of a revenue center identifies the difference between the actual and the budgeted costs. It is important to consider the flexible budget variance and the sales volume variance. Management needs to know what amount of the variance relates to the difference between the actual and budgeted amounts due to sales volume and the amount related to the sales prices.

- **Profit center**—Responsibility in this center is for revenues and expenses, and ultimately profits or net income. The performance report compares the actual to the budgeted revenues and expenses. When there is a centralized Service Department that benefits various profit centers there should be an allocation of these costs to each center. The expense associated with the service received should be included in the performance report, even though the manager of the profit center may not be able to control the allocated service costs.

Review Exhibits 24-4 through 24-6 (pp. 1162–1163) for examples of performance reports for cost, revenue, and profit centers.

 Use ROI, RI, and EVA to evaluate investment centers.

An example of an investment center would be a separate large division of a company. It has revenue and expenses like a profit center but it also has separate identifiable assets that are used to generate profit. The investment center must be held accountable to generate an acceptable level of return on the assets invested.

The **return on investment (ROI)** is one of the tools of financial performance. It measures the operating income compared to the total assets. The higher the ROI the better.

$$ROI = \frac{\text{Operating income}}{\text{Total assets}}$$

The **residual income (RI)** compares the operating income of the division with that expected by management, given the assets of the investment center.

$$RI = \text{Operating income} - (\text{Target rate of return} \times \text{Total assets})$$

The **economic value added (EVA)** evaluates the return on assets from the stockholders' and long-term creditors' viewpoint. The minimum rate of return required by these stakeholders is the weighted average cost of capital (WACC).

$$EVA = \text{Operating income (after taxes)} - [(\text{Total assets} - \text{Current liabilities}) \times \text{WACC \%}]$$

Review Exhibit 24-8 (p. 1171) for a summary of the investment center performance measures.

Demo Doc 1

Performance Management and Evaluation

Learning Objective 4

Coffee Café (within Better Books) had the following results during the month of May 2013:

COFFEE CAFÉ Performance Evaluation Report For the Month Ended May 2013				
	Actual	Flexible Budget	Flexible Budget Variance	Percentage Variance*
Sales revenue	$98,000	$94,000		
Cost of goods sold	24,500	23,500		
Gross profit	73,500	70,500		
Operating expenses	22,250	24,000		
Income from operations before				
Service Dept. charges	51,250	46,500		
Allocated Service Dept. charges	12,240	12,000		
Income from operations	$39,010	$34,500		

*Round % to two decimal places.

Requirements

1. Complete the performance evaluation report.

2. Based on the report, what type of responsibility center is used?

Demo Doc 1 Solutions

4 Use performance reports to evaluate cost, revenue, and profit centers

Requirement 1

Complete the performance evaluation report.

Part 1	Part 2	Demo Doc Complete

The actual results should be compared to the flexible budget. If the difference between the actual and the budget amounts results in income from operations being higher than budgeted, it is a positive, favorable difference. Those that cause income to be lower are negative, unfavorable differences.

COFFEE CAFÉ Performance Evaluation Report For the Month Ended May 2013				
	Actual	Flexible Budget	Flexible Budget Variance	Percentage Variance*
Sales revenue	$98,000	$94,000	$4,000	4.26%
Cost of goods sold	24,500	23,500	(1,000)	(4.26)
Gross profit	73,500	70,500	3,000	4.26
Operating expenses	22,250	24,000	1,750	7.29
Income from operations before				
Service Dept. charges	51,250	46,500	4,750	10.22
Allocated Service Dept. charges	12,240	12,000	(240)	(2.00)
Income from operations	$39,010	$34,500	$4,510	13.07

*Round % to two decimal places.

When sales revenue is higher than budgeted, it results in higher income from operations and so the difference is positive. When expenses such as cost of goods sold are higher than budgeted, it results in lower income from operations and so the difference is negative.

The % variance is calculated as the flexible budget variance amount divided by the flexible budget amount. For example, the sales revenue % variance is,

$$\text{Sales revenue \% variance} = \frac{\$4,000}{\$94,000}$$
$$= 4.26\%$$

Requirement 2

Based on the report, what type of responsibility center is used?

Part 1	Part 2	Demo Doc Complete

The performance report for Coffee Café within Better Books shows both revenue and expenses. The café is within the bookstore and does not have separate assets. Coffee Café is a profit center.

Part 1	Part 2	Demo Doc Complete

Demo Doc 2

ROI, RI, and EVA to Evaluate Investment Centers

Learning Objective 5

The Vas Company has two large divisions with separate facilities that produce specialty coffees and teas. Some key financial information for the past year is shown for these two divisions:

Division	Sales	Operating Income	Total Assets	Current Liabilities
Coffee	$3,800,000	$ 750,000	$2,700,000	$250,000
Tea	5,200,000	1,200,000	4,000,000	500,000

Vas's management has specified a target 10% minimum rate of return. The company's weighted average cost of capital is 7% and its effective tax rate is 25%.

Requirements

1. Calculate each division's ROI.

2. Top management has extra funds to invest. Which division will most likely receive those funds? Why?

3. Can you explain why one division's ROI is higher? How could management gain more insight?

4. Compute each division's RI. Interpret your results.

5. Compute each division's EVA. Interpret your results.

Demo Doc 2 Solutions

5 Use ROI, RI, and EVA to evaluate investment centers

Requirement 1

Calculate each division's ROI.

Part 1	Part 2	Part 3	Part 4	Part 5	Demo Doc Complete

$$ROI = \frac{\text{Operating income}}{\text{Sales}} \times \frac{\text{Sales}}{\text{Total assets}} = \frac{\text{Operating income}}{\text{Total assets}}$$

Coffee Division = ($750,000/$2,700,000)

= 27.8%

Tea Division = ($1,200,000/$4,000,000)

= 30.0%

Requirement 2

Top management has extra funds to invest. Which division will most likely receive those funds? Why?

Part 1	Part 2	Part 3	Part 4	Part 5	Demo Doc Complete

Top management would invest extra funds in the tea division. The higher the ROI the better. The tea division has a higher ROI, 30.0%; the coffee division is 27.8%.

Requirement 3

Can you explain why one division's ROI is higher? How could management gain more insight?

Part 1	Part 2	Part 3	Part 4	Part 5	Demo Doc Complete

The tea division ROI may be higher because they may earn more operating income for every dollar of sales. The ROI may also be higher for the tea division because it is operating more efficiently than the coffee division, generating more sales per dollar of assets.

Requirement 4

Compute each division's RI. Interpret your results.

Part 1	Part 2	Part 3	**Part 4**	Part 5	Demo Doc Complete

$$\text{RI} = \text{Operating income} - (\text{Target rate of return} \times \text{Total assets})$$

$$\text{Coffee Division RI} = \$750,000 - (.10 \times \$2,700,00)$$
$$= \$480,000$$
$$\text{Tea Division RI} = \$1,200,000 - (.10 \times \$4,000,000)$$
$$= \$800,000$$

A positive amount indicates that the divisions have met the minimum required return. The tea division has a higher RI than the coffee division.

Requirement 5

Compute each division's EVA. Interpret your results.

Part 1	Part 2	Part 3	Part 4	**Part 5**	Demo Doc Complete

$$\text{EVA} = \text{After-tax operating income} - [(\text{Total assets} - \text{Current liabilities}) \times \text{WACC \%}]$$

$$\text{Coffee Division EVA} = [(\$750,000 \times (100\% - 25\%)] - [(\$2,700,000 - \$250,000) \times .07\%]$$
$$= \$562,500 - \$171,500$$
$$= \$391,000$$
$$\text{Tea Division EVA} = [(\$1,200,000 \times (100\% - 25\%))] - [\$4,000,000 - \$500,000) \times .07\%]$$
$$= \$900,000 - \$245,000$$
$$= \$655,000$$

These EVA calculations show that both divisions have generated wealth in excess of expectations for the company's investors and long-term debt-holders. The tea division has the higher EVA.

Part 1	Part 2	Part 3	Part 4	Part 5	**Demo Doc Complete**

Quick Practice Questions

True/False

_____ 1. The advantages of decentralization usually outweigh the disadvantages.

_____ 2. Benchmarking is the process of comparing a company's practices against the best practices in the industry.

_____ 3. Financial results tend to be leading indicators.

_____ 4. The balanced scorecard measures only the operational performance of a company.

_____ 5. Key performance indicators help a company assess whether they are achieving their goals.

_____ 6. Customer satisfaction surveys can be used to assess key performance indicators.

_____ 7. "Service department charges" on a performance report indicate that centralized services have been shared by units.

_____ 8. A shortcoming of financial performance measures is their long-term focus.

_____ 9. The Accounting Department of a company is considered a profit center.

_____10. Centralization increases the difficulty of achieving goal congruence.

Multiple Choice

1. Which is *not* an advantage of decentralization?
   a. Unit managers can more readily see the "big picture"
   b. Motivates employees
   c. Improves customer relations
   d. Frees up top management

2. The Men's Suit Department of Macy's is considered to be what type of center?
   a. Revenue
   b. Cost
   c. Profit
   d. Investment

3. The Advertising and Sales Promotion Department of the Kellogg's Corporation is considered to be what type of center?
   a. Revenue
   b. Cost
   c. Profit
   d. Investment

4. Gross margin growth and return on investment are two indicators used in the balance scorecard, focusing on which perspective?
   a. Financial
   b. Customer perspective
   c. Internal business
   d. Learning and growth

5. Warranty claims and repair time are two indicators used in the balance scorecard, focusing on which perspective?
   a. Financial
   b. Customer perspective
   c. Internal business
   d. Learning and growth

6. If a profit center has sales revenue of $900,000 and a flexible budget of $950,000, which of the following is true?
   a. An unfavorable variance of 5.55% results.
   b. A favorable $50,000 variance results.
   c. A favorable variance of 5.26% results.
   d. None of the above is true.

7. Which of the following is used to compute all of the performance measurements of ROI, RI and EVA?
   a. Current liabilities
   b. Weighted average cost of capital (WACC)
   c. Target rate of return
   d. Total assets

8. The Wyss Company has a target rate of return of 10%, a weighted average cost of capital of 8%, an effective tax rate of 20% and the following financial information:

Operating income	$350,000
Total assets	955,000
Sales......................................	975,000
Current liabilities	85,000

   What is the ROI percentage?
   a. 36.6
   b. 35.9
   c. 27.3
   d. 24.3

9. Using the data in Question 8, what is the RI?
   a. $252,500
   b. $254,500
   c. $263,000
   d. $273,600

10. Using the data in Question 8, what is the EVA?
    a. $210,400
    b. $254,500
    c. $263,000
    d. $280,000

Quick Exercises

24-1. Identify and explain the advantages and disadvantages of decentralization.

24-2. Describe the benefits of a performance evaluation system.

24-3. Explain what a balanced scoreboard is and the four types of perspectives.

24-4. The following performance evaluation report for Anderson Company is incomplete.

a. Complete the performance evaluation report.

ANDERSON
Performance Evaluation Report

	Actual	Flexible Budget	Flexible Budget Variance	Percentage Variance*
Salaries and wages	$ 59,000	$ 68,000		
Payroll benefits	20,500	21,500		
Payroll taxes	7,000	7,500		
Depreciation—furniture and fixtures	12,000	12,000		
Supplies	1,250	1,000		
Misc. expense	13,240	12,000		
Total	$112,990	$122,000		

*Round % to two decimal places.

b. Based on the report, what type of responsibility center is used?

24-5. McNeil Company has two large divisions with separate facilities that produce shirts and pants. Some key financial information for the past year is shown for these two divisions:

Division	Sales	Operating Income	Total Assets	Current Liabilities
Shirts	$4,800,000	$ 950,000	$3,200,000	$400,000
Pants	7,200,000	1,260,000	5,900,000	680,000

McNeil management has specified a target 12% minimum rate of return. The company's weighted average cost of capital is 10% and its effective tax rate is 30%.

a. Calculate each division's ROI.

b. Calculate each division's RI.

c. Calculate each division's EVA.

Do It Yourself! Question 1

The Grab and Go concession at the local municipal pool had the following results during the month of July 2013:

GRAB AND GO Performance Evaluation Report For the Month of July 2013				
	Actual	Flexible Budget	Flexible Budget Variance	Percentage Variance*
Sales revenue	$75,000	$78,000		
Cost of goods sold	25,000	26,000		
Gross profit	50,000	52,000		
Operating expenses	20,350	24,000		
Income from operations before				
Service Dept. charges	29,650	28,000		
Allocated Service Dept. charges	11,340	12,000		
Income from operations	$18,310	$16,000		

*Round % to two decimal places.

Requirements

4 Use performance reports to evaluate cost, revenue, and profit centers

1. Complete the performance evaluation report.

4 Use performance reports to evaluate cost, revenue, and profit centers

2. Based on this report, what type of responsibility center is used?

Do It Yourself! Question 2

The Fullerton Food Company has separate divisions and facilities for its sales to government and food service (restaurant) customers. Some key financial information for the past year is shown for these two divisions:

Division	Sales	Operating Income	Total Assets	Current Liabilities
Government	$5,300,000	$725,000	$6,000,000	$975,000
Food Service	6,600,000	640,000	4,800,000	550,000

Fullerton's management has specified a target 9% minimum rate of return. The company's weighted average cost of capital is 10% and its effective tax rate is 30%.

Requirements

5 Use ROI, RI, and EVA to evaluate investment centers

1. Calculate each division's ROI.

5 Use ROI, RI, and EVA to evaluate investment centers

2. Top management has extra funds to invest. Which division will most likely receive those funds? Why?

5 Use ROI, RI, and EVA to evaluate investment centers

3. Can you explain why one division's ROI is higher? How could management gain more insight?

5 Use ROI, RI, and EVA to evaluate investment centers

4. Compute each division's RI. Interpret your results.

5 Use ROI, RI, and EVA to evaluate investment centers

5. Compute each division's EVA. Interpret your results.

Quick Practice Solutions

True/False

_____T_____ 1. The advantages of decentralization usually outweigh the disadvantages. (p. 1152)

_____T_____ 2. Benchmarking is the process of comparing a company's practices against the best practices in the industry. (p. 1154)

_____F_____ 3. Financial results tend to be leading indicators.

False—Financial results tend to be lagging indicators. (p. 1155)

_____F_____ 4. The balanced scorecard measures only the operational performance of a company.

False—The balanced scorecard measures operational *and financial* performance. (p. 1155)

_____T_____ 5. Key performance indicators help a company assess whether it is achieving its goals. (p. 1156)

_____T_____ 6. Customer satisfaction surveys can be used to assess key performance indicators. (p. 1156)

_____T_____ 7. "Service department charges" on a performance report indicate that centralized services have been shared by units. (p. 1157)

_____F_____ 8. A shortcoming of financial performance measures is their long-term focus.

False—A shortcoming of financial performance measures is their *short-term* focus. (p. 1155)

_____F_____ 9. The Accounting Department of a company is considered a profit center.

False—The Accounting Department of a company is considered a *cost* center. (p. 1153)

_____F____10. Centralization increases the difficulty of achieving goal congruence.

False—Decentralization increases the difficulty of achieving goal congruence. (p. 1152)

Multiple Choice

1. **Which is not an advantage of decentralization?** (p. 1171)
   a. Unit managers can more readily see the "big picture"
   b. Motivates employees
   c. Improves customer relations
   d. Frees up top management

2. The Men's Suit Department of Macy's is considered to be what type of center? (p. 1153)
   a. Revenue
   b. Cost
   c. Profit
   d. Investment

3. The Advertising and Sales Promotion Department of the Kellogg's Corporation is considered to be what type of center? (p. 1153)
   a. Revenue
   b. Cost
   c. Profit
   d. Investment

4. Gross margin growth and return on investment are two indicators used in the balance scorecard, focusing on which perspective? (p. 1166)
   a. Financial
   b. Customer perspective
   c. Internal business
   d. Learning and growth

5. Warranty claims and repair time are two indicators used in the balance scorecard, focusing on which perspective? (p. 1158)
   a. Financial
   b. Customer perspective
   c. Internal business
   d. Learning and growth

6. If a profit center has sales revenue of $900,000 and a flexible budget of $950,000, which of the following is true? (p. 1163)
   a. An unfavorable variance of 5.55% results.
   b. A favorable $50,000 variance results.
   c. A favorable variance of 5.26% results.
   d. None of the above is true.

7. Which of the following are used to compute all of the performance measurements of ROI, RI and EVA? (pp. 1166–1170)
   a. Current liabilities
   b. Weighted average cost of capital (WACC)
   c. Target rate of return
   d. Total assets

8. The Wyss Company has a target rate of return of 10%, a weighted average cost of capital of 8%, an effective tax rate of 20% and the following financial information:

Operating income	$350,000
Total assets	955,000
Sales	975,000
Current liabilities	85,000

What is the ROI percentage? (p. 1166)
a. 36.6
b. 35.9
c. 27.3
d. 24.3

9. Using the data in Question 8, what is the RI? (p. 1168)
a. $252,500
b. $254,500
c. $263,000
d. $273,600

10. Using the data in Question 8, what is the EVA? (p. 1169)
a. $210,400
b. $254,500
c. $263,000
d. $280,000

Quick Exercises

24-1. Identify and explain the advantages and disadvantages of decentralization. (pp. 1152–1153)

As companies expand it is often necessary to split them into different divisions or subunits. Generally the advantages outweigh the disadvantages of decentralization. The advantages include:

- Provides top management with more time to focus on the overall direction of the company.
- Allows individuals with various expertise to be employed in management positions to best use their specific skills.
- More management among the subunits permits closer relations with customers and faster servicing.
- Permits management training in the organization before being promoted to top management positions.
- Allows lower management to make decisions and exercise power within their subunits, which increases employee morale and retention.

The disadvantages of decentralization include:

- Some centralized services may now be split off and duplicated resulting in additional costs.
- Difficulty in communicating and ensuring that the company's set of goals is acknowledged throughout the organization.

24-2. Describe the benefits of a performance evaluation system. (pp. 1154–1155)

Performance evaluation systems help top management to control what is happening throughout the company in a decentralized environment. This system helps to ensure goal congruence and coordination, mesh expectations, motivate management, and provide feedback and benchmark. Benchmarking is comparing the company's performance to those performances of other companies that are considered the best in the industry.

24-3. Explain what a balanced scoreboard is and the four types of perspectives. (pp. 1155–1159)

The balanced scoreboard is a system that measures and evaluates the financial performance *as well as* the operating performance of the organization. It is necessary to evaluate the lead indicators as well as the lag indicators to keep the entity on track for the long-term. Four perspectives are considered in the balanced scoreboard:

- Financial perspective answers the question, "How do we look to stockholders?" Some of the typical indicators would be the financial ratio analysis discussed in this and previous chapters.
- Customer perspective answers the question, "How do customers see us?" Customer survey ratings are commonly used to assess how satisfied the customer is.
- Internal business perspective answers the question, "At what business processes must we excel to satisfy customer and financial objectives?" Adequate internal systems must be in place to reach these objectives.
- Learning and growth perspective answers the question, "Can we continue to improve and create value?" Maintaining an educated, skilled, and informed workforce provides a necessary linchpin to achieving all of these objectives.

24-4. The following performance evaluation report for Anderson is incomplete. (pp. 1162–1163)

a. Complete the performance evaluation report.

ANDERSON
Performance Evaluation Report

	Actual	Flexible Budget	Flexible Budget Variance	Percentage Variance*
Salaries and wages	$ 59,000	$ 68,000	$9,000	13.24%
Payroll benefits	20,500	21,500	1,000	4.65
Payroll taxes	7,000	7,500	500	6.67
Depreciation—furniture and fixtures	12,000	12,000	0	0
Supplies	1,250	1,000	(250)	(25.00)
Misc. expense	13,240	12,000	(1,240)	(10.33)
Total	$112,990	$122,000	$9,010	7.39

*Round % to two decimal places.

b. Based on the report, what type of responsibility center is used? (p. 1153)

Only costs appear in the performance center report. Therefore it must be a cost center.

24-5. **McNeil Company has two large divisions with separate facilities that produce shirts and pants. Some key financial information for the past year is shown for these two divisions: (pp. 1166–1171)**

Division	Sales	Operating Income	Total Assets	Current Liabilities
Shirts	$4,800,000	$ 950,000	$3,200,000	$400,000
Pants	7,200,000	1,260,000	5,900,000	680,000

McNeil management has specified a target 12% minimum rate of return. The company's weighted average cost of capital is 10%, and its effective tax rate is 30%.

a. Calculate each division's ROI.

$$\text{Shirts} = \frac{\$950,000}{\$3,200,000}$$
$$= 29.69\%$$

$$\text{Pants} = \frac{\$1,260,000}{\$5,900,000}$$
$$= 21.36\%$$

b. Compute each division's RI.

Shirts = $950,000 – ($3,200,000 × .12)
      = $566,000

Pants = $1,260,000 – ($5,900,000 × .12)
      = $552,000

c. Calculate each division's EVA.

Shirts = $950,000 × (100% – 30%) – [($3,200,000 – $400,000) × .10]
      = $665,000 – $280,000
      = $385,000

Pants = $1,260,000 × (100% – 30%) – [($5,900,000 – $680,000) × .10]
      = $882,000 – $522,000
      = $360,000

Do It Yourself! Question 1 Solutions

The Grab and Go concession at the local municipal pool had the following results during the month of July 2013:

Requirements

1. Complete the performance evaluation report.

<table>
<tr><td colspan="5" align="center">GRAB AND GO
Performance Evaluation Report
For the Month of July 2013</td></tr>
<tr><td></td><td align="center">Actual</td><td align="center">Flexible
Budget</td><td align="center">Flexible
Budget
Variance</td><td align="center">Percentage
Variance*</td></tr>
<tr><td>Sales revenue</td><td>$75,000</td><td>$78,000</td><td>($3,000)</td><td>(3.85%)</td></tr>
<tr><td>Cost of goods sold</td><td>25,000</td><td>26,000</td><td>1,000</td><td>3.85</td></tr>
<tr><td>Gross profit</td><td>50,000</td><td>52,000</td><td>(2,000)</td><td>(3.85)</td></tr>
<tr><td>Operating expenses</td><td>20,350</td><td>24,000</td><td>3,650</td><td>15.21</td></tr>
<tr><td>Income from operations before</td><td></td><td></td><td></td><td></td></tr>
<tr><td> Service Dept. charges</td><td>29,650</td><td>28,000</td><td>1,650</td><td>(5.89)</td></tr>
<tr><td>Allocated Service Dept. charges</td><td>11,340</td><td>12,000</td><td>660</td><td>5.50</td></tr>
<tr><td>Income from operations</td><td>$18,310</td><td>$16,000</td><td>$2,310</td><td>14.44%</td></tr>
</table>

*Round % to two decimal places.

2. Based on this report, what type of responsibility center is used?

The performance report for the center contains revenues and expenses. The Grab and Go is a profit center.

Do It Yourself! Question 2 Solutions

The Fullerton Food Company has separate divisions and facilities for their sales to government and food service (restaurant) customers. Some key financial information for the past year is shown for these two divisions:

Division	Sales	Operating Income	Total Assets	Current Liabilities
Government	$5,300,000	$725,000	$6,000,000	$975,000
Food Service	6,600,000	640,000	4,800,000	550,000

Fullerton's management has specified a target 9% minimum rate of return. The company's weighted average cost of capital is 10%, and its effective tax rate is 30%.

Requirements

1. Calculate each division's ROI.

$$\text{Government ROI} = \frac{\$725,000}{\$6,000,000}$$
$$= 12.08\%$$

$$\text{Food Service ROI} = \frac{\$640,000}{\$4,800,000}$$
$$= 13.33\%$$

2. Top management has extra funds to invest. Which division will most likely receive those funds? Why?

Food Service would be the division most likely to receive the extra funds. The ROI of food service is 13.33%; higher than the 12.08% ROI for government.

3. Can you explain why one division's ROI is higher? How could management gain more insight?

The food service division ROI may be higher because they may earn more operating income for every dollar of sales. The ROI may also be higher for the food service division because it is operating more efficiently than the government division, generating more sales per dollar of assets. Management could gain more insight by computing separately the two elements of ROI; operating income divided by sales and sales divided by total assets.

4. Compute each division's RI. Interpret your results.

$$\text{Government} = \$725{,}000 - (6{,}000{,}000 \times .09)$$
$$= \$185{,}000$$

$$\text{Food Service} = \$640{,}000 - (4{,}800{,}000 \times .09)$$
$$= \$208{,}000$$

The food service division has a higher RI.

5. Compute each division's EVA. Interpret your results.

$$\text{Government} = [\$725{,}000 \times (100\% - 30\%)] - [(\$6{,}000{,}000 - \$975{,}000) \times .10]$$
$$= \$507{,}000 - \$502{,}500$$
$$= \$5{,}000$$
$$\text{Food Service} = [\$640{,}000 \times (100\% - 30\%)] - [(\$4{,}800{,}000 - \$550{,}000) \times .10]$$
$$= \$448{,}000 - \$425{,}000$$
$$= \$23{,}000$$

The food service division has a higher EVA.

The Power of Practice

For more practice using the skills learned in this chapter, visit MyAccountingLab. There you will find algorithmically generated questions that are based on these Demo Docs and your main textbook's Review and Assess Your Progress sections.

To go to MyAccountingLab, follow these steps:

1. Direct your URL to www.myaccountinglab.com.
2. Log in using your name and password.
3. Click the MyAccountingLab link.
4. Click Study Plan in the left navigation bar.
5. From the table of contents, select Chapter 24, Performance Evaluation and the Balanced Scorecard.
6. Click a link to work tutorial exercises.

Glindex

A Combined Glossary/Subject Index